Teaching about Teaching:
Purpose, Passion and Pedagogy in Teacher Education

Edited by

John Loughran and Tom Russell

The Falmer Press

(A member of the Taylor & Francis Group)
London • Washington, D.C.

UK   Falmer Press, 1 Gunpowder Square, London, EC4A 3DE

USA   Falmer Press, Taylor & Francis Inc., 1900 Frost Road, Suite 101, Bristol, PA 19007

First published in 1997

A catalogue record for this book is available from the British Library

ISBN 0-7507-0708-9 cased
ISBN 0-7507-0622-8 paper

Library of Congress Cataloging-in-Publication Data are available on request

Jacket design by Caroline Archer

Typeset in 10/12 pt Times by
Graphicraft Typesetters Ltd., Hong Kong.

Printed in Great Britain by Biddles Ltd., Guildford and King's Lynn on paper which has a specified pH value on final paper manufacture of not less than 7.5 and is therefore 'acid free'.

Every effort has been made to contact copyright holders for their permission to reprint material in this book. The publishers would be grateful to hear from any copyright holder who is not here acknowledged and will undertake to rectify any errors or omissions in future editions of this book.

Teaching about Teaching

Contents

Acknowledgments   vii

Foreword by Gary D. Fenstermacher   viii

Introduction   1

Chapter 1 An Introduction to Purpose, Passion and Pedagogy   3
             John Loughran

**Section 1: Principles and Practices Which Shape Teaching
about Teaching**   11

Chapter 2 Practicing Theory and Theorizing Practice in Teacher
             Education   13
             Robert V. Bullough, Jr.

Chapter 3 Teaching Teachers: How I Teach IS the Message   32
             Tom Russell

Chapter 4 Teacher Education as a Process of Developing Teacher
             Knowledge   48
             Jeff Northfield and Richard Gunstone

Chapter 5 Teaching about Teaching: Principles and Practice   57
             John Loughran

Section 2: Challenges in Teaching and Learning about Teaching   71

Chapter 6 Teaching Teachers for the Challenge of Change   73
             Anna E. Richert

Chapter 7 Learning to Teach Prospective Teachers to Teach
             Mathematics: The Struggles of a Beginning Teacher
             Educator   95
             Cynthia Nicol

Chapter 8 Teaching and Learning in Teacher Education: Who is
             Carrying the Ball?   117
             Peter Chin

Contents

Section 3: Rethinking Teacher Educators' Roles and Practice   131

Chapter 9   Learning about Learning in the Context of a Science
Methods Course   133
Garry Hoban

Chapter 10   Teaching to Teach with Purpose and Passion: Pedagogy
for Reflective Practice   150
Vicki Kubler LaBoskey

Chapter 11   Advisor as Coach   164
Anthony Clarke

Section 4: Conversations about Teacher Education   181

Chapter 12   Obligations to Unseen Children   183
*The Arizona Group: Karen Guilfoyle, Mary Lynn
Hamilton, and Stefinee Pinnegar*

Chapter 13   Storming through Teacher Education: Talk about
Summerfest   210
*Allan MacKinnon, Michael Cummings and
Kathryn Alexander*

Section 5: Conclusion   227

Chapter 14   Becoming Passionate about Teacher Education   229
Tom Russell

Notes on Contributors   236

Author Index   239

Subject Index   241

Acknowledgments

We are most grateful for the time, help and support from Airlie and LaVerne.

We would also like to acknowledge the support of our Deans of Education (Rena Upitis and Richard White) who also share the passion for teacher education which is so important for our pre-service programs to continue to attempt to address the needs and concerns of pre-service teacher candidates.

John Loughran and Tom Russell
September, 1996

Foreword

Gary D. Fenstermacher

In these times, it is much in vogue to speak of silenced voices. The reference is typically to the voices of teachers, women, children, or members of minority groups. It also applies to the voices of teacher educators. We hear the voices of university researchers, of law makers, and of policy analysts, speaking about what teacher educators do or fail to do, but we do not often hear the voices of teacher educators themselves. This book begins the remedy for lopsided talk about teacher education.

In the chapters that follow, you will 'hear' teacher educators discussing their own work. They describe their aspirations for the teachers they teach, their methods for realizing these aspirations, the concepts and theories that ground these methods, and the tribulations and triumphs encountered in the course of their work. These are remarkable essays, for they are at once intellectually engaging and refreshingly personal. This duality of thoughtful abstraction and personal experience permits the reader who has taught teachers to both identify with and learn from the authors. These chapters can be read for profit and for pleasure, a treat too often absent from academic literature.

When the editors asked if I would prepare some prefatory material for this book, I agreed not so much because I have a high opinion of forewords (I do not), but because I wanted to read these writers as quickly as I could lay my hands upon their work. I know most of them, professionally if not personally, and I anticipated with pleasure the receipt of their manuscripts. Not only was I not disappointed in what I read, I was delighted with what I learned for my own teaching. The manuscripts arrived just as I was putting together a foundations course for secondary level teacher education students. The course I designed is different from the ones taught previously because of the work contained here.

Having said that, I know I should tell you how it is different, but I will not. At least, not yet. You see, like so many teachers I know, I am more comfortable talking to you about my efforts after I have tried them. They do not have to succeed; they simply have to be — to get a life, if you will — before I will talk much about them. The reason for my stance becomes evident as one reads these chapters. We learn by doing and by reflecting on what we are doing. In some ways, we may be said not to know what we are doing until we have done it. As we engage in an activity, it becomes increasingly clear to us what we are about, providing we do not go about it naively or thoughtlessly. Thus I will refrain from telling you what I am trying to do, because I am not yet sure just what it is.

After it is underway or nearly finished, when I am clear enough about it to attach words to what I am doing, then I will tell you. I will be sad if it fails, though that will not keep me from telling you about it. Whether I succeed or fail is not what keeps me from revealing what I am doing; it is, rather, the absence of sufficient experience with the activity to be able to express it clearly. As I try out the ideas gained from this book, and gain sufficient feel for them to attach reasonably accurate descriptive terminology to my activities, I create the conditions for reflection. Some will argue with this phrasing, saying that reflection need not or should not await the right words (here is where such notions as tacit, pre-cognitive, ineffable, and pre-conscious are tossed into the mix). We need not contest the point here, however, for all are likely to agree that reflection cannot be long sustained without expression in words. By naming what I am doing, I create the basis for sharing it with others, for analysing it myself, for asking others for their help or advice, and for changing my practice.

Now we venture on to contested ground, for there are those who would argue that the naming itself is the act of critical engagement, whereas others contend that how we are engaged in the naming is the act of critical engagement. There are vital differences here. These differences speak to the sense of wonder these essays evoked for me. Let me see if I can capture my puzzlement with sufficient clarity that you come to share it with me.

Within the community of teacher educators, there are a number of families. One of these families is concerned with preparing teachers who will impart their content efficiently and expertly, accompanied by high levels of acquisition by the students. Another family believes that teachers must know how to assist students to develop a critical understanding of society, so that they do not merely reproduce the given culture. A third family contends that the construction of meaning is the essence of teaching and of learning; members of this family prepare teachers to assist students in becoming makers of meaning. Still another family consists of those who believe that the essence of teaching is in reflecting on experience and reconstructing practice following reflection. This book consists primarily of work from members of this fourth family. They might be called the Schön family, after the person who appears to have given identity and coherence to this family. However, it includes members who exhibit varying degrees of consistency with Schön's ideas, so it might be more accurate to call them the Reflectivist family.

Although it is of some value to understand that the contributors to this volume exhibit sufficient commonality to be grouped into a family, that is not an insight of much significance. What is worth more, I believe, is understanding how the families differ from one another. Of particular interest to me is how the Reflectivist family differs from a fifth family, one I will call the Analyst family.

The Analysts hold a high regard for reflection, but are not content with the mere act of reflection. Instead, they insist on standards for reflection. These standards vary from one family member to another. Some Analysts argue for a standard of truth, or at least validation by agreement between the initial claimant and other observers of the same phenomenon. Others contend for an analytic framework, wherein the activity of reflection is held accountable to some standards of procedure and outcome. Still others press for the transitive nature of reflection, averring that reflection must always be about something in particular before we can assess it as a process or a product. The Analysts are an odd lot, insofar as they have quite different ideas about how reflection is subjected to analysis. They are, however, united into family membership by the belief that reflection is an instrumental good, not a good-in-itself. Hence the analysts require standards, criteria, or analytical frameworks for the activity of reflection, and will not give much credence to reflection devoid of these tools.

Reflectivists and Analysts have been known to spar over their positions, as occurs, for example, when Tom Russell and Gary Fenstermacher get on the same symposium at the annual meeting of the American Educational Research Association. With the utmost respect for one another's position, they argue the benefits of their own views and the liabilities of the other's views. Allow me to demonstrate how well I have listened by arguing for the Reflectivist family position.

The beauty of the Reflectivist position is that it keeps intact the thinking and deliberation of the person reflecting. The Reflectivist, as one sees so clearly in the chapters of this book, cares deeply about getting the agent to deliberate on what he or she is doing or seeing others do. The Analyst, on the other hand, risks corruption of the deliberation of the one reflecting by pressing these deliberations into an analytical mold of some sort, be it a standard for truth, logical coherence, or moral discernment. The Reflectivist is not without standards, though these are, by and large, standards derived from the process of reflection itself, not standards derived elsewhere against which the quality of the reflection is measured.

By imposing a scheme or model of some sort, the Analyst engenders something of the same situation Heisenberg describes in the uncertainty principle: Any attempt to measure the momentum and position of subatomic particles runs afoul of the process used to measure them, for the act of measuring itself disturbs either position or momentum. Analysts have a similar predicament, for in imposing some framework or standard, they risk altering the deliberations so that they become more representative of the framework or model than of the person doing the deliberating.

If I have fairly and accurately represented the Reflectivist position *vis-à-vis* the Analyst position, perhaps I might now be permitted to examine a puzzling aspect of Reflectivism. To what end is the reflection undertaken? If reflection is an end-in-itself, the answer is obvious. One undertakes reflection in order to be reflective. If, on the other hand, reflection is viewed as an instrumental benefit, then there is something more that must be provided. What is it?

It is a theory of education. Such a theory specifies what we mean when we speak of education, of an educated person, and of receiving an education. The theory contains a moral dimension, setting forth the proper contribution of education to moral development; an epistemic dimension, providing a basis of making claims to knowledge or informed opinion; and a practical dimension, setting forth a conception of skilled performance in matters common to the life of the species (e.g., political, consumer, and parent practices). Such a theory then serves as the framework for reflection. It provides both structural substance for reflection as well as a standard against which to determine whether one's deliberations are gaining or losing ground for the person reflecting.

With the publication of this book, members of the Reflectivist family have created the occasion for teacher educators of all family backgrounds to express themselves on the personal and professional aspects of their practice. I hope we will be able to continue and enlarge this discussion by fashioning a working theory of education against which the work of all the families might be appraised. What a magnificent achievement that would be for teacher educators everywhere.

Before that can happen, books like this one must happen. Voices must be found, passions revealed, purposes uncovered. These are the things that will form the families of teacher education into the community of teacher educators. The task will not be easy, for those outside teacher education seem more preoccupied with marginalizing than with advancing it. For decades teacher education has been the deprived stepchild of the academy. The pursuit of any form of educational studies within institutions of higher education, at least in much of the English-speaking world, has always been somewhat suspect. Within educational studies itself, the activity of teacher education has been even more suspect.

Those who labor in teacher education may feel righteous indignation at their place on the academic pecking order, but it is well to recall that there was a time when the ranking may have been deserved. I think, for example, of my own experience as a student in teacher education. It began when I was in my early twenties, a baccalaureate degree in hand, and the prospect of mandatory military service ahead. When poor eyesight disqualified me for officer training, I learned that my local draft board was imagining what I would look like in a soldier's uniform. My choices were clear: A private in the Army or a graduate student. The latter looked to be the better part of wisdom, though not valour, and I found myself knocking on the door of my *alma mater*.

An admissions officer said I was too late for the coming Fall, that I might be considered for Spring, but most likely admission would not come until the following Fall. Had I followed their advice, I would probably have been policing the 38th parallel in Korea, or perhaps included in the first contingent of military 'advisers' in Viet Nam. Such thoughts gave rise to greater inventiveness on my part. I went looking for the school of education, thinking it an easy mark for my tale of *travail*. The people there were exceptionally nice, but firm on this point: While I could not be admitted to a master's degree program in such haste, I could get into the teacher preparation program. Were I in such a thing, I asked, would I still be considered an enrolled student? (Were it not so, my draft board would soon have a real picture of me in uniform.) Oh, yes, they said; of course you will be a regular, enrolled student. My next question was where to sign.

My questions about admission and student status were among the last I would ask for that month, indeed, for the entire semester. I was handed a course program, stipulating in unambiguous detail what to take, when, where, and with whom. I recall reading it and silently asking whether I had in fact been drafted, as my days, weeks, and months were mapped with the same kind of precision I was sure would go into planning an assault on a military target. Even so, I began my courses eagerly, thinking that though my choices had been so grossly instrumental to this point, I liked the idea of becoming a teacher. That sense of anticipation began to dissolve as I attended my first classes. As it became clearer to me what this activity called teacher education was all about, despair began to displace anticipation.

When I was an undergraduate major in government, I was often asked for my views on matters of consequence. Few professors liked what I said, and graded me accordingly, but I was flattered to be asked. As a student in teacher education, no one seemed interested in what I thought, save as a way of saving me from error. I was not asked for my views, but instead told that certain views were required in order to succeed. These were views about childhood learning, about parent involvement, about teaching methods, and about relating to other teachers and administrators. Recall that it was the early 1960s, when professors (especially, it seemed to me, education professors) seemed very sure of their ground. No discovering your own meaning here, no post-Enlightenment relativity, no narrative or story, no reflection, no personal or practical knowledge, no authority of experience, no allowances for context or culture; just pure logic, truth, and goodness. It was as if we were being initiated into the priesthood, with the noble task of ensuring that the magnificent attainments of western civilization were passed without corruption to the young. In hindsight, I suppose we were expected to feel as one might on being asked to carry the Olympic torch and light the great flame.

That is not what I felt. Instead, I felt my flame getting smaller and smaller, in danger of being extinguished. To the extent the instruction was practical, I failed to understand it because I had no experiential basis for making it real or concrete. To the extent the instruction was theoretical, I saw it as so far removed from what I would be doing that I dismissed it as the leisured meanderings of the theory class. I had a few interesting and engaging professors, but I recall finding them interesting on intellectual grounds, not on the likelihood of their being helpful to me when it came time to teach.

Near the end of that first semester, I asked my adviser if I might take some courses in the college of arts and sciences. He was delighted to have me do so, and signed all the necessary papers. At the time, I was unaware that I would not again take an education course until after being admitted to the doctoral program. In the process of learning to become a teacher, I became something else. What I became was neither a teacher or a teacher educator.

I did not return to teacher education until encouraged to do so by the dean of the college where I took my first position. It was John Goodlad, then Dean of UCLA's School of Education, who convinced me of the importance of teacher education. He understood its peripheral status within research universities, indeed within his own school of education, and sought to nurture a faculty that would take teacher education seriously as both an arena for serious inquiry and a place to take pride in one's own teaching. The results of his immediate efforts were mixed, given the scale of the challenge (one need only examine the experiences of so many of the institutions that are participating in the Holmes Group to understand the enormity of the challenge Goodlad faced in the late 1960s).

Teacher education has lived and, to a considerable extent, still lives on the margins of academic life, where it has little or no scholarly space or professional voice. By scholarly space, I mean a program of formal inquiry that is accorded respect through the usual academic trappings: departments, journals, associations, 'invisible colleges', publishers, and doctoral programs. By 'professional voice' I mean intellectually grounded conversations among colleagues about their work, framed within a discourse that permits the participants to learn from one another, to advance the larger activity in which they are mutually engaged, and to gain the regard of those engaged in different, but pertinent, conversations.

This volume makes a vital contribution to the creation of scholarly space and the finding of professional voice for teacher education. It reveals the delight, the frustrations, and the rewards of being a teacher educator. It gives to teacher educators what they have had too little of, a public voice that speaks of personal experience and grounded theory with passion and with purpose. While it is true that these voices are raised within the same family of teacher educators, that is a benefit in this case. For those I have here identified as members of the Reflectivist family are among the most passionate, most concerned teacher educators. They are the ones who have so willingly engaged in the study of their own and one another's professional practices. They are the ones who have organized conferences on teacher education, created new and different literatures about teacher education, and brought so many different elements of reflective scholarship to bear on its study and its practice. In this book we witness the fruits of their good labors. I trust it is as much a treat for you as it has been for me.

Gary D. Fenstermacher

Introduction

1 An Introduction to Purpose, Passion and Pedagogy

John Loughran

During the Fall term of 1995, I had the good fortune of spending my sabbatical leave at Queen's University in Canada. One of the major reasons for going to Queen's was to work with teacher educators and student teachers and to experience a different approach to pre-service teacher education from the one in which I teach in the School of Graduate Studies at Monash University. Tom Russell hosted my visit and initiated a research project so that we could actively pursue a study of teaching in teacher education. Through this project I was invited into all of Tom's classes as well as those of his colleague Peter Chin.

My collaboration with Tom and Peter largely focused on 'unpacking pedagogy' in a manner similar to that in a school-based professional development in-residence program I had been involved in for the previous four years (Loughran, 1994). The project at Queen's included pre-teaching discussions about what was planned for a class and why, observation of the class, and an extended period of de-briefing to develop alternative perspectives on the events of the class. In short, we engaged in a collaborative form of reframing (Schön, 1987). During each teaching session I would move around the class as appropriate, joining in with different groups of student teachers as they worked on their activities. This helped to broaden my understanding of their views on the teaching episode. An important aspect of this involvement was the rich range of data on which to base our discussions in the de-briefing sessions as we explored the 'real' teaching and learning events that had unfolded during each class.

Not surprisingly, then, throughout the Fall semester, Tom, Peter and I spent numerous hours passionately discussing pedagogy and purpose in pre-service teacher education. We were continually striving to better understand how these student teachers learnt about teaching. We pushed each other to better understand the impact that teaching about teaching had on new teachers' learning about teaching. We also unpacked some of the principles of pedagogy that underpinned the teaching about teaching practice used. One important aspect of this work that continually surfaced in our discussions was the recognition of the *developing understanding of pedagogy* in teaching about teaching. It seemed to us that there was an important transition in understanding required of all teachers of prospective teachers. The three of us are experienced high school teachers, but the knowledge of pedagogy we acquired by teaching was not in itself sufficient for the task of teaching about teaching. Nevertheless, it was clearly an essential starting point. What became more and more apparent was the professional knowledge of teaching about teaching that we had developed through our experiences teaching pre-service teachers. This professional knowledge included an understanding of:

- student teachers' needs and concerns in their transition from student to teacher;
- appropriate ways and times of challenging their beliefs about teaching and learning;
- a range of school teaching situations (content, year level etc.); and
- approaches and practices in supervision; pedagogy; and, teaching about teaching.

As we regularly revisited different aspects of practice, we began to recognize an important knowledge of *teaching about teaching* that we were always returning to and articulating as we discussed the teaching and learning episodes being created for the student teachers in the pre-service education classes. The *content* of this knowledge encompassed both a knowledge of pedagogy as well as a knowledge of the subject matter content. Hence, in teacher education, helping student teachers to learn about and experiment with pedagogy for particular subject matter knowledge involves a knowledge of *pedagogy* that might bring this knowledge to the fore. It could therefore be that this *special knowledge of teaching about teaching* is tacit knowledge, knowledge easily overlooked by others, taken for granted by teacher educators themselves, and consequently neither sufficiently understood nor valued.

During a break in my discussions with Tom and Peter, when their students were teaching in schools, I travelled to Vancouver to visit the University of British Columbia and Simon Fraser University. Having spent so much time discussing *learning about teaching* and *teaching about teaching*, it was inevitable that my discussions with Tony Clarke, Cynthia Nicol, Allan MacKinnon and others also focused on this theme. It seemed that, even though pre-service teacher education is the starting point for beginning teachers to learn about teaching and learning, there is minimal 'institutional' value or understanding of approaches to the pedagogical reasoning and purpose inherent in pre-service teacher educators' practices. While it has been recognized for some time that many faculty institutions responsible for teacher preparation have an interest *in* teacher education but are not actively concerned *with* teacher education (Borrowman, 1965), there has been little progress in developing our collective understanding of the pedagogy unique to pre-service teacher education.

Beginning teachers' views of the teaching profession, as well as their understanding of the role of Schools of Education, are necessarily influenced by their experiences during their studies in initial teacher education programs. These experiences need to be seen as relevant and appropriate, just as the teaching they experience needs to model 'good practice'. When this is the case, our best efforts to educate teachers in ways that reinforce the importance of the links between teaching and learning are modelled through our teacher education programs. The need for teacher educators to practice what they preach seems obvious.

That the relationship between theory and practice should be apparent *within* the teaching and learning episodes we create is central to learning about teaching. There seems little point in telling student teachers about the benefits of group work if those benefits are not demonstrated through our teaching practice. Similarly, it is counterproductive to lecture on higher-order questioning skills, wait-time or the benefits of interpretive discussions if these important aspects of teaching cannot be demonstrated through our own practice. It is even worse if our practice 'in action' is contradictory. As teachers of teachers we need to be able to understand our pedagogy from differing perspectives so that our roles in improving the preparation of prospective teachers can be meaningful and fruitful both for our student teachers and for ourselves.

Teaching about teaching is no easy task, and learning about teaching is equally demanding. For student teachers to learn about teaching, they need to operate constantly at two levels, as do their teachers. One level concerns the need to learn about learning through the experiences they are offered in pre-service teacher education programs. The other level concerns the simultaneous learning about teaching. We believe it is woefully inadequate to assume that learning about teaching occurs only in practice teaching placements. Within the context of the teaching we do in pre-service courses, we must attend to learning about teaching as well as learning about learning. Only in our own classrooms do we have the opportunity to control and explore the significance of the teaching strategies we adopt. In the teaching and learning episodes in which we engage our teacher candidates, they need to reflect on their cognitive and affective development as learners as a result of our pedagogy, while also reflecting on the pedagogy itself — how and why it is used, adapted, understood and developed. Through all of this, the attentive teacher educator also needs to be cognisant of these perspectives and to be ready, willing and able to respond to each as appropriate and as necessary. This is far from an easy task, but we believe that investing effort in this domain promises to improve the effectiveness of teacher education programs as well as the images of teacher education carried away by beginning teachers.

Van Manen (1995) offers insight into ways of understanding different perspectives on teaching and learning episodes through his conception of anecdotes. For many practicing classroom teachers, his anecdotes are a powerful tool for reconsidering pedagogy and for reconsidering familiar situations by helping us see the 'taken for granted' in new ways. The following anecdote was written by a student teacher enrolled for the Graduate Diploma in Education at Monash University in response to being asked to write about a personal experience during the pre-service program.

A Lesson on Policy

The tutorial room was quiet. Only the professor's voice broke the silence. I had to say something. I disagreed with what he was saying. I spoke up. That's what I thought we were supposed to be learning to do. To be actively engaged in our learning. To question our understanding. We're certainly expected to be doing that with our students in school.

'I don't think that policy has to be about change!' I said, and I gave some examples to support my point of view. With that, others in the class also started to contribute.

'This is what the definition is! Reputed researchers agree!' was his rather forceful response.

Faced with that, what else could I say? He was the expert. He would take it as a personal insult if I again raised issues, so I kept my mouth shut. As the rest of the monologue surged forth, the class returned to its earlier silence. I opened my note book and wrote furiously, 'I disagree, I disagree.'

We had just been talking about including people in discussions, accepting others' point of view, inclusion, understanding. I don't think that classrooms should be lecture theatres. Teaching is not a one-way process.

This anecdote goes to the heart of the central concerns of the contributors to this book. Chin, Hoban, LaBoskey, Nicol, and Richert all write about their approaches to their teaching in ways that demonstrate the importance of the relationship between teaching and learning. They show how program intentions must be supported and reinforced through the teaching practice if the intended effects are to be achieved. Teaching about teaching as Bullough demonstrates, requires a genuine commitment to pedagogy, a pedagogy that is underpinned by principles of practice that overtly shape actions. The importance of these principles of practice are extended through the work of Guilfoyle, Hamilton and Pinnegar, MacKinnon, Cummings and Alexander, Northfield and Gunstone, and Russell.

It is difficult to believe that the student teacher (above) who wrote the anecdote on policy learnt much of what the professor 'intended'. The anecdote clearly demonstrates the 'real' impact of the session and the obvious learning as a result of the teaching approach. Students of teaching should not suffer learning about teaching as contradiction, it is certainly not a productive way to engender a sense of valuing pedagogy. Pedagogy, must surely portray discretion, judgment, caution and forethought (van Manen, 1994), regardless of the setting in which it occurs.

Learning about teaching does not occur only in university classrooms. A great deal of learning through experience occurs when our student teachers explore their learning about teaching in the 'real world' of schools. Clarke takes up this point as he unpacks his approach to supervision during the teaching practicum. In this setting, the role of the teacher educator needs to again be carefully considered. It needs to be considered in ways that highlight the importance of support, understanding and guidance so that learning through the experiences may be meaningful and valuable. Here again the teacher educator's role is crucial, even more so when student teachers find themselves in vulnerable situations. Our actions in situations of vulnerability will influence not only new teachers' learning about teaching but also their views of the profession they seek to enter and the profession that 'nominally' supports their learning to teach.

Consider the learning significance of the messages about teaching and learning to teach embedded in two more anecdotes, one by a student teacher and one by a teacher educator.

The First Lesson

It was the first day of my first-ever teaching round. I was excited but anxious, so to keep calm I concentrated on my breathing. I was down for lesson one, two and three! I was, needless to say, fairly nervous. 'This must be ordeal by fire,' I thought to myself.

My stomach was churning and I was beginning to wonder what I was about to undergo. First up would be Chemistry. Yay! The excitement was giving way to fear as the minutes ticked by. I snapped to attention the second my supervising teacher came to collect me on his way to class. The waiting was over. 'OK, here goes. It can't be that bad surely.'

I followed my supervising teacher across the yard to the classroom. 'So how do you think you'll go?' he asked. 'Oh, OK,' I said a little hesitantly. Then I blurted, 'But I am really nervous!'

When we arrived at the class he introduced me and wrote my name on the board. It was spelt wrong! Then he squinted, his eyes focusing in on me, and I looked down sheepishly.

'Now', he started, 'Be nice to Miss. She's a bit nervous.' Twenty-six pairs of devilish and now intrigued eyes turned on me. Aagh! Am I even the size of an ant? I don't think so.

This anecdote comes from the student teachers' perspective, but in teaching about teaching, there are times when the demands of teaching and learning are equally as frustrating and contradictory for the teacher educator. Dick Gunstone offered the following anecdote as a vivid memory of just such a situation.

Because the Teacher Says

They were a great group — mostly! All but Mary. I found her to be rather prickly, and, judging by some of the interesting group dynamics, it seemed that the rest of the group had somewhat similar feelings. It was therefore a little reassuring to think that it wasn't just me.

Mary's major problem with me and the other group members was her inability to hear ideas that did not agree with the position she already held. We were about four months into the course, and the students had had their first taste of teaching. Three weeks with their own classes isn't a lot, but it had given most of them a sense of reality. I was into my third or fourth group session of interactive, discussion-based consideration of all this research about the ideas children bring to science classes. We had even dropped the magic term 'alternative conceptions' and had linked this with notions like 'superficial learning' and 'passing tests but not learning'. Now we were looking at teaching approaches and materials produced by science teachers I had been working with for a number of years.

It all got to be too much for Mary. 'I don't care what you say. When I tell kids something, they will believe me because I am the teacher.'

That was too much for me. My response was, unfortunately, not delicate. 'Well I'm the teacher here and I say you are wrong!'

Notice, of course, that Dick's response failed to take Mary's position as an 'alternative conception', and in a situation such as this, a constructive response would have been extremely difficult. Perhaps teaching about teaching is inevitably problematic simply because teaching comprises a complex array of skills, attitudes, actions and meanings. Because teaching prospective teachers demands time, effort and commitment, perhaps it is not a field that is easy to study or understand. Perhaps this is why models of imparted learning underlie most traditional pre-service teacher programs (Sumison, 1996). Perhaps it is simply easier to 'tell' prospective teachers how to teach than it is to model for them how to learn about teaching and to design experiences that reveal the inner nature of teaching. In this context, the importance of documenting the purpose, passion and pedagogy of teacher educators becomes increasingly important.

At a time when teachers' professional knowledge is starting to be recognized and valued in both the teaching profession itself and in Faculties of Education, we find it important to also recognize the goal of teacher educators' professional knowledge: enhancing pre-service teachers' pedagogical knowledge, practice, reasoning and development. In a recent paper in which Hargreaves (1996) 'revisits voice', he concludes that there are important reasons why teachers' voices need to be represented and heard through educational research. His third point, '. . . that as a principle of professionalism, we should not dismiss or diminish the words of wisdom of trained individuals . . .' (p. 16) is particularly compelling and equally appropriate for researching teaching in teacher education.

In this collection, we have assembled the insights and understandings of a range of teacher educators who share a commitment to the importance of pedagogy in teacher education. They all associate pedagogy with both purpose and passion. We see each author as committed to the ongoing development of personal understanding and practice in teaching about teaching, and in so doing, as better able to help student teachers prepare themselves for the problematic nature of teaching throughout their teaching careers. Not only did each prospective author respond positively, but, following an initial meeting at the AERA meeting in New York, each also worked quickly to produce a full draft of the book in very short time. Their commitment to teaching about teaching was translated directly into their commitment to articulating and disseminating their ideas clearly and on time — perhaps that old and important teacher trait of getting work back on time still lingers.

The contributors to this volume represent a range of levels and types of experience in teacher education, from method lecturers to program directors. All consider their involvement in pre-service education to be important in shaping the purpose, philosophy and approach to teaching that will challenge their student teachers. They are also pedagogues who continue to reflect on their own practice as they strive to create better learning about teaching opportunities for their students of teaching. Although it may once have been the case that, 'teachers of teachers — what they are like, what they do, what they think — are typically overlooked in studies of teacher education' (Lanier and Little, 1986, p. 528), we hope that the contribution by the authors in this book demonstrate why teachers of teachers, their knowledge and practice, can no longer be overlooked.

References

BORROWMAN, M.L. (1965) 'Liberal education and the professional education of teachers', in BORROWMAN, M.L. (Ed) *Teacher Education in America: A Documentary History*, New York, Teachers College Press, Columbia University.

HARGREAVES, A. (1996) 'Revisiting voice', *Educational Researcher*, **25**, 1, pp. 12–19.

LANIER, J.E. and LITTLE, J.W. (1986) 'Research on teacher education', in WITTROCK, M.C. (Ed) *Handbook of Research on Teaching*, 3rd ed., New York, Macmillan Publishing Company.

LOUGHRAN, J.J. (1994) 'Professional development for science teachers: A school based approach', *Science Education International*, **4**, 4, pp. 25–8.

SCHÖN, D.A. (1987) *Educating the Reflective Practitioner: Toward a New Design for Teaching and Learning in the Professions*, San Francisco, Jossey-Bass.

SUMISON, J. (1996) 'Empowering beginning student teachers: Challenges for teacher educators', *Asia-Pacific Journal of Teacher Education*, **24**, 1, pp. 33–46.

VAN MANEN, M. (1994) 'Pedagogy, virtue, and narrative identity in teaching', *Curriculum Inquiry*, **24**, 2, pp. 135–92.

VAN MANEN, M. (1995) 'Pedagogical politics?: Political pedagogy?', in MIEDEMA, S., BIESTA, G., BOOG, B., SMALING, A., WARDEKKER, W. and LEVERING, B. (Eds) *The Politics of Human Science*, Brussels, VUBPRESS.

Section 1

Principles and Practices Which Shape Teaching about Teaching

2 Practicing Theory and Theorizing Practice in Teacher Education

Robert V. Bullough, Jr.

Introduction

Principles emerge from practice; we practice our principles, and in practicing and confronting our limitations often we discover just what those principles are. And so the initial question posed by the editors of this volume, 'Why teach teachers as you do?' necessitates a two-phased response, beginning with practice and ending with principles, guiding assumptions or fundamental beliefs, which, hopefully, wraparound and inform and sustain my practice. The first phase inevitably takes a biographical turn because practicing teacher education, like other teaching relationships, involves testifying — to teach is to testify; to bear witness of a way of being in and understanding the world; a life is an argument — and because, like teachers, teacher 'educators' work . . . appears to be significantly shaped by prior experiences' (Hatton, 1994). I begin, then, with a story that represents my initial grounding, the argument I brought with me to teacher education. Then I address their second question, 'What principles underpin your practice?' and their third, 'How do I know what I do makes a difference?'

Grounding in Biography

I never intended to be a teacher. I was not called to teach. Growing up my father was a junior high school art teacher who always worked at least one, and usually two, jobs after school in order to take care of his family. He scooped ice cream. Swept floors. Pumped gas. My mother saved change, ever hoping to purchase a needed item, a piece of furniture, a lamp, tires for the car. A penny saved was a penny earned. Frugality was a necessary virtue. We ate a good deal of macaroni and cheese — the high cholesterol kind, orange and slippery. Lacking adequate medical insurance, a small accident could spell disaster. I broke a collar bone, my sister broke an arm, and months of payments followed. No, I had no desire to be a teacher; and my father did his part to steer me elsewhere.

The Viet Nam War loomed over and stood in the way of my efforts and those of other young men to realize what Levinson and his colleagues (1978) called 'The Dream', a dream of the 'kind of life they want to lead as adults', a vision 'of self-in-adult-world' (p. 91). Many a young man's Dream was cut short in far away rice paddies. Like many others of my generation, I became increasingly disillusioned with the prospects of working in government service and corporate America was out; no one dreamed there. My academic studies shifted from ancient history to South Asian studies as though it was a natural move, a fateful slide that was supposed to be. All the while, I wondered what to do, what the future did hold for me, assuming there would be a future after my draft deferment ended.

By default, I enrolled in an education course. Although I did not want to be a teacher, when compared to other options teaching seemed noble, an honorable vocation driven by a service ideal that resonated deeply. Ironically, the implicit vow of poverty that had so profoundly and negatively impacted my family only added to teaching's nobility. The course was dreadful. The professor was inexperienced, overly concerned with appearing professorly but the cap sat awkwardly, and the gown hung uncomfortably. It was a bad role play. Options limited, I enrolled in additional education courses, which only added to my growing disillusionment. Reconsidering my options, I decided to withdraw from teacher education.

I clearly recall sitting in a methods course taught by Flo Krall, drop card in my shirt pocket. I only needed her signature and I was out of there for good. I approached her and waited as she addressed other students' questions. My turn came, she looked up, and before I could say a word, stated in her direct, no nonsense, way, 'I've been watching you.' I remember wondering what I had done. I expected trouble. She asked if I would like to complete the certification requirements by working in an alternative program she had recently begun in a local high school for 'disaffected' students. Initially stunned, I jumped at the offer, and not only because it signaled the end of my formal, and to that point dreadful, teacher education. Call it fate or call it synchronicity with Jung, but at that moment my life changed.

Within days I found myself working at East High School with three other university pre-service teachers, half days, in an evolving program that had no other purpose, initially, than to provide something of educational value that would keep thirty students in school. There were no clear policies to guide our work. If there were administrative boundaries, we only discovered them after crossing over. Drawing on Paulo Freire's book, *Pedagogy of the Oppressed* (1972), we began exploring ways of organizing curricula thematically. No topics were off limits, at least none I can recall. Topics arose from the students — war, power, sex, ecology — and flowed into one another as we sought to locate content and create the conditions needed to realize our incipient understanding of critical consciousness. Friendships developed. Issues were confronted. Students stayed in school. It was, in the parlance of the time, an educational 'happening'.

That Spring I failed my draft physical — freed to dream. That Fall I was hired to direct and continue to teach in the program. Eventually, we worked with two groups of about thirty or thirty-five students, one group in the morning and the other in the afternoon. In addition to curriculum development and administrative responsibilities, I worked with pre-service teacher education students who, like me the year before, were seeking certification. I did all this despite being virtually ignorant of teacher education, which seemed at the time a kind of virtue, not a vice.

Interdisciplinary teams were formed that assumed responsibility for planning and implementing the curriculum with the public school students. The curriculum evolved but continued to be organized thematically. At times, visitors from the university who were interested in the program would remind us that our units needed to be purposeful, that we had a tendency to get overly excited about an activity or a unit just because it was engaging and not because it was educationally powerful. Happenings were that way. Reminiscent of early attacks on progressive education in the United States, we sometimes engaged in activity for activity's sake. Our intention was to create a responsive curriculum, one within which the students would feel a measure of ownership and find place. This intention aside, sometimes we lost our way and the aim of producing an engaging curriculum shoved aside more educational purposes, ones associated with helping students gain the intellectual tools and understanding needed to meaningfully make their own ways in the world.

After two years I quit. Perhaps I became overly involved in the lives of my students. I found myself engaging in a good deal of student counselling, without training, testifying in court, working with and visiting parents and parole officers and much more. The program consumed me. I had chronic headaches. Although to the end the work remained exciting, I realized I needed a change; failing to pace myself, I flickered, and burned out. I left East High School somewhat puzzled by what had happened to me but still believing that teaching was a noble profession, one that could improve the wider society. Increasingly, I found myself interested in social theory and in the role of schools in society.

I enrolled in a Ph.D. program at The Ohio State University to pursue a degree in foundations and curriculum. This move was prompted by a number of factors, and not only the realization that a degree in history emphasizing South Asian studies was not worth much. Even while teaching art, my father had continued his formal university studies. After twenty-three years of college he completed a doctorate and assumed a position as an assistant professor of education. His excitement about research touched me. Then there was Flo Krall, whose professional life — more a life force — exemplified praxis. She was a formidable presence, one who understood deeply the social responsibilities that attend professing and the importance of providing contexts within which younger people can confront and perhaps transcend their own limitations. Her interpersonal style was unique, simultaneously confrontational yet nurturing. Together with sizeable chunks of my father and of Flo, I took with me to Ohio parts of several of my teachers and professors whose lives testified that ideas matter and have social consequences.

Just prior to leaving for Ohio, I received a phone call from a faculty member at Ohio State who informed me that prior to the beginning of the school year a series of meetings would be held to plan the curriculum for the methods course I would be involved in teaching as part of my assistantship. He used the word 'competency', and my heart sank. I knew what that word meant, and that the intention was to develop a list of skills, complete with performance indicators, that would serve as the objectives for the course. 'The student will be able to . . .' was and still is foreign to my way of thinking. Program aims would be established in advance, and, ignoring Dewey's profound discussion of the relationship of aims and means, means would be prescribed. Controlling learning outcomes was the aim. Themes? Interdisciplinary units? A responsive curriculum? All nonsense, or so I feared. I debated whether to withdraw and go to one of the other schools interested in having me as a student but, being a person who must read a book to its end, and despite my misgivings, I packed my few belongings and headed east for Columbus, Ohio.

Once there, I soon discovered that I was not alone in my misgivings. While some faculty were anxiously working to develop a competency-based program, others had serious doubts, among them Paul Klohr, who became my advisor. Themes, interdisciplinary units, and a responsive curriculum all made sense to him. He admired Freire, and being historically grounded in the work associated with the Eight Year Study (Aikin, 1942) and the lab school at Ohio State (see Alberty and Alberty, 1962; University School Faculty, 1952), he could nudge my thinking along in fruitful ways. He pushed me, for example, to read extensively in the history of American progressivism and in curriculum theory and development. Moreover, he was exploring work in continental philosophy and was chewing at the edges of the disciplines, seeking deeper insight into the personal and philosophical foundations of education (Klohr, 1978). He was especially interested in the problem of meaning making, of hermeneutics. Well before the constructivist revolution, Klohr understood that meaning is constructed and constructed in terms of past experience, a point first understood, I suspect, through his careful study of the writings of John Dewey and Boyd Bode.

Having lived long enough to see this competency movement fade, and eventually return in the different guise of outcome-based or performance-based education, I am less ruffled by the winds of change than I was when I first arrived in Columbus. Mercifully, winds shift and a few educators have memory enough to recognize it.

Graduating from Ohio State, I assumed a position at the University of Utah, my home, as an assistant professor in the Department of Education. The foundations faculty was housed in Educational Administration, so I soon found myself living schizophrenically. Formally, educational foundations were separated from methods courses. Mostly I taught a skills-based course like the one I had taught at Ohio State. The program itself was disjointed. Students often and rightly complained of redundancy and irrelevance. Professors, like their students, dropped in and out of the program, and no faculty member was responsible for helping students make sense of what was happening to them. Continuity was lacking, but more importantly, so was caring. Unlike my experience at East High School, I felt disconnected. I had difficulty even remembering student names from one quarter to the next, let alone feeling connected to them in any significant way. Yet I feared spending too much time with them because of needing to prove myself as an academic through publishing and at least appearing somewhat expert, when clearly I was not. Expertise encourages disengagement and distance. Like my first education professor, mine was a bad role play.

In his study of teacher education, *Teachers for our Nation's Schools* (1990), John Goodlad accurately and painfully portrayed the problems of teacher education in research institutions, problems I came to know well. Within universities the norms of the arts and sciences dominated, and in the pursuit of an illusive prestige, education faculty often distanced themselves from teacher education and the concerns of teachers. Adjunct faculty increasingly bore the burden of teacher education. External agencies set teacher education policies and there was comparative little 'curricular autonomy' (Goodlad, 1990, p. 93). Programs lacked coherence. Relationships with schools were often strained, and placements were made for practice teaching with comparatively little regard for cooperating teacher quality. Preparation programs did little to influence the beliefs and expectations about teaching that beginning teachers brought with them: 'Their preparation programs are simply not powerful or long enough to dissuade them from what has already been absorbed from role models' (Goodlad, 1990, p. 149). Little attention was given to socializing students to a professional ideal; surprisingly little attention was given to the moral and ethical issues that ought to command the attention of educators. As I said, foundations and methods were separated. Instead, the values of individualism dominated: 'They come through their preparation as individuals . . . likely to take responsibility only for their individual classrooms and assume that someone else will take care of the rest' (Goodlad, 1990, pp. 265–6). Students entered and left their programs with a 'very practical orientation — an orientation that leads them to judge all education courses by utilitarian, instrumental criteria' (Goodlad, 1990, p. 213). Accordingly, the 'socialization process appeared to nurture the ability to acquire teaching skills through experience rather than the ability to think through unpredictable circumstances' (Goodlad, 1990, p. 215). Technique mattered, and learning to fit into and survive within 'an operational role in the classroom' mattered most (Goodlad, 1990, p. 251).

These were, and to a degree still are, the problems of teacher education. They certainly were weaknesses of the program within which I served. But at that point I did not think of myself as a teacher educator. They were not *my* problems. My research interests had taken a turn and in the late 1970s and early 1980s I was part of a study group that slowly and carefully worked its way through the writings of Karl Marx and then those of Jurgen Habermas. We produced a book, *Human Interests in the Curriculum: Teaching and Learning in a Technological Society* (1984), and also a few papers that sought to ground the insights we were gaining in a critique of schooling. Central to our argument was that the desire for control embedded in instrumental reason and expressed in the pursuit of ever more powerful teaching techniques, had overwhelmed and undermined the concern for education and human emancipation. Marx's discussion of alienation and of species being were especially important to our analysis, as were Habermas' concepts of human interests and of the 'ideal speech situation', where the aim is communication without domination (Habermas, 1979).

I began teaching introductory foundation courses following a merger of the foundations faculty with the education department and the formation of a new Educational Studies Department. But mostly I continued to teach curriculum and methods courses. The more I taught, the more frustrated I became. Eventually I realized I could not flee teacher education, that the problems of the program were, after all, *my* problems. There was no escaping that conclusion, which was forced on me not only by my teaching assignment but also by my study of Marx and critical theory. Theory could not be separated from practice; there was no escape. I knew this, Dewey and Boyd Bode had taught me this lesson before, but knowing the good and doing it are not the same: 'It is a good divine that follows his own instructions: I can easier teach twenty what were good to be done, than be one of the twenty to follow mine own teaching' (Shakespeare, *Merchant of Venice*, Act I, Scene II).

Ironically, in 1983 I was elected chair of secondary education and, almost despite myself, became intimately involved in program development. Through the dean's efforts, the department became involved in the early days of the Holmes Group, which brought numerous opportunities to further think about teacher education. Just prior to becoming chair, the program had been reorganized around cohorts of students. Secondary education students would stay together for a year and, under the guidance of a professor and a teaching associate, would complete curriculum and methods courses, practice teach, and participate in a weekly problem-solving seminar. This was the program I administered. My first 'cohort' proved to be a difficult teaching assignment, but I became increasingly interested in the problems of teacher education, especially of how to integrate social theory and methods. This lesson I had learned when doing a section of my dissertation on Bode: 'educational practice which avoids social theory is at best a trivial thing and at worst a serious obstruction to progress' (1937, p. 74).

Spending a year with a group of students inevitably forced me to attend to developmental issues. I noticed that some students seemed able to ignore what I taught while others grabbed hold of it easily, as though what I had to say confirmed but failed to challenge beliefs. While struggling with this issue, I began exploring the role of life history as the backdrop against which students become teachers. Paul Klohr planted that seed when I was a graduate student, a seed that grew in the hands of the reconceptualists in curriculum theory (Pinar, 1975) and has since grown mightily (Richardson, 1996).

My second cohort changed me, fundamentally. I bonded with this group quickly. I found myself heavily invested in their learning and in their school successes. Their disappointments became my disappointments. I worked very hard with, and on behalf of, this group but when the year ended I felt a measure of disappointment, although I did not know why. After school ended, and while on the way with my family to vacation in West Yellowstone, I decided to conduct a case study of one of the students in the cohort as a way to begin rethinking my work. Returning home, I contacted Kerrie Baughman and began the series of studies that led to the publication of *First Year Teacher: A Case Study* (1989). I also completed a series of essays that formed *The Forgotten Dream of American Public Education* (1988), which was an attempt to settle my thinking about education and to present foundational issues in ways accessible to beginning teachers and others interested in education. Other studies followed, most notably *Emerging as a Teacher* (1991), that involved writing a series of case studies of first-year teachers along with meeting them in a weekly seminar to discuss their concerns. From each study I learned a great deal, and simultaneously the problems of teacher education became more intriguing. I also began gathering data from students in my cohorts, and I used the data to rethink content, instruction, and class organization. With my students I openly explored what we were doing and why and solicited feedback and criticism. Exit interviews were conducted and written evaluations invited. A series of articles resulted from this work, some touching on life history and others with teaching metaphors as means for helping beginning teachers think about themselves as teachers (Bullough, 1991). Still others explored what I came to call Personal Teaching Texts (PTTs), case records of a sort, as means for helping beginning teachers take greater responsibility for their development and for building program coherence (Bullough, 1993). The initial focus on metaphors came from spending a year and a half in Kerrie Baughman's classroom and coming to realize how central nurturing and mothering were to how she thought about teaching. Only later would I realize that others were working along similar lines. Recently, the results of this work were brought together in a single volume *Becoming a Student of Teaching: Methodologies for Exploring Self and School Context* (1995), written with Andrew Gitlin. By 1990 I realized I had become a teacher educator, almost despite myself.

Private Theories and Principles

Telling this story as a way of beginning to address the question 'Why teach teachers as you do?' was necessary because actions become meaningful by placing them in a narrative, or a narrative form, by imposing order. The order we impose is grounded in the beliefs we hold, the tacit knowledge (Polanyi, 1958) that underpins our sense of the world, our world view. To create a story is thus to engage in narrative reasoning, which plays a central role in a teacher's efforts to create a teaching self, a moral orientation to the world of which we testify when we teach. Principles come later.

> Personal identity can be brought to self-awareness through narrative self-reflection. Self-knowledge not only assumes that one can establish one's own personal identity by means of stories, but also assumes that one can be accountable narratively for how one has developed as a person — for how one has become what one has become. . . . Self-knowledge is related to the search for one's own life story. Thus, by engaging in such narrative 'theorizing' teachers may further discover and shape their personal pedagogical identity, and through such stories they can give accounts of the way they have developed over time into the kind of persons they are now. (Van Manen, 1994, p. 159)

Story telling, then, is a way of getting a handle on what we believe, on the models, metaphors and images that underpin action and enable meaning making, on our theories. Through story telling, personal theories become explicit, and in being made explicit they can be changed, where change is warranted, and a new or different story results; we behold differently. The 'critical root' of the word theory, as

Robert Coles reminds us is '"I behold", as in what we see when we go to the theatre' (1989, p. 20).

It is important that theory emerge from practice, as David Hunt observes, because 'unless theories come from practice, they will not apply to practice' (1987, p. 109). Hunt's assertion presents a problem, however. In teacher education, a gulf divides theory from practice, as Goodlad's study demonstrated so forcefully. It is common among teacher educators to talk about the need for linking theory with practice, yet foundations courses continue to precede field work; those who teach these courses seldom venture into the field. We speak of learning from experience but not *in* experience. Those who spend a majority of their time working in the field with beginning teachers often speak as though time spent in schools equates with learning, forgetting Dewey's insights that for experience to have educational value, one must 'extract its net meaning' through reflection (Dewey, 1916, p. 7) and that not all experience is educative, indeed some experiences are 'miseducative' and impede future growth (Dewey, 1938, p. 13). Doing without 'undergoing the consequences of doing' does not count as experience at all (Dewey, 1916, p. 323). Consequences matter because it is through attending to them that theories are tested, as Dewey remarked: 'An ounce of experience is better than a ton of theory simply because it is only in experience that any theory has vital and verifiable significance' (Dewey, 1916, p. 169). It is little wonder the preponderance of evidence suggests that when making instructional decisions teachers rarely value and perhaps seldom draw upon the kind of theory — what Griffiths and Tann (1992) call 'public theory' — that is presented to them in teacher education. Ironically, there is good evidence to suggest that teacher educators similarly ignore public theory and instead rely on personal experience and implicit theory, on common sense, when making decisions (Hatton, 1994; see also Eisner, 1984). Like our students, we face the daunting challenge of becoming our own best theorists, as Hunt would say, and this requires attending to our experience as teacher educators and reflecting on it.

My story points in the direction of an answer to the question, 'Why teach teachers as I do?', but a richer response necessitates digging into the story to uncover theories that underlie my practice, my principles. While the principles I identify initially arose from thinking about my practice, my experience of being a teacher educator, it is important to note that public theory has played a prominent part in nurturing, refining, and in some cases undermining them. Public theory has on occasion helped me to know what to look for and helped me better to see, to anticipate consequences. Freire's *Pedagogy of the Oppressed* played such a role early on when I taught at East High School, and Dewey's writings, among others, continue to challenge and to inspire my thinking as is readily apparent from what I have written here. Through seeking an active conversation between private and public theory, played out in my classroom, I have come to behold teacher education more richly and more fully, albeit still only partially. It is for this reason that Dewey asserted that 'Theory is in the end . . . the most practical of all things, because [of the] widening of the range of attention beyond nearby purpose and desire . . .' (Dewey, 1929, p. 17).

The following set of principles arise from my experience and underpin my work which is driven by one fundamental aim: to help prepare teachers who are disposed to be students of teaching, who are morally grounded in the practice of education as the practice of freedom, who are at home with young people, and who possess the skills and knowledge needed to design potentially educative environments characterized by civility, inviting the young to work at the edge of their competence. At present, my principles include these:

1   Teacher identity — what beginning teachers believe about teaching and learning and self-as-teacher — is of vital concern to teacher education it is the basis for meaning making and decision making. Teachers, like Flo Krall, teach themselves. Teacher education must begin, then, by exploring the teaching self.

2   Because selves are formed in context, the exploration of teacher identity necessitates the study of schooling and the wider social context and the ways in which those contexts both enable and limit meaning, privilege and suppress knowledge (Bullough, in press). One hears the echoes of various critical theorists here.

3   To identify ways in which contexts enable and limit meaning requires an understanding of social philosophy and the aims of education in a democracy.

4   Reflecting a life-time investment, self conceptions are deeply resistant to change, as my determined flight from the problems of teacher education illustrates. Yet self-study can be risky and is fraught with danger. Teacher education must be powerful enough to challenge beliefs that potentially might be miseducative in their effects, while the immediate context of teacher education must be supportive and respectful of the individual as an adult learner fully capable of making reasonable judgments about his own learning and the direction of that learning.

5   Part of building a trusting and respectful learning environment is to openly articulate the reasons lying behind program decisions. Purposes, I have learned, must be explicit and open to scrutiny before they are found compelling.

6   All education is ultimately indirect, as Dewey argued; teachers can create the conditions for learning while learning itself is the responsibility of those who chose either to embrace or reject the opportunity. Many of my students have rejected my offerings but some, I have discovered, find value in them later.

7   Educational outcomes are inevitably unpredictable and aims flexible. While there may be a minimal level of acceptable student performance in teacher education, the most important learning outcomes will be personal, idiosyncratic, and probably unmeasurable. There is no one best teaching style, personality or model that can serve as a standard for evaluation. Competency models inevitably oversimplify teaching and impoverish teacher education and teachers. Nevertheless, quality judgments of some

kinds must be made because of teachers' ethical responsibilities to serve young people.

8   Each person makes teacher education meaningful in her own way, a point illustrated by my story and in each of the case studies I have written of beginning teachers.

9   Program continuity is not just a matter of sensibly sequencing courses and content but of creating means that enable students to forge their own sense of continuity through attending, systematically and over time, to their experience of teacher education and development as teachers. This point is consistently supported by the richness and diversity of the Personal Teaching Texts my students produce.

10   Coming to feel part of a profession not only requires learning the language of teaching but learning and applying it with others who are similarly invested in professional education and in situations that have genuine educational consequences.

11   To teach is to testify and also to care about, converse, and connect with others whose experiences differ from our own. To teach is to enable boundary crossing while seeking to build a sense of belonging to a wider and ethically grounded community. Lastly, and now going outside the story presented, seeking to develop teaching skills and eventually artistry in teaching necessitates opportunities to teach, to test and explore methods and techniques under the guidance of thoughtful teacher-critics while at the same time engaging in ongoing data-driven self-evaluation.

Operationally, these eleven principles, taken as fundamental working assumptions, are not distinct. They intertwine. The cohort organization provides the context within which the principles find expression and plays an important role in creating the 'shared ordeal' (Lortie, 1975) so often missing in teacher education. Although disconnected from work done in the subject matter areas, which is unfortunate, the considerable amount of time given to the cohort has enabled a measure of experimentation impossible under other conditions. Moreover, experimentation has been encouraged by a kind of institutional benign neglect. Within this context and with the involvement of the students themselves, it has been possible to explore questions of purpose, content, and process.

The Principles in Practice

The curriculum is composed of content, activities, and processes or methodologies, each grounded in the principles as I currently understand them. The formal content includes published research, methods materials, a Personal Teaching Text — a student produced case record — (Bullough, 1993), and written and video cases. Running across the year, the methodologies which often require work in the field, include writing life histories, metaphor analysis, student shadow studies, interviewing teachers, classroom ethnographies, textbook analysis, action research, peer observation of, and conversation about, teaching, and writing a periodic Review of the products of the other methodologies to assess professional development and the direction of that development (see Bullough, Knowles and Crow, 1992, Chapter 10; Bullough and Gitlin, 1995).

Life History

The year begins with students writing life histories as a point of departure for self-study. These are not elaborate literary creations, but are intended to get the students thinking about how they have come to hold their current beliefs about teaching and themselves as teachers. This chapter begins with part of my life-history. The assignment reads as follows:

> Write an 'education-related' life history. In the life history describe how you came to your current decision to become a teacher. Especially identify important people or 'critical incidents' that significantly influenced your decision and your thinking about the aims of education, the proper role of teachers, and about yourself as teacher. Consider your 'experience of school', how school felt, and how you best learned and when you felt most valued, connected, and at peace — or least valued, most disconnected and at war with yourself and with school.

The life histories are discussed, shared, and themes identified that hold out the possibility of challenging student views of teaching. They become the first entry into the Personal Teaching Text, and are returned to throughout the year.

Metaphor Analysis

Drawing on the life histories, students are asked early in the year to identify and describe a Personal Teaching Metaphor that captures the essence of how they think about themselves as teachers. With secondary education students expert metaphors are very common. Nurturing metaphors are also prevalent. Throughout the year we return to the metaphors which are updated to reflect current thinking. Through discussing and comparing metaphors and changes in metaphors students are helped to think about their thinking about themselves as teachers, to consider factors influencing their development, and to entertain alternative conceptions of teaching. The later point is particularly important for students who have only vague or contradictory conceptions of the kind of teacher they wish to become. Such persons appear especially vulnerable to institutional pressures to conform (see Bullough, Knowles and Crow, 1992).

Through this work, I was prompted to explore my own teaching metaphors, which revealed something of a struggle between the desire to be a conversationalist and at times function as an expert (Bullough and Stokes, 1994). Teaching is conversation is a particularly powerful metaphor in part because, as John Dewey remarked at his 90th birthday party, democracy begins in conversation — so does professional community.

Student Shadow Studies

Teacher education students shadow a public school student seeking to capture a portion of what the school day is like for students and to recall their own lives as students. They are expected to shadow students quite unlike themselves. The studies are used as a basis for considering and criticizing current school practices and for identifying the sources of student satisfaction and dissatisfaction and for making comparisons of school experience. Such comparisons are crucial to boundary crossing. Factors that make for good teaching and student learning are identified and explored in relation to some of the available research literature.

Teacher Interviews and Classroom Ethnographies

To begin participation in the professional conversation of teachers, early in the year and after observing a variety of teachers, students interview a potential cooperating teacher (the list of teachers available to serve as cooperating teachers is limited, and approval of the building principal and cohort leader is required before a placement is finalized. Depth of experience is valued over breadth so students work in a single school for the entire year). Aside from facilitating conversation, the purpose of the interview is to identify sources of satisfaction and dissatisfaction with teaching in anticipation of a more careful study of the work context. In addition, the interview enables the student to compare and contrast his thinking with the teacher being considered as a cooperating teacher. Again, the results of the interviews are shared and comparisons made between teacher views and student-teacher conceptions of teaching and learning.

The study of the context of schooling begins with a classroom ethnography. The writing assignment reads as follows:

> Ethnography, simply stated, is the 'work of describing a particular culture' (Spradley, 1980, p. 3). The challenge is to grasp how those within a culture understand it, how they make sense of their experience. Identify a class that you will be student teaching and that you find interesting or challenging. Your task is to gather data through observations, informal and formal interviews, and whatever other ingenious means you can come up with, that will enable you to describe how the classroom environment is understood and recreated by the teacher and students. What are the *formal* and *informal rules*, the *norms*, that give order do the classroom? In what ways are they enabling and limiting of meaning? What roles do the students and the teacher play and what is the relationship of these roles to one

another? How do the students and the teacher experience the classroom? What are the key words, metaphors, ideas, concepts, that they use to give meaning to the classroom and to structure their experience? Try to get *underneath* surface appearances by asking not only what do I see these people doing, *but what do these people see themselves doing?*

Additional directions and helpful hints are given. The focus initially is on understanding how roles are negotiated and bounded and then attention is shifted to identifying ways in which cultures can be shaped and changed, made more or less friendly to teacher conceptions of good teaching.

With some cohorts, the classroom ethnography has been introduced by videotaping a portion of a class session, viewing the video, and then exploring the guiding questions as they relate to my teaching. Although a bit threatening, the results are inevitably interesting. Such an approach has the added benefit of underscoring for my students that I am seriously studying my practice.

Textbook Analysis

Given the prevalence of textbooks in American education and of how profoundly they influence the curriculum and teaching, teacher education students obtain a textbook or a curriculum guide commonly used in their area of expertise. Using a set of guidelines, they criticize the text seeking signs of bias, and identify and explore assumptions about teaching, learning, and the good life embedded within it. The aim is to help them develop a set of conceptual tools useful for becoming critical consumers and producers of curricula.

Action Research

To enable the study of practice, students practice teach half, not full, day. Encouraged to work in teams, students identify and frame an issue and go about the complicated process of gathering data through a variety of means, including audio and video-taping, peer and cooperating teacher observation, questionnaires and reviews of pupil work, and proposing, implementing, and evaluating a plan designed to ameliorate the problem or build on perceived strengths. Students understand that I collect data on my own teaching as a means for better understanding my practice in order to improve it and that I expect them to do the same now and in the future.

Peer Observation and Conversation

During winter term when students engage in a short-course during which time they teach a unit to a class in anticipation of student teaching and in student teaching itself, they observe one another teach and talk about their observations. Electronic mail is a tool we are exploring as a means of extending and enriching this conversation. The students are observers, not critics. When they share observations the aim is to explore their practice in relationship to their intentions. An exception to this is when peer observation is used as a means for gathering data for an action research project.

Personal Teaching Text

All the written work from the year is gathered to form a Personal Teaching Text (PTT). At the end of each quarter the students are asked to review their texts, and assess their development and its direction. A recent Review assignment read as follows:

> Re-read the contents of your Personal Teaching Text for the entire year. Based upon this reading, assess your development as a teacher. Are you pleased with what you have accomplished so far? Any disappointments? Has your resolve to become a teacher strengthened or weakened? Why? Has your view of yourself as a teacher changed during the course of the year? If so, what has prompted the change? If not, why not? Are you on course for becoming the kind of teacher you imagine yourself capable of becoming? Be specific, and give examples.

The Personal Teaching Text is a record of development, one that seems to help them become increasingly responsible for their own professional growth, to recognize the value of teacher education, and to bring a sense of closure to their preservice preparation (see Bullough, 1993).

How Do I Know It Makes a Difference?

I have been deeply troubled from time to time by the question, 'What difference does it make?' This concern, joined with the inevitable hope that my work had value, led me to begin the ongoing study of my practice. Here I mention just a few studies. Based upon an analysis of student work, interviews and questionnaires, Bullough and Stokes (1994) presented strong evidence that students not only changed as they progressed throughout the cohort year, but changed in some dramatic ways. Their conceptions of teaching became increasingly complex and sometimes sophisticated. Their views of student learning and understanding of students similarly became more complex. Naive optimism about themselves as teachers was replaced by a more mature self-confidence, an outcome prompted by the ongoing study of teaching metaphors, a method that was judged useful by nearly all of the twenty-two student participants. Moreover, twelve of the students presented evidence of engaging in critical reflection, where they attended to issues that required that they step outside of themselves for a time and think about education contextually.

Case studies of my students have demonstrated the importance of the focus on self in teacher education, and how issues related to self profoundly influence the experience of the first year of teaching (Bullough, 1992; Bullough, Knowles and Crow, 1992). In Bullough and Baughman (1993) we explored how metaphors evolve over time and in relationship to life history and school context and how ongoing teacher education may influence this development. Evidence from this study underscores that powerful teacher education requires the joining of pre-service with in-service teacher education.

As already noted, exit interviews are conducted routinely with students who complete the cohort, and I send anonymous follow-up questionnaires to obtain additional data. Data from one of these questionnaires, sent out in November during the first year of teaching to a group of recent cohort graduates, follows. This questionnaire was sent in part in response to the challenge of Gary Fenstermacher, issued in his presidential address to the American Association of Colleges for Teacher Education. He asserted that in the face of the overwhelming power of the 'systemics' of schooling on beginning teachers, colleges of education should 'diminish [their] involvement in pre-service teacher education and increase . . . involvement in in-service teacher education' (Fenstermacher, 1992, p. 5). 'Systemics' are the socializing and legitimating functions of schooling including grading, tracks, tests, texts and the like. They are the 'forms and structures, processes and procedures, put in place to carry out the business of schooling' (Fenstermacher, 1992, p. 2). Systemics emphasize training over education. Fenstermacher doubted that pre-service teacher education was worth the investment. In response, I found myself wondering anew if what I did had value. Thus I chose November — three months after the beginning of the school year — to send out the questionnaire because I thought that many of my former students would still be struggling with systemics. I thought some would feel overwhelmed and that they might be especially critical of the program and doubtful of its value. I worried about what I might discover.

The questionnaire was sent to seventeen students. One student could not be located. Fifteen questionnaires were returned. Included in the questionnaire were items intended to identify the power of 'systemics' in shaping these teachers' thinking and practice during the first few months of the school year. My expectation was that systemics would be the dominating concern, issues of establishing control and fitting into the school, yet I hoped there would be evidence of holding onto and working toward the attainment of more educational purposes. Items also sought to identify if there was a preferred teacher role in the school and whether or not the role, if there was one, was congenial — consistent with the teacher's conception of self as teacher. Additionally, information was sought that described how the beginning teacher responded to the discovery of tension between an institutionally preferred role and the teacher's professional and personal identity, their metaphor(s). Questions asked the beginning teachers to judge the value and influence of the cohort. And finally, questions were asked that sought indirect evidence about whether or not these former students still felt a sense of connection to their cohort colleagues and of professional community.

The first cluster of questions asked the beginning teachers to rate on a 1 (negligible) to 7 (very high) scale the value and influence of the cohort experience. The first question read, 'Rate the overall value of the cohort experience.' Results were as follows: The mean was 5.5; the median six; and the mode seven. There was one three rating and six seven ratings. The second question read, 'Rate the influence of the cohort experience on *how* you now think about teaching.' For this question the mean was 5.7 and the median and mode six. The third question read, 'Rate the influence of the cohort experience on your teaching practice.' The mean for this question was 5.9, the median six and the mode seven.

The beginning teachers were asked to rank in 'order of priority . . . the three most helpful activities or assignments undertaken in the cohort. The results of this question were surprising. I had expected that all would mention student teaching, but eight did not. In fact, sixteen different responses were given that ranged from a unit on cooperative learning to the focus on metaphors, the Personal Teaching Text and even the Life History assignment. Perhaps the question was ambiguous, and some students did not think of student teaching as an 'activity', but this seems unlikely. Additional data are needed to illuminate this apparent anomaly.

Question 13 stated: 'Identify your most serious teaching problem or concern at the beginning of your first year of teaching (please explain).' And Question 14 stated: 'Identify your most serious teaching problem or concern now (please explain).' The idea was to see if there had been any change in concerns or problems. I anticipated that virtually all the beginning teachers would say that systemics — discipline and management, specifically — were primary early concerns. I wondered if there would be any sign of an increased emphasis on educational concerns with the passage of time. Fourteen of the fifteen beginning teachers mentioned management or discipline related issues in response to question thirteen. The one exception appears indirectly related to systemics. Although not clear, this beginning teacher seemed concerned about classroom authority. These results were expected.

Six of the beginning teachers mentioned concerns related to systemics in their responses to Question 14, but nine did not. For the six, grading (including issues of fairness), lesson pacing, and firming up initial management plans dominated. The others mentioned a range of concerns that relate more directly to the educational purposes of schooling. Responses included, 'making the lessons [more] understandable', creating a better, more productive, classroom climate, setting up better science labs, 'making the content fun for students', 'planning meaningful lessons that teach something worthwhile for students', and motivating lower level students. These results were somewhat surprising. In part they suggest that for some of the beginning teachers, systemics, while still undoubtedly claiming a good deal of energy, has diminished in importance and energy was being directed toward the educational purposes of schooling: These teachers seemed to be thinking seriously about the educative ends of teaching. The responses to the first cluster of questions relating to the value and influence of the cohort, and Question 11, that will be discussed shortly, suggest that there is at least indirect evidence that the cohort had a hand in bringing about this shift in concerns.

Question 17 asked the following: 'In your school is there a preferred teaching role? If so, what is it? What is your relationship to this role (Does it fit you? Have you created a different, perhaps contrary, role for yourself?' The responses revealed remarkable diversity, suggesting that context differences matter a great deal. In one school, for example, the beginning teacher reported having difficulty with a dominating administrator and being unwilling to fit into the role of 'teacher as Gestapo'. She reported that she was functioning as a 'quiet rebel', seeking to maintain her ideal of herself as a teacher and shape the work context. In the same school, another beginning teacher characterized the preferred teaching role as that of 'strict disciplinarian'. She stated: 'This role does not fit me, but I understand why most of the teachers [buy into it]. Some of the kids are amazingly horrible, mean, rebellious. I find myself fitting into this role more and more, though I'm not sure I like it . . .' Another reported that the preferred role emphasized student involvement, and that this role 'fits. . . . However, I am not as involving as I wish to be because of the amount of time necessary to prepare such lessons.' Eleven reported either that there was no preferred role or if there was one they had not yet discovered it. Typical comments included, 'The English Department head is great about letting everyone do their own things' to 'teachers have a great amount of autonomy, and I feel I fit into my school well'. These beginning teachers felt, in varying degrees, that they could become the kind of teachers they imagined themselves becoming during the cohort, although they were aware of having to make some compromises. Several reported that the focus on self in the cohort was a source of strength and confidence as they sought to establish themselves in a new role.

Finally, Question 11 asked if they were in contact with other cohort members. With the exception of two beginning teachers (one of them took a job out of state), all fifteen teachers (including one teaching out of state) answered that they had been in contact with others. Some met frequently to share experiences and work together developing curriculum. Friendships were formed through the cohort, but more importantly it appears that a sense of community was built that has extended into the first year of teaching and eased the transition, somewhat. However, whether a wider conception of community will emerge is uncertain.

Admittedly, the data from the questionnaire are more suggestive than convincing but, when coupled with other cohort-related research, I have good reason to continue pushing along the lines presented here. The principles, of course, are subject to revision as I continue to act and undergo and think about the consequences of my action, as I experience teacher education and seek to make my experience more fully educative. Soon the university will be moving from a quarter to a semester system and, with changing structures, I will have additional opportunities to reconsider my work. The public schools within which we place students are also changing as we struggle to better understand what a professional development school might contribute to pre-service teacher education (Bullough *et al.*, in press). By necessity and by design, I have become a student of teaching and teacher education. The work has become more interesting and challenging than I ever imagined it could be, especially when I think back to when I was fleeing from it. I am now convinced that the future of teacher education is dependent on the willingness of teacher educators to practice theory and to theorize our practice and to put the results of our efforts before a frequently hostile public. We must make a compelling case that what we do has value.

References

AIKIN, W.M. (1942) *The Story of the Eight-year Study*, New York, Harpers.

ALBERTY, H.A. and ALBERTY, E.J. (1962) *Reorganizing the High-school Curriculum*, 3rd ed., New York, Macmillan.

BODE, B.H. (1937) *Democracy as a Way of Life*, New York, Macmillan.

BULLOUGH, R.V.JR. (1989) *First Year Teacher: A Case Study*, New York, Teachers College Press.

BULLOUGH, R.V.JR. (1991) 'Exploring personal teaching metaphors in preservice teacher education,' *Journal of Teacher Education*, **42**, 1, pp. 43–51.

BULLOUGH, R.V.JR. (1992) 'Beginning teacher curriculum decision making, personal teaching metaphors, and teacher education,' *Teaching and Teacher Education*, **8**, 3, pp. 239–52.

BULLOUGH, R.V.JR. (1993) 'Case records as personal teaching texts for study in preservice teacher education,' *Teaching and Teacher Education*, **9**, 4, pp. 385–96.

BULLOUGH, R.V.JR. (In press) 'Self and social location of teacher education,' in BIDDLE, B.J., GOOD, T.L. and GOODSON, I.F. (Eds) *The International Handbook of Teachers and Teaching*, Dordrecht, The Netherlands, Kluwer Academic Publishers.

BULLOUGH, R.V. JR. and BAUGHMAN, K. (1993) 'Continuity and change in teacher development: First year teacher after five years,' *Journal of Teacher Education*, **44**, 2, pp. 86–95.

BULLOUGH, R.V.JR. and GITLIN, A. (1995) *Becoming a Student of Teaching: Methodologies for Exploring Self and School Context*, New York, Garland.

BULLOUGH, R.V.JR., GOLDSTEIN, S. and HOLT, L. (1984) *Human Interests in the Curriculum: Teaching and Learning in a Technological Society*, New York, Teachers College Press.

BULLOUGH, R.V.JR. and STOKES, D.K. (1994) 'Analyzing personal teaching metaphors in preservice teacher education as a means for encouraging professional development,' *American Educational Research Journal*, **31**, 1, pp. 197–224.

BULLOUGH, R.V.JR., KAUCHAK, D., CROW, N.A., HOBBS, S. and STOKES, D.K. (in press) 'Professional development schools: Catalysts for teacher and school change,' *Teaching and Teacher Education*, **13**, 2.

BULLOUGH, R.V.JR., KNOWLES, J.G. and CROW, N.A. (1992) *Emerging as a Teacher*, London, Routledge.

COLES, R. (1989) *The Call of Stories: Teaching and the Moral Imagination*, Boston, Houghton Mifflin.

DEWEY, J. (1916) *Democracy and Education*, New York, Macmillan.

DEWEY, J. (1929) *The Sources of a Science of Education*, New York, Horace Liveright.

DEWEY, J. (1938) *Experience and Education*, New York, Macmillan.

EISNER, E. (1984) 'Can educational research inform educational practice?,' *Phi Delta Kappan*, **65**, 7, pp. 447–52.

FENSTERMACHER, G.D. (1992) 'Where are we going? Who will lead us there?,' Presidential address to the annual meeting of the American Association of Colleges for Teacher Education, February.

FREIRE, P. (1972) *Pedagogy of the Oppressed*, Harmondsworth, Penguin.

GOODLAD, J.I. (1990) *Teachers for Our Nation's Schools*, San Francisco, Jossey-Bass.

GRIFFITHS, M. and TANN, S. (1992) 'Using reflective practice to link personal and public theories,' *Journal of Education for Teaching*, **18**, 1, pp. 69–84.

HABERMAS, J. (1971) *Knowledge and Human Interests*, Boston, Beacon Press.

HABERMAS, J. (1979) *Communication and the Evolution of Society*, Translated by Thomas McCarthy, Boston, Beacon Press.

HATTON, E. (1994) 'Work experience as a solution to the problems of relevance and credibility in teacher education,' *Australian Journal of Education*, **38**, 1, pp. 19–35.

HUNT, D.E. (1987) *Beginning with Ourselves: In Practice, Theory, and Human Affairs*, Cambridge, MA, Brookline Books.

KLOHR, P.R. (1978) 'Emerging foundations for curriculum theory,' *Educational Considerations*, **6**, 1, pp. 17–19.

LEVINSON, D.J., DARROW, C.N., KLEIN, E.B., LEVINSON, M.H. and McKEE, B. (1978) *The Seasons of a Man's Life*, New York, Alfred A. Knopf.

LORTIE, D.C. (1975) *School-teacher: A Sociological Study*, Chicago, University of Chicago Press.

PINAR, W. (Ed) (1975) *Curriculum Theorizing: The Reconceptualists*, San Francisco, McCutchan.

POLANYI, M. (1958) *Personal Knowledge: Towards a Post-critical Philosophy*, Chicago, University of Chicago Press.

RICHARDSON, V. (1996) 'The role of attitudes and beliefs in learning to teach,' in SIKULA, J. (Ed) *Handbook of Research on Teacher Education*, 2nd ed., New York, Macmillan, pp. 102–19.

SPRADLEY, J.P. (1980) *Participant Observation*, New York, Holt, Rinehart and Winston.

UNIVERSITY SCHOOL FACULTY (1952) *A Description of Curricular Experiences: The Upper School*, Columbus, Ohio, The Ohio State University.

VAN MANEN, M. (1994) 'Pedagogy, virtue, and narrative identity in teaching,' *Curriculum Inquiry*, **24**, 2, pp. 135–70.

3 Teaching Teachers: How I Teach IS the Message

Tom Russell

Introduction

I am a teacher who teaches teachers. When I use that description to introduce myself, it always seems awkward, highlighting the complexity, the ambiguity, and the apparent contradictions of the enterprise of teacher education. This chapter is an account of how I teach teachers, why I teach them that way, and how I came to hold the views and display the practices I do. To start at the beginning makes as little sense as starting at the end. And so I begin somewhere in the middle, work my way back to the beginning to indicate the origins of some of my beliefs and practices, and then return to the present, acknowledging debts and treasured connections made along the way.

I write to the people I teach, about their work and my own work. One significant piece of writing more than four years ago was rediscovered recently by virtue of the fact that a beginning physics teacher, Paul Tarc, from my 1991–2 class, returned to Queen's in 1995–6 as a full-time M.Ed. student after three years of teaching. In 1991–2 I taught a physics class in a local high school (Frotenac Secondary College). Paul had watched me teaching in the school and had offered some thoughtful critiques of that teaching. In so doing, Paul also made it clear to me that he attended carefully to his own learning experiences. My final assignment each year in my science methods course is to write a personal 'story of learning to teach'. It seems to be an unusual assignment, and I tell those in my class that I want them to have it so that in two or three years' time they can look back and see how far they have progressed since their pre-service courses and teaching experiences. Here is what I wrote to Paul in 1992, in response to elements of his 'story of learning to teach' assignment:

> The obvious point, then, as I look at it, is that save for exceptional people like you (and we should learn from the exceptions!), people come [to teacher education programs] to be told how to teach X so that they can go forth and teach X for the next thirty-five years and collect their pensions and retire from teaching X. The TELLING cycle can't be broken, for most people. I like to think I've broken it myself, but I don't think I did when I was teaching at Frontenac! I've figured out how to break it in the McArthur

[McArthur Hall, the building which houses the Faculty of Education at Queen's University] context, but all around me are enough colleagues who still follow the TELLING cycle so that I have no assurance that the signal I'm trying to send appears as signal rather than noise when all is said and done.

[There is] an interesting dilemma in your reluctance to make anything of the practice teaching rounds. 'Mini-experiences' is a good way to describe them. I guess you are pushing me to say to myself that, until we get a truly different practicum arrangement, we are not going to produce people who have learned to teach before they get their own full-time classes, and we are not going to produce people who understand what has happened to them. It is so much more than length of time in a classroom, though what I dream of can't happen in two or three weeks. Two months is probably a minimum. And time alone won't do it. [Teacher candidates] had three months in England, but they didn't do anything with it. The Waterloo people are very different, but little is being done with their time in schools, so again what could happen is not. Unless we train people to do things that will document and show them what is happening to them in the world of practice, and then make something of the data when they return from practice, I'm going to continue to fall short of my goal of having the profession understand where its knowledge comes from. When I try to push that goal at experienced teacher educators, it comes across as noise — it doesn't mean anything.

I find this piece from my personal 'paper trail' fascinating because it confronts me with some of the key features of my teaching as it has evolved over my twenty-two-year teacher education career:

- I began my work in pre-service education with the challenge of doing less 'telling' how and what to teach than most teacher educators seem to do in their teaching. A group of experienced teachers sensitized me to this issue just before I moved into pre-service work.
- I returned to the secondary school classroom in a significant way (one-third time, for two half-years) in 1991–3 (after twenty-four years away from it!). I fell far short of my own 'ideals' for science teaching, and I learned a great deal about what I am trying to help new teachers to learn.
- Understanding how we learn from experience continues to be a fundamental theme in my approach to teaching people how to teach.
- My view of the importance of 'understanding where our knowledge comes from' is one that I try to practice myself, as this excerpt illustrates. Four years ago, I had no way of knowing that, at the 1993 AERA conference, the Self-Study of Teacher Education Practices (S-STEP) Special Interest Group would be formed, and that I would see the pre-service program at Queen's University transformed, profoundly, to a design with 'early extended teaching practice' that promises to remedy the 'making something of the experiences' shortcomings that I mention in my letter to Paul.

I try to be a teacher educator who walks his own talk. Only recently have I begun to recast this to see that, in the special context of learning to teach, the most powerful initial influence on each new teacher's classroom practices may be the millions of images of teaching that go with them into the practice teaching setting. Against these images, there is little hope for significant influence from any generalizations about learning they may have drawn from their own student experiences. Cultural maxims (such as 'Don't smile until Christmas' or 'Keep it simple') may be remembered, but I see little hope for influence from what I *say* in class or what teacher candidates *read* in books and research about good teaching. Recently I have found it useful to think in terms of getting our practices to catch up to what we say and write, and to catch up to what we say we believe about teaching and learning. It is also a matter of learning how to make our beliefs influence our practices, recognizing all the while that the central matter is 'listening to our practices' — learning what words mean when we express them in our actions, and learning what ideas do to the people we are teaching. These are major challenges for experienced teachers and teacher educators. Those who are new to teaching may not even see the issue, because they have not had access to the experiences of teaching that are essential to understanding just how easy it is to separate actions from beliefs and goals at the front of a classroom.

Collecting 'Backtalk' by Early Necessity: Why Do Teachers So Rarely Ask Directly for Students' Comments about the Learning Experience?

When I started at Queen's in 1977–8, I had two classes of twenty-five to thirty people in secondary science methods. The room was a 'pedagogical nightmare', with eight huge lab benches firmly fastened to the floor, and a central corridor leading to the front, where a ninth 'demonstration' bench blocked the route to the chalkboard. Simply to get closer to the people I was teaching, I moved to the back of the room where there was a smaller but closer chalkboard. After only a few weeks, I sensed that my students were having reactions I needed to know about that were not being vocalized to me. In fact, this was one of my earliest reactions to pre-service teaching: it was so lacking in any kind of evidence of how my teaching would ultimately affect their teaching. I began to invite groups of five or six people for pizza at my home, where I could hear about, and we could discuss, the confusions I was creating by deliberately reducing the amount of talking I did.

Later, I found ways to collect 'backtalk' on paper and share it with my students, and I invented (for myself) a 'mid-course evaluation' in which people supplied strengths, weaknesses, and suggestions. These were compiled, printed, and returned at the next class for all to read and discuss. It became a powerful way of showing them how many features of teaching are appreciated by some but not by others. I also found that the data were vital to establishing an 'agenda' that I very much wanted to introduce, but which seems rare in most teaching: 'Why does the teacher teach in particular ways?' The mid-course evaluation became an important opportunity for me to raise a new set of issues for the remainder of the course. Students did not always accept my explanations, but they respected them and could learn more from my classes once they had started to think about why I was doing (and not doing) things in particular ways. The classic comment came in December, 1978, during the discussion of the mid-course evaluation, when one particularly frustrated individual demanded, in a tone verging to frantic, 'Why didn't you *tell* us you weren't going to *tell* us?' The irony was obvious, both in the question itself and in the fact that I *had* told them but they had not known what my words meant. I continue to emphasize small-group discussion and leadership from within the group, but that comment convinced me, forever, just how powerful and important it can be to resist the basic teacher tendency to fill classroom silence with talk. Of course all teachers do this because they have seen all their own teachers do it.

Master of Rote Learning: Do Most People Never Realize that Alternatives Exist?

How much of what we do as teacher educators is in reaction to our own experiences of schooling? Don't most of us enter the profession to make teaching even better than the teaching at which we were so successful? Don't teachers who move into teacher education do so to improve the process of learning to teach? As I look back, it is fairly obvious that I was good at mastering 'school knowledge'. I completed secondary school in New York State, where the long-standing system of 'Regents exams' continues almost forty years later. In each course, the mark on the New York State Board of Regents examination in a subject was my final mark for the course. For some reason I have never parted with the copy of the April 1959 issue of *American Heritage* magazine, given to me by the man who taught me American History in Grade 12. A small card inside states, 'To the highest Senior in American History Regents in June, 1959. Tom Russell, 98 percent.' Although I did not see it that way at the time, having the highest average in my graduating class meant that I had fairly good skills of 'rote learning'. Science and mathematics were my most obvious strengths, so how do I explain the success in history? I can still remember my history teacher explaining that if we memorized his thirty-four outlines for common topics on the Regents examination, then we would be well prepared for any essay question that might be presented to us. I must have taken him at his word. In 1993, when I returned to Cornell University for a conference thirty years after completing my first degree, I sat in the quadrangle where statues of Ezra Cornell and Andrew Dickson White face each other, and made notes to myself about how little I had understood the learning process itself and about how dependent I had been on recall rather than conceptualization of what I was trying to learn. A course in American History at Cornell had quickly 'brought me up short' as I discovered that I was expected to know several different interpretations of a set of events, along with the names of the individuals who developed them. Memory was no longer the key; understanding mattered. It was little wonder, then, that my early years of teaching (1963–7) saw me fascinated by the 1960s critiques of learning in schools. Today, in my science methods classes, I am far more likely to be asking questions such as 'What is the point of teaching density?' and 'Now that we have demonstrated what happens, what's the point?'

Teaching without Formal Pre-service Teacher Education: Only Teaching Experience Can Generate the Essential Learning-to-Teach Questions

From Cornell, I stepped directly into the Peace Corps, five months before JFK was shot. As Africa's most populous country, Nigeria was a prime destination for volunteers who could teach, and experience or formal training were welcome but not required. Physics was a scarce subject, so off I went to Nigeria, wondering where my first meal would come from. My two-month training program was held in New York City, and preparation for teaching was only a modest part of the overall 'orientation' to a new set of cultures. Two weeks of each of three different languages was more than my rote learning skills could master. The training program did provide me with two opportunities to stand before children taking Summer school courses in science, but I seem to remember more about the elevators to get us out of the subway station than I do about those first moments of teaching. In Nigeria, my students and I survived my 'teaching myself how to teach' — an experience that confirmed that virtually anyone with more than fifteen years of experience as a student has seen enough of teaching to be able to make 'teaching-like moves' at the front of the classroom. Some of my earliest teaching moves were horrendous, yet I doubt that prior training would have made a big difference. I remember starting with science and math to the younger students, and one day in a math class I said something that caught their attention but not mine. When algebra teachers need examples with letters other than x, they usually choose y and z, but no one had told me that Nigerian English, like the Queen's, required me to say 'zed' rather than 'zee' when I worked a problem on the board. This was hardly a profound issue, but it certainly mattered to my students! Once I moved into a decently equipped science lab to teach physics, I had no hesitation about making good use of the equipment, but I did not understand the importance of helping students make sense of their lab data. Today, Peter Chin and I speak of the difference between 'What?' and 'So what?' but then I think I worked with a sense that the phenomena somehow 'spoke for themselves' and made a case on their own for the law or theory being illustrated. Some physics teachers may recall a refraction experiment (in the unit on light) in which pairs of straight pins are used on both sides of a rectangular glass block to infer the path of the light ray through the block. It was one thing to show students how to line up the pins, and it was quite another to know how to unpack the assumption that light travels in straight lines. In hindsight, I was fortunate to begin my science teaching with students who had, I eventually learned, an innate scepticism about western science. In a non-western culture, there are many non-scientific explanations for natural phenomena, and these can predispose students to doubt the truth of what the science teacher sees so clearly. My own career as a student had never suggested the possibility that learning could involve multiple sets of explanations for the same events; small wonder that the external examinations tended to yield high failure rates. In western culture, students learn 'H_2O' as a substitute for 'water' long before they could possibly know its chemical meaning. In Nigeria, they had every reason to ask what such a term could possibly mean, yet they had no guarantee that their teacher would reward their scepticism.

When I returned from Nigeria to do my teacher education in an M.A.T. program at Harvard, I had two important reactions. I realized that I had many more questions than my colleagues who had no prior teaching experience, and I realized that it would have been wonderful to experience that program of pre-service education after just one year of teaching. I kept thinking how differently I would have taught in my second year, just completed in Nigeria. In the summer of 1966, after finishing at Harvard, John Holt published 'The Fourth R — the Rat Race' in the *New York Times Magazine* on a Sunday when I happened to buy the newspaper. Holt was teaching in a private school on Commonwealth Avenue in Boston, and I managed to make telephone contact with him and then meet him at the school. I still have my $1.85 paperback copy of *How Children Fail* (Holt, 1964), the book that had a profound influence on my next year of teaching, in 1966–7. In hindsight, Holt's ideas on 'Fear and Failure' and 'Real Learning' became the first 'theory' that I tried to express in my teaching 'practice'. This was not theory in a formal research sense, but 'theory' in the form of conclusions about learning drawn from personal teaching experience. Here is a paragraph marked as one that I noticed thirty years ago, before starting my third year of teaching:

> The invention of the wheel was as big a step forward as the invention of the airplane — bigger, in fact. We teachers will have to learn to recognize when our students are, mathematically speaking, inventing wheels and when they are inventing airplanes; and we will have to learn to be as genuinely excited and pleased by wheel-inventors as by airplane-inventors. Above all, we will have to avoid the difficult temptation of showing slow students the wheel so that they may more quickly get to work on the airplanes. In mathematics certainly, and very probably in all subjects, knowledge which is not genuinely discovered by children will very likely prove useless and will be soon forgotten. (Holt, 1964, p. 125)

It was the era of discovery learning, and I was teaching from the second edition of the PSSC Physics course. Holt speaks about mathematics teaching, but the wheel-and-airplane example transfers readily to the physics context. Holt's issues and examples were powerful ones for a new teacher, simply because I had never thought about 'slow students' and how teaching them might mean more than 'slowing down the pace of my teaching'. I recall clearly saying over and over again to my students that year: 'What matters most to me is what you are going to remember about these ideas five years from now.' That was my personal translation of Holt's message, intended to signal that I really did want to focus on 'real learning'. I still do. Perhaps that indicates one of the reasons why some teacher candidates find my approach 'less than comfortable'. If a teacher educator aims for the long haul while a new teacher seeks only the basics needed for the next teaching assignment, missed messages become more and more likely in both directions.

In-service Teacher Education before Pre-service Work: A Captive Audience Working for High Grades Cannot 'Talk Back'

My career in teacher education began with three years (1974–7) at the Ottawa Valley Field Centre of the Ontario Institute for Studies in Education, where I worked closely with David Ireland and others on short-term and long-term activities for teachers and principals. Three years with an in-service focus before any pre-service experience convinced me of a powerfully important difference between the two: when teachers can vote with their feet, they will! Ongoing in-service work is only ongoing as long as the teachers feel that their time invested is justified in the value of the activities. Pre-service teacher education is fundamentally different because those learning to teach are enrolled in university programs and cannot 'vote with their feet'. I was astonished when I learned that some of my colleagues made attendance compulsory or included attendance as an element of their marking schemes. Yes, I believe each and every one of my classes is important, and I try to make each one as valuable and productive as possible. Yet it is important to me that teacher candidates be able to 'vote with their feet' in the ways that university students usually assume that they can. Increasing numbers of absences can be the clearest indication that something is not right and there are issues to be addressed sooner rather than later. In such situations, teacher educators have an invaluable opportunity to model how a teacher can deal with such a situation, and a range of issues come to mind:

- How can a teacher respond most constructively when 'problems' become apparent?
- What prevents students from speaking directly about their concerns?
- What are the risks to students and teacher, and when do the risks outweigh the potential benefits?

I have dim memories, as well as vivid ones, of times when I explored these issues in front of my classes, with no idea whether the result would be positive or negative. In 1995–6, the mid-course evaluation in my M.Ed. course on action research seemed to provide a way to move forward, but something went wrong as I tried to unpack the issues the class had expressed as strengths and weaknesses in our first six weeks. Although we all felt set back by that discussion, the positive and constructive responses from the class members in the following weeks led, quite unpredictably from my perspective, to an intense and successful conclusion for many in the group. Our journey into assumptions about teaching and learning had moved many people forward in their personal understandings of the complexities of teaching.

Research on Reflective Practice (Schön) and the Authority of Experience: Learning Is *in* the Experience, and Reflection *Can* Link Learning Back to Action

I began teaching pre-service courses (in secondary science methods) in 1977, and by my fourth or fifth year at Queen's I had a basic pattern established that got me from one end of the academic year to the other without major protests to the Dean's office or major shortcomings on my course evaluations. My attention continued to focus on the theory–practice interface in teacher education: Does what *we* do in 'the crystal palace' (where it all sounds so easy) have any impact on what *they* do in classrooms? I developed ways of encouraging the people in my science methods course to tell me about their experiences in practice teaching placements, and their honest replies were clear: practice teaching is what matters, and so does the style of the associates or cooperating teachers who receive them into classrooms, share resources, and offer their voices of experience.

In 1983, I read Schön's (1983) *The Reflective Practitioner* just before my first sabbatical leave; I treasured the opportunity to work with those ideas in another setting, with 'space' away from the intense experiences of my first six years of pre-service teaching. My first research grant followed soon after, and since 1985 Hugh Munby and I have pursued a series of research grants related to the development of teachers' professional knowledge. Funding from the Social Sciences and Humanities Research Council of Canada continues to be a treasured resource that facilitates progress with new ideas, perspectives, and practices. By 1988, Hugh and I were using the phrase, 'the reflection is in the action', to express our sense of Schön's much-debated 'reflection-in-action', which we interpret as indicating that coming to see events of practice in new ways is a first step which must be followed by expression of that new perspective in changed practices. More recently, we have begun saying 'the learning is in the experience', rather than 'from' the experience. If we think of learning as something that 'happens later', then we shortchange ourselves and those we teach. The 'here and now' is what we share and what we have to work with. What we learn can always be reinterpreted later, but it is important that people leave any and every class with a sense that they have learned something.

One of the great flaws in my own interpretation of the history of teacher education relates to this issue. We speak to teacher candidates as though they can understand our words as we do, yet they have little experience of teaching to guide their understanding of, or to promote their challenging of, what we say. Then we wonder later why they have 'difficulties' with their earliest teaching experiences. When this happens, I tell myself that what they learned was not what I intended them to learn, and I reassess my own teaching with a view to designing in-class events and experiences that will generate more of the learning I intend. Of course, critiques of teaching in schools seem to deal with similar issues.

Action Research — From the Ford Teaching Project and Douglas Barnes to Jack Whitehead, Jean McNiff, and the Ontario Public School Teachers' Federation: Teacher Research by and for Teachers Is Coming of Age

My earliest introduction to Action Research came from the work of John Elliott and Clem Adelman on the Ford Teaching Project in England in the mid-1970s. That work is still classic in its respect for teachers' thinking about their work and in its efforts to show what is possible in thinking about teaching (Elliott, 1976–7). I encountered this work as I was engaging in 'in-service work before pre-service teaching', in which we were showing several groups of teachers how to study their own teaching (Ireland and Russell, 1978). As they came to understand their teaching, they became eager for 'respectable alternatives' to 'traditional' teaching in which curriculum content is presented, practiced, reviewed and tested. Douglas Barnes (1976) had just published *From Communication to Curriculum*, and his accounts of the potential benefits of students working in small groups appealed to many of the teachers. Barnes' contrast between 'transmission' and 'interpretation' still influences the thinking of many who work in teacher education. The work of Barnes and of Elliott and Adelman supported my growing interest in teachers' abilities to understand their own practices, and paved the way for my eager response to Schön's (1983) *The Reflective Practitioner* six years into my work in pre-service programs.

For reasons that remain unclear, I did not follow closely the literature of action research in education and teacher education during the 1980s. I knew it was there, but no individual contributions or personal contacts drew me in. In 1992, I 'reconnected' with Action Research by meeting Jack Whitehead (University of Bath, UK) in Stanford at a Teacher Research conference related to the imminent publication of *Teacher Research and Educational Reform* (Hollingsworth and Sockett, 1994). A conference on 'teacher research' seemed unusual and promising. While that conference and the associated book are, in my view, early 'landmarks' in the field of teacher research, it was Jack Whitehead who provided me with a personal reintroduction to action research. His frequent asking of the question, 'How can I improve the quality of my students' learning?' always strikes me as going to the heart of what every teacher and teacher educator should be asking. Jack has introduced me to a range of people in England, including Pam Lomax and Jean McNiff, who with Jack are co-authors of *You and Your Action Research Project* (McNiff, Lomax, and Whitehead, 1996). Jack has been able to join me in supporting exciting developments in action research in my own province of Ontario, where the Ontario Public School Teachers' Federation has just completed a stimulating and promising one-year project encouraging teachers to explore the potential of action research in their classrooms (Halsall and Hossack, 1996).

**Returning to the Physics Classroom, Twice:
Why Didn't I Think of It Sooner?**

What is teaching? Only in recent years have I paid particular attention to the way beginning teachers seem predisposed, by most of their experiences as students, to assume that a teacher's greatest challenge is to be able to answer every question students may ask. Perhaps many teacher educators make that assumption, just as many teachers do. Six history teachers in Ottawa in 1976 taught me otherwise, and the lesson fits with my interpretation of my own past as student and teacher. Most teachers quickly become very good at answering all the questions, far better than they were when writing examinations themselves. How do you keep the challenge in teaching once you can answer all the questions? For me, the essential challenge of teaching follows from realizing that teaching's greatest mystery is the fact that we have no control over what our students make of what we say and do as we teach, and this is as true for learning to teach as it is for learning subjects. In teacher education, it may be far more important to be able to 'tune in' to, and work with, each individual. After at least fifteen years at school and university, and perhaps years of experience in other work settings, the intending teacher is a unique 'bundle' of experiences, images, and beliefs about teaching. While coming to understand one or more disciplines accumulates over most of two decades, the transition to teaching is usually limited to a year or two. I incline increasingly to the view that I need to know as much as possible about each individual with whom I work.

A sabbatical leave at the University of York (UK) provided access to practices and experiences of pre-service teacher education in a different social and political context, stimulating extensive questioning of a program structure that had become quite familiar. Re-entering the physics classroom personally appeared to be an appropriate and promising professional move, and I was fortunate to be able to make the administrative arrangements quite easily. When I returned to the physics classroom, seventy-five minutes every day from September 1991 through January 1992, and again in 1992–3, I discovered that I first had to prove to myself, my students, and the other science teachers in the school that I could cover the curriculum and achieve the same class averages that they could. Beyond that, and much more fully in the second year, I was able to focus on what the physics students were making of the curriculum and what the beginning teachers in my physics methods class were constructing from my teaching — in a school and at the university. Interestingly, that group of new physics teachers in 1992–3 gave me some very frustrating messages about what they were making of my teaching in two contexts, one of which was intended to help them bridge the gap between theory and practice. To make sense of their backtalk, I began to think of 'barriers to learning to teach' which, in varying degrees, exist between the students themselves and their pre-service teacher education program experiences. In summary form, those barriers are as follows:

1   Teaching can be told.
2   Learning to teach is passive.

3   Discussion and opinion are irrelevant.
4   Personal reactions to teaching are irrelevant.
5   Goals for future students do not apply personally during teacher education.
6   'Theory' is largely irrelevant to learning to teach.
7   Experience cannot be analyzed or understood.

While the majority of teacher candidates disagree with most of these statements if asked directly for reactions, their own *actions* in my classes appear to contain at least some elements of these statements, and those who are least happy with my teaching tend to be those who enact those 'barriers', even as they may disown them in what they say and write. These barriers to understanding what is required in the actions of learning to teach tend to be consistent with society's views of teaching (as an 'easy' profession) and with the images of the relationship between words and actions conveyed in school and university classrooms. Returning to the classroom to teach the same course twice had a profound impact on how I understand my own work with new teachers (Russell, 1995a, 1995b, 1995c). I realized that the teaching role I enacted was very different from the one to which I aspire and hope that new science teachers will eventually enact. I lived and breathed the countless constraints on teaching options that fade when one's teaching experience is limited to teaching within 'the crystal palace', as one teacher fondly described the Queen's University Faculty of Education. That 'crystal palace' reality is changing as this book goes to press, as we pilot a new pre-service program design with sixty-two individuals prior to expanding it to all 700 teacher candidates in 1997–8. On September 3, 1996, at a 7.30 am staff meeting prior to students arriving for the first day of school, six new teachers and I were introduced to a school staff of seventy, and the new teachers began the first day of fourteen weeks of teaching that will precede most of their course work in education. I am truly fortunate to work in an organization that is enacting many of the principles that I have discovered for myself over two decades.

Backtalk, P.O.E. and PEEL: Teaching Is Long Overdue for Shock Treatment

I know of only one sustained 'assault' on the general assumptions about teaching and learning that I have been trying to question and challenge in my own teaching practices over the years, and that is the Project for Enhancing Effective Learning (Baird and Mitchell, 1987; Baird and Northfield, 1992) centred in the state of Victoria in Australia. This project seeks to unite teachers and students in having students take more responsibility for, and assuming a more active role in, their own learning. The project appears to be a forerunner of the growing interest in teacher research and action research in education. When a group of teachers in one school joined together to encourage 'good learning behaviors' as antidotes to students' 'poor learning tendencies', their professional lives were touched forever, and not always positively. Changing the patterns of teacher–student and student–student interaction is no easier in Grade 3 or in Grade 10 than it is in a teacher education classroom. Yet the initial ideas of the project have stood the test of time and spread to a network of schools that take turns producing issues of a newsletter, *PEEL SEEDS*, now in its thirty-fourth issue of alternative teaching strategies and associated student work.

'Backtalk' is a strategy quite consistent with encouraging more personal responsibility for learning, and providing backtalk to teachers certainly would count in my book of good learning behaviors. The single most powerful strategy that I have taken from PEEL that I can use readily in my teaching is the 'P.O.E.', short for Predict–Observe–Explain. While it may be most easily described in the context of science teaching, it can be applied across the school curriculum. Science classes often involve demonstrations in which students are given opportunities to observe phenomena as an explanation is given. Observations are selected for the students by the teacher, and so the students' sense of involvement and engagement is often quite limited. The P.O.E. strategy involves having the students make predictions before they are permitted to observe the phenomenon, and the effect of this apparently modest change can be very dramatic, even shocking! However, in addition to this, the explanation part of this strategy is also very important. No matter whether the prediction is correct or incorrect, the participants need to explain their prediction in light of the observation. Hence, the total P.O.E. strategy causes an engagement in understanding the phenomenon beyond that which is 'normal' for a classroom demonstration. In fact, some of my fondest memories of my classes relate to times when those I am teaching generate a P.O.E. experience for the class and my own personal prediction is shown to be incorrect. For example, in last year's class, two people prepared identical balloons inflated to different levels and then clamped off, but the balloons were connected by a piece of tubing. They asked for predictions of what would happen when the clamps were released so that air could move freely between the balloons. I was very sure that the air would move so that the balloons would both become the same size, and so I was speechless when they released the clamps and the small balloon shrank, increasing the size of the larger one.

Do backtalk and P.O.E. merit the term 'shock treatment'? Is that what teaching and teacher education require? In teacher education, as in teaching at any level, our responsibilities as teachers include understanding how people learn and change, treating learners with respect, and accepting responsibility for helping individuals and groups to learn more about their own learning. Is it unkind to suggest that the teaching strategies most of us remember focused on (1) getting us to think we understood, and (2) getting us to think that learning is easy? I see backtalk and P.O.E. as samples of simple, elegant, cross-curricular teaching strategies that can bring refreshing winds of change to any teaching-learning context. They appeal because they focus on the unexpected, which is often the trigger for new understandings. Backtalk, P.O.E., and similar 'shocking' strategies have much to contribute to teacher education.

The Content Turn and then the Pedagogical Turn: Learning to Teach Is a Two-step Process

While John Loughran was visiting Queen's University for the Fall term of 1995, he paid me the professional compliment of sitting in on every class I taught that term. Our discussions afterwards were among the most exciting of my career because they were about my personal practices as well as the general issue of how we help teachers learn to teach. One day's discussion led to the idea that becoming a teacher educator (or teacher of teachers) has the potential (not always realized) to generate a second level of thought about teaching, one that focuses not on content but on *how* we teach. Most people who begin a teaching career seem to focus, naturally and understandably, on *what* they teach. Most seem to report that the earliest years of teaching a subject (or age group, if elementary) generate significant rethinking of subject matter (or how children of a particular age think about their world, across the curriculum). I began to refer to this, in the secondary context, as the 'content turn', following Schön's (1991) 'reflective turn'. People who move on to work in a teacher education context must continue to think about how teaching affects one's understanding of what one teaches, but a new dimension also appears. When individuals find themselves recommending particular teaching strategies for particular purposes, they start to realize that their own teaching must be judged similarly. This new perspective constitutes making the '*pedagogical turn*', thinking long and hard about *how* we teach and the messages conveyed by how we teach. This began to happen to me in 1977 when I wanted to model 'less teacher talk' to new teachers, who were accustomed to being taught by teachers who did most of the teaching.

I have come to believe that learning to teach is far more complex than we have ever acknowledged within teacher education or within society generally. The content turn seems to come naturally, because preparing and presenting familiar material to those who find it unfamiliar seems to lead most people to 'fill in the gaps' in their own understanding of a topic. The conditions for entering into and surviving the pedagogical turn are far less clear. Little is written about it, few people seem to talk about it, and many teacher educators seem not to recognize its significance. Perhaps these three conditions are interrelated. There is and always will be a 'content' of teacher education, and teacher educators will make a content turn as they come to terms with presenting that content. For some, and perhaps for many, that may be enough. Others go further, moving beyond the various content pieces of the formal teacher education curriculum to begin to make the pedagogical turn, realizing that how we teach teachers may send much more influential messages than what we teach them.

As the letter early in this chapter and the letter that follows indicate, some teacher candidates do find themselves drawn, early on, into the pedagogical turn. Others seem to see no need at all for attention to the effects of *how* we teach, and so they may leave my course feeling frustrated by how I taught it. They may wonder why I went to the effort of teaching in unexpected ways. They may wonder why I did not include some of the topics they expected me to 'cover'. Speaking of a content turn followed by a pedagogical turn that may or may not occur helps me to understand my enterprise and my reasons for persisting to call attention to how I teach. I believe that schools already offer extensive resources for developing the content of teaching and surviving the content turn. I believe that teacher education has a responsibility for indicating the possibility of moving into the pedagogical turn as one's career unfolds. This is, of course, a message more easily conveyed when people have significant teaching experience before their courses in a pre-service teacher education program, and it is very encouraging that the program within which I teach will provide extensive early teaching experience for all teacher candidates from the 1997–8 academic year.

How I Teach IS the Message: Is Anybody Watching? Listening? Hearing?

Everything comes together for me, as a teacher educator, when my efforts to challenge people's premises and assumptions about learning come full circle and appear later in their subsequent teaching. Schools and universities have similar 'cultures' which tend, quite unwittingly, to suppress discussion of the learning process. P.O.E., backtalk, and the idea of barriers to learning to teach share the property of calling attention to the learning process itself. While I believe that it is essential for teacher education to place each teacher candidate's own learning in bold relief, if there is to be any hope that they will make similar moves as teachers, there are always some who resist my efforts to bring the individual learning process into the mental spotlight. Some class groups resist these efforts more than others, and the 1994–5 group is one I remember in that way. Thus it was very special to receive, as I was preparing this chapter, the following thoughts from one member of that class as he completed his first year of teaching at an international school in Europe:

Date: 20 Jun 96 09:42:13 EDT
To: Tom Russell <RUSSELLT@QUCDN.QueensU.CA>
Subject: End of Year
Hi Tom,
Well I've made it. I am tired and feel as though I deserve a vacation. I am looking forward to next year, when I know that I will change many things. Today was the last day with students, and tomorrow we have to hand in our report cards, so I have to get working. I was thinking of you today as I received an email from a student of mine. I have attached it at the end. *I think that I took many things away last year from your teaching style* [my emphasis]. I was very open with many of my students, very flexible, trying to let them learn what they wanted to learn. I know that this did not work with all students, and I will modify my approach next year to try to take into account a greater variety of learning styles (some kids definitely need more direction with step-by-step instruction). However, I know that for some students, this year was a very successful one. Anyway, I just wanted

to share this with you. I will be in Canada for two days in July, and a week in August. I hope to stop by and say hello. Have a great summer, and I hope that you find yourself well prepared for the major changes taking place in the teacher education program in Ontario.

From a student in my grade 8 class:

Well, here we are, at the end of the year. You know, this year I have learned many things, and I want to thank you for giving me the liberties and privileges that you have. I have really enjoyed the course, and I wish I could stay another year.

Learning the HTML language was one of my primary goals, and what I've learned gave me hours of enjoyment at home making my own pages at my house. Giving me the N:\> drive access was really cool, and it gave me a feeling of authority.

I was just writing this note since I wanted to thank you for teaching the course. I'll try to keep up my work with the crusader when I'm in Japan. When you do send me the files in Japan through Compuserve, they'll need to be text files, since I don't have Pagemaker. Thanx for the cool year! (JH, personal communication, June 20, 1996)

When JH and I parted company at the end of his pre-service teacher education program, I had little evidence that he had attended to how I taught the class. There had been some 'rocky moments' with his class, and I was not feeling I had done my best when we finished the year. After only a few exchanges by electronic mail over the year, it was an 'unexpected treasure' to learn that he attributed some of his first year successes to the manner in which I taught his class. I am pleased that he himself received encouraging backtalk from a student and will always be grateful that he then made the effort to share that with me. Comments such as this make the risks and the uphill efforts worthwhile. Learning from time to time, usually in unexpected ways at unexpected moments, that some new teachers did 'catch the message in my teaching' and express it in their own teaching sustains my conviction that how I teach *should be* the message that teacher candidates take from my classroom. If they also remember how much teacher education consumes me as it also fascinates and puzzles me, then I have successfully shared my professional passion for teacher education.

References

BAIRD, J.R. and MITCHELL, I.J. (Eds) (1987) *Improving the Quality of Teaching and Learning: An Australian Case Study — The PEEL project*, Melbourne, Monash University Printery.

BAIRD, J.R. and NORTHFIELD, J. (Eds) (1992) *Learning from the PEEL Experience*, Melbourne, Monash University Printery.

BARNES, D. (1976) *From Communication to Curriculum*, Harmondsworth, UK, Penguin.

ELLIOTT, J. (1976–7) 'Developing hypotheses about classrooms from teachers' practical constructs: An account of the Ford Teaching Project,' *Interchange*, **7**, 2, pp. 2–22.

HALSALL, N.D. and HOSSACK, L.A. (Eds) (1996) 'Act, reflect, revise . . . revitalize: Action research: Moving beyond problem-solving to renewal,' Mississauga, Ontario, Ontario Public School Teachers' Federation.

HOLLINGSWORTH, S. and SOCKETT, H. (1994) *Teacher Research and Educational Reform*, Chicago, University of Chicago Press.

HOLT, J. (1964) *How Children Fail*, New York, Dell.

IRELAND, D. and RUSSELL, T. (1978) 'The Ottawa Valley curriculum project,' *Journal of Curriculum Studies*, **10**, pp. 266–8.

McNIFF, J., LOMAX, P. and WHITEHEAD, J. (1996) *You and Your Action Research Project*, Bournemouth, Hyde Publications and London, Routledge.

RUSSELL, T. (1995a) 'A teacher educator and his students reflect on teaching high school physics,' *Teacher Education Quarterly*, **22**, 3, pp. 85–98.

RUSSELL, T. (1995b) 'Reconstructing educational theory from the authority of personal experience: How can I best help people learning to teach?,' *Studies in Continuing Education*, **17** (1 and 2), pp. 6–17.

RUSSELL, T. (1995c) 'Returning to the physics classroom to re-think how one learns to teach physics,' in RUSSELL, T. and KORTHAGEN, F. (Eds) *Teachers Who Teach Teachers: Reflections on Teacher Education*, London, Falmer Press, pp. 95–109.

SCHÖN, D.A. (1983) *The Reflective Practitioner: How Professionals Think in Action*, New York, Basic Books.

SCHÖN, D.A. (Ed) (1991) *The Reflective Turn: Case Studies in and on Educational Practice*, New York, Teachers College Press.

4 Teacher Education as a Process of Developing Teacher Knowledge

Jeff Northfield and Richard Gunstone

Introduction

There are at least two fundamental purposes for teacher education. Firstly it must be concerned with assisting teachers to learn and apply important ideas about teaching and learning. Secondly, teacher education must be presented in ways that achieve some balance between the existing context and role of teaching and the possibilities for improving teaching and learning. As well as preparing teachers for schools and existing curriculum demands there is an expectation that teacher education will encourage a critical perspective on schooling.

Each of these purposes seem trite and self-evident, but may be worth exploring in more detail. How do we believe teachers learn about teaching and learning? What are we expecting teachers to get better at as they undergo teacher education? How do we prepare teachers for existing conditions and still provide a vision of what might be possible for teachers and schools? This last question is very important when there are clearly expressed concerns about the way teachers and teaching are regarded (Smyth, 1995, p. 1). There appears to be little confidence and support for teachers to implement policies and provide leadership in education. Munby and Russell (1994) would also suggest that teachers have reservations about the nature and quality of their own knowledge, experience and capacity to shape educational improvement. Teacher education may make its greatest contribution by enhancing the way teachers value their own knowledge generation and dissemination. Kessels and Korthagen (1996) are quite clear about the teacher education implications of enhancing the value of teachers' knowledge.

> (A teacher educator) is there to help the student see, not to teach the student a number of concepts. One is there to help the student refine his or her perception not to provide the student with a set of general rules. One is there to help the student make his or her own tacit knowledge explicit, to help the student capture the singularities of the experience, to find the rightness of tone and the sureness of touch that only holds good for a particular situation. One is not there to lecture about educational theory, to instruct given rules, or extensively discuss instructional principles. (Kessels and Korthagen, 1996, p. 21)

As a pair of teacher educators, our own personal learning has been long and difficult as there is always a tendency to overestimate what we were able to tell teachers and underestimate the importance of, and our ability in, providing conditions for teachers to be learners about teaching. Our challenge has been to develop teacher education courses (both pre-service and in-service) in ways that reflect this developing insight that it is teachers who have to be learners and then appreciate the nature and significance of their knowledge and experience.

This chapter argues a set of principles which form a basis for an approach to teacher education which is designed to enhance teachers' capacities to affect their situations. These principles are developed from a set of assumptions about teacher education and those who practice as teacher educators.

- Teacher education programs should model the teaching and learning approaches being advocated and promote the vision of the profession for which they are preparing teachers.
- Teacher education must be based on a recognition of the prior and current experiences of teachers and encourage respect for teacher knowledge and understanding.
- Teacher educators should maintain close connections with schools and the teaching profession. They need to be advocates for the profession and supporters of teachers' attempts to understand and improve teaching and learning opportunities for their students.
- Learning about teaching is a collaborative activity and teacher education is best conducted in small groups and networks with ideas and experiences being shared and discussed.
- Teacher education involves the personal development, social development as well as the professional development of teachers.

The interaction of these three aspects of education in science teacher education is well expressed by Bell and Gilbert (1996).

> Social development . . . involves the renegotiation and reconstruction of what it means to be a teacher . . . It also involves the development of ways of working with others that will enable the kinds of social interaction necessary for renegotiating and reconstructing what it means to be a teacher of science. Personal Development . . . involves each individual teacher constructing, evaluating and accepting or rejecting for himself or herself the new socially constructed knowledge about what it means to be a teacher . . . and managing the feelings associated with changing their activities and beliefs . . . particularly when they go 'against the grain' of the current or proposed socially constructed and accepted knowledge. Professional development as a part of teacher development involves not only the use of different teaching activities but also the development of the beliefs and conceptions underlying the activities. It may also involve learning some science. (Bell and Gilbert, 1996, p. 15)

This need for teacher education to be concerned with the personal, social and professional development of individuals is a constant theme as we outline the pedagogical implications of the ideas and assumptions introduced in this section.

Towards a Set of Principles to Guide Teacher Education

The following set of principles have been discussed and modified and interpreted over almost two decades of our collaborative reflection on our own practice. The ultimate test of the principles lies in their compatibility with the values and assumptions outlined above and the direction they provide for the implementation of teacher education programs. We state the principles as assertions and each is further developed with implications and some of the experiences that have been associated with our trying to apply them in different teacher education situations. The first assertion focuses on the background and prior experiences of those who participate in teacher education.

Assertion 1
The teacher has needs and prior experiences which must be considered in planning and implementing the program. The nature and intensity of these needs should shift throughout the teacher education program.

At pre-service level the work of Hall and Hord (1987) which focused on stages of concern was very significant when making decisions about sequencing ideas and activities. The self, task and impact concerns offered a rationale for initial activities and reminded us of the personal development agenda that has to be part of any teacher education effort (Bell and Gilbert, 1996). The personal concerns of new teachers had to be addressed and our latest effort is in the form of a first unit 'Images of Education' which acknowledges the experiences of education that students bring to the course from their own schooling and the media presentation of teaching and education. These 'images' are the basis for beginning to form an image of themselves as a teacher. The further development of this self image as a teacher will require opportunities to begin teaching where feedback and support are available from colleagues as well as teacher educators.

At this early stage of professional education it is clear that personal development is going to require working with a small group of colleagues and a staff member where a level of trust and confidence can be established quickly. Peer teaching and micro-teaching can then be opportunities to begin teaching in ways that allow participants to see themselves as others see them in teaching situations and provide constructive responses to their colleagues as they begin teaching. One to one teaching opportunities with pupils are also designed to take away the threats of teaching new subject matter to large groups of unknown pupils. Confidence is likely to be increased as the new teacher is able to form a relationship with individuals and small groups of pupils and feel that their contribution is valued by the pupils.

Assertion 2

The transition to teacher as a learner of teaching is fundamental and difficult and is facilitated by working in collaboration with colleagues.

The isolating effects of teaching cannot be allowed to limit the ways teachers learn about teaching. At pre-service level it is important to introduce teaching as a collaborative activity. It is inconceivable that new teachers can develop an image of themselves as teachers in the absence of others' views of their ideas and practices as they begin teaching. This is most likely to occur if the prospective teacher can build a level of trust and confidence in those who are working with them. Beginning the study of teaching within a small group of fifteen to twenty new teachers and one or two staff members for a large proportion of time would seem to introduce students to the way in which teaching is conducted in schools The ability to work with colleagues is an important part of the personal and social development required of teachers. It provides conditions where teachers can share and shape ideas and teacher knowledge and understanding is seen as the way of addressing teaching and learning challenges.

Of greater importance is the message to teachers that knowledge about teaching and learning is to some extent an outcome of their experience and their effort in interpreting that experience. Knowing and implementing system and school policies with some understanding of fundamental educational ideas is only the first level of teacher professional development. It forms the knowledge and ideas which are essential for teachers but in themselves and in the way this knowledge is generally delivered it only forms part of what teachers need to know and be able to do. Table 4.1 sets out one view of what professional development could mean for teachers. The four levels beyond the first all require interaction with colleagues and it would seem important for all new teachers to experience each of the levels of professional development. The second level highlights the importance of teachers developing personal understanding and accepting their responsibility to be independent learners about teaching and learning. Level 3 highlights the ability of teachers to develop teaching and assessment strategies — the important 'second wave' of activity as new educational programs and policies are introduced to schools. There needs to be recognition that it is only teachers who can turn the policies

Table 4.1: The meaning of professional development

1	Knowing and implementing system and school policies	— DELIVERY
2	Understanding and modifying changes with experience	— FOLLOW UP
3	Developing new teaching and assessment strategies	— TEACHER RESEARCH
4	Acknowledging their own and their colleagues' achievement	— PD part of TEACHER ROLE
5	Documenting and sharing experiences	— THE TEACHER VOICE

and ideas into practice. Teachers also need to have the confidence and skills to understand new innovations and generate the strategies to make them work. This respect for their own knowledge and expertise by teachers must begin with teacher education and providing conditions to experience and learn for this part of the teacher role.

Levels 4 and 5 show aspects of professional development which require high levels of support and teacher interaction with colleagues if they are to become part of the teacher role which allows them to have shaping and leadership roles in their profession. Any teacher education program must include opportunities for teachers to work together as they reflect on their teaching experiences and endeavor to understand and communicate their ideas to others.

Assertion 3

The teacher is a learner who is actively constructing ideas based on personal experience. This learning must occur in at least the following areas:

1   Ideas about the teaching and learning process
2   Ideas in relevant knowledge discipline areas
3   Understanding of self
4   The social structures within the profession and in school communities.

This is a comprehensive agenda for teacher education but each of the components needs to be addressed in the process of learning about teaching. The nature of teaching and the experiences of teachers mean that teachers gain their knowledge and understanding in some unique ways. Table 4.2 sets out a tentative list of features of teacher knowledge which seem to emerge from working with teachers who have explored ways of communicating their experiences and understanding to other teachers. These features provide directions for those who are committed to forms of teacher education which have the generation and dissemination of teacher knowledge as an outcome. Our experience suggests that teachers tend to have long-term concerns about teaching and learning as a basis for the things they wish to know about and study. Improving children's understanding of ideas, increasing children's self-image as learners, increasing motivation and interest are examples

Table 4.2: Some unique characteristics of teacher knowledge and research

1   Long term concerns are the source of teacher interest.
2   Teachers require confidence and gain support. They need to gain respect for their won experience and knowledge.
3   Complex classroom contexts and issues often exemplify a significant vignette.
4   Teacher research findings and teaching demands become interwoven.
5   Findings are not always good news for the teacher.
6   Teachers have to live with the implications and consequences of their findings.
7   Communication of findings is difficult.
8   Make the tacit explicit: communication and sharing ideas with others is a critical part of teacher research.

of the broad concerns that teachers have and there is a reluctance to specify these more precisely into more manageable questions for study. Their concerns match the nature of the teaching demands that they face.

The second point in Table 4.2 is crucial if teachers are to value their own knowledge and understanding. Munby and Russell (1994) use the phrase 'authority of their own experience' to describe the recognition and confidence teachers can achieve about their own knowledge and experience. Dealing with teaching demands does not depend on external sources of knowledge and ideas (or the elusive promise of these) but can be addressed by analyzing their own experience and sharing ideas with colleagues.

The importance of reviewing experiences with other teachers over extended periods of time must therefore be an essential part of any teacher education effort. The consideration of experience can extend to the description of significant events by teachers to represent important issues (Point 3 in Table 4.2). We have noted the way teachers tend to use incidents to highlight an area of concern. The complexity of the issue can be put to one side to allow a vivid vignette which is significant for the teacher. 'Here is how it is'. . . . 'Let me give you an example'. These vignettes are indicators of teacher knowledge that deserve to be more widely considered as case examples to perhaps affirm other teachers' work and ideas or further clarify common areas of concern. The teacher still remains very aware of the complex context of the classroom and the difficult task of responding effectively but finds a way of exemplifying an important area of concern.

The remaining four characteristics in Table 4.2 are concerned with the way teachers have to respond to their new understandings. New insights have to be incorporated almost immediately into the teaching tasks. Teachers have to deal with findings and adjust their classrooms so that new knowledge and daily teaching become interwoven. However, the demands of teaching mean there is little time to reflect and find ways of communicating findings to others and perhaps sharing experiences with colleagues.

There are clear implications for teacher education. Beginning at pre-service level it is important that the teacher role be introduced with opportunities and encouragement to review and reflect on their growing experience. Maintaining journals, contributing to discussions, acknowledging teacher experience when introducing topics are more obvious ways of showing respect for teacher knowledge. Requiring teachers to prepare case studies or represent their ideas as portfolio items emphasizes the importance of 'writing for understanding'. Insisting that ideas and drafts be reviewed by peers presents teaching as, ideally, a collaborative profession despite the isolating pressures on teachers and the dailiness of the role.

At the in-service level the same implications and possibilities are important but the limiting factor of time for professional development must be acknowledged. However, a more subtle factor is the apparent lack of respect for teacher knowledge and understanding when we tend to rely on 'up-front', 'one-off', delivery modes for communicating policies and ideas to teachers. It seems obvious that teacher education should be presented in ways that model the principles underlying the program, a proposition which can be expressed as Assertion 4.

Assertion 4
Teacher education should model the teaching and learning approaches being advocated in the program.

How do we believe the new teacher becomes an expert teacher? This fundamental question is the starting point for Farnham-Diggory (1994) to outline three predominant models — the behavior, apprenticeship and development models — which seem to be evident in teacher education. Associated with underlying assumptions of these models about how a novice becomes a teacher are assumptions about the nature of knowledge in teaching and learning.

A teacher education program derived from a behavior model will place priority on what teachers need to know and are able to apply in the school situation. The apprenticeship model would emphasize school experience with teachers being socialized to fit into the existing school contexts. The development model would set out to build teacher confidence in their own learning, and their understanding of experiences. In the latter model, teacher educators need to be seen to be learners, monitoring their own experiences and supporting teacher research efforts and valuing teacher knowledge and experience. The problem with establishing a set of principles for teacher education is that the purposes embedded in the principles will only be communicated if the practice models the aspirations. A teacher development perspective would seem to imply a teacher education approach where the teacher educator is able to form a long-term relationship with a small group of teachers assisting them to interpret their own experiences (similar to the cohort approach used by Bullough, in press; see his chapter in this book). If possible the value of collegial learning must be demonstrated while acknowledging that teaching has isolating pressures and working and sharing with others will require levels of trust and confidence which are not always possible in school contexts. Teacher educators should demonstrate their willingness to work in collaboration with each other as well as with teachers. In short, teacher educators must model continual learning if such a priority is to be evident in their teacher education programs.

From another perspective, a commitment to improvement means that teachers (and teacher educators) must be prepared to question existing practices. Being prepared to make the 'taken for granted' problematic requires a willingness to move away from everyday practices and the confidence to review accepted approaches. The pedagogy of teacher education must also include a willingness to review and revise teacher education experiences and an expectation that the teacher participants have a responsibility to shape the program they are engaged in. Learning about teaching requires the consent and active participation of all involved in the process.

Assertion 5
Teacher participants should see the teacher education program as a worthwhile experience in its own right.

This assertion is most likely to be achieved if the teacher education program has personal social and professional development (Bell and Gilbert, 1996) as the purposes for its agenda. Placing value on teacher knowledge and experiences and accepting a view that experience precedes understanding of teaching and learning puts the teacher at the centre of the teacher education effort. Requiring participants to reflect on the purposes of their teacher education and the relationship of these purposes to the pedagogy being used means that all have to accept responsibility for the processes and outcomes.

The evaluation of teacher education must extend beyond what is taught and include the quality of understanding that has been achieved by participants.

Assertion 6
Teacher education programs are by definition incomplete.

If one accepts that teacher programs can only make a contribution towards increasing prospective teachers' understanding of teaching and learning, then it becomes clear that teacher education is a starting point with a focus as a career long learner about teaching and learning. Therefore, a teacher education program is inevitably inadequate in 'preparing teachers' because it is the starting point in a career and not an end unto itself. Clearly then, making progress towards understanding must be seen as the optimum outcome when teacher education activities and experiences are reviewed. Each participant should be encouraged to test their growing understanding in their classrooms and with colleagues. The emphasis on personal development of ideas must be balanced by a willingness to test these ideas as they practice their profession. A teacher education program must provide opportunities to test new ideas and underline their incompleteness in at least some respects.

Conclusion: Towards a Pedagogy of Teacher Education

A coherent pedagogy of teacher education requires addressing the question, 'What do you expect the teacher to get better at?' This in turn requires considering how teachers learn about teaching and what it means to know and understand teaching and learning. In this chapter we have introduced a series of related assertions which begin with the concerns and experiences of teachers, a view of teacher knowledge and understanding, and a wish to place a high value on teacher experience and understanding in meeting educational challenges. The implications of the assertions or principles that follow from our position continue to require defending, and our reviewing of the way our teacher education is structured and presented. As teacher educators we are required to defend what we do to each other and the teachers with whom we work. The defence and maintenance of our programs do not become easier. Long-term relationships with smaller numbers of teachers must be balanced against cutbacks and pressure for more 'efficient' delivery of programs with fewer staff and resources. Universities are places which do not easily reward the long-term contacts that are maintained with students. Quality teaching is seen as often quality delivery of knowledge by acknowledged experts. Research and publication records are important and, in teacher education, long term studies in teaching and learning within their own teaching programs and with teachers in school settings have been rare and not highly regarded (Fensham and Northfield, 1993).

In this case we have indicated a pedagogy that is easier to argue than implement in the conditions for teacher education which exist at pre-service and in-service levels. It requires considerable commitment and energy to align practice with principles but we would argue that no coherent pedagogy of teacher education can be developed without first addressing fundamental questions about teacher knowledge and learning.

References

BELL, B. and GILBERT, J. (1996) *Teacher Development: A Model from Science Education*, London, Falmer Press.

BULLOUGH, R.V. (In Press) 'Practicing theory and theorizing practice in teacher education', in LOUGHRAN, J.J. and RUSSELL, T.L. (Eds) *Teaching about Teaching: Purpose, Passion and Pedagogy*, London, Falmer Press.

FARNHAM-DIGGORY, S. (1994) 'Paradigms of knowledge and instruction', *Review of Education Research*, **64**, 3, pp. 463–77.

FENSHAM, P.J. and NORTHFIELD, J.R. (1993) 'Pre-service science teacher education: An obvious but difficult arena for research', *Studies in Science Education*, **22**, pp. 67–84.

HALL, G.E. and HORD, S.M. (1987) *Change in Schools: Facilitating the Process*, New York, SUNY Press.

KESSELS, J.P.A.M. and KORTHAGEN, F.A.J. (1996) 'The relationship between theory and practice: Back to the classics', *Educational Researcher*, **25**, 3, pp. 17–22.

MUNBY, H. and RUSSELL, T.L. (1994) 'The authority of experience in learning to teach: Messages from a physics methods course', *Journal of Teacher Education*, **45**, 2, pp. 86–95.

SMYTH, J. (1995) 'Introduction', in SMYTH, J. (Ed) *Critical Discourses on Teacher Development*, London, Cassell, pp. 1–19.

5   Teaching about Teaching: Principles and Practice

John Loughran

Introduction

As a high school teacher I planned lessons that I thought were interesting in the hope that it would help my students come to better understand the content we were studying. However, over time, I came to recognize that, despite these good intentions, another crucial shaping force which had an impact on my students' approach to learning was assessment. Sadly, almost regardless of how I taught, if the assessment strategies I used did not reflect my espoused beliefs about my approach to teaching, then my efforts were blunted. This was never more obvious than in the senior years of schooling where external examinations were the driving force of the curriculum and, therefore, a major determinant of 'school learning'. Although I wanted my students to understand the content I was teaching, the need for them to be able to cope with (and succeed in) the forms of assessment they would face at the end of the year eventually influenced their view of learning and their understanding of what was 'important' to learn, which also inevitably affected how they learnt.

In many ways, then, when I began teaching pre-service teacher education students, a similar dilemma arose. Despite what I thought was important about teaching, if I did not teach in ways that reflected my beliefs, my student-teachers' ideas about what was important to learn and how to apply themselves to learning about teaching would be shaped more by my practice than my philosophy. For example, there was little value in encouraging student-teachers to consider using the jigsaw group-work strategy in their teaching if they did not experience it as learners. Hence, a lecture on the 'jigsaw' would lead to, at best, a superficial understanding of the teaching and learning aspects of the approach, but more likely simply be counterproductive. Clearly, if it was worth knowing about the jigsaw method, the best way of 'knowing' would be through experiencing the strategy in action. Similarly, as a science-teacher educator, my concern about the way science teaching is often depicted as the presentation of a long list of propositions delivered by the teacher, then digested and regurgitated by students in an examination, could not be challenged if my teaching did not offer alternative experiences of being engaged in science. Therefore my teaching through the use of strategies such as Prediction–Observation–Explanation (P.O.E.), concept maps, Venn diagrams and a variety of other teaching approaches designed to probe students' understanding (White and Gunstone, 1992) has become not only fundamental to my beliefs about teaching science, but also imperative in my practice of teaching about science teaching and learning.

In the transition from a teacher of school students to a teacher of student-teachers I have also been confronted by the need to better understand my own pedagogy. I have come to recognize that teaching about teaching by using engaging strategies is in itself not sufficient. I have come to understand that I must also be able to articulate my understanding of my practice; purpose and intent.

This need to articulate the thinking which underpins my pedagogy is primarily borne of the student-teachers' need to know 'why'. Just because I was an experienced high school teacher was not sufficient reason for them to simply accept my views, or for me to believe that the authority of position (Munby and Russell, 1994) was sufficient reason for their learning; it was important that they actively questioned my views and brought to bear the authority of their own developing experience. Therefore, my once tacit views of student learning and the way they linked to, or influenced my teaching, have become much more explicit as I have felt a need to be able to communicate these to my student-teachers.

This desire to be able to articulate my understanding about my pedagogy has become increasingly important to me because I want my student-teachers' learning about teaching to be more than the absorption of propositions about teaching. If learning about teaching *is* simply the absorption of a teacher educator's pedagogical knowledge, then it seems to me most likely that it will be learnt in a manner that encourages digestion and regurgitation in practicum experiences then, more likely than not, rejected in their own post-university teaching practice when the pervading influence of their being assessed is removed. I want my student-teachers to be engaged in their learning about teaching. I want them to consider their own developing practice and to make informed decisions about their teaching, and I want this to be based on an explicit 'knowing about practice' which they develop through their own active and purposeful learning about teaching.

It has been through thinking about learning about teaching based on the dilemmas, hopes and challenges outlined above that my understanding and practice in teacher education has developed. What follows then is my understanding of the 'why' of teaching about teaching; for me, this 'why' is based on a number of principles which I continue to better understand and articulate as I reflect on my teaching with prospective teachers.

Principles of Pedagogy in Teacher Education

Differentiating between 'telling' and 'teaching' needs to be clear if the following principles of pedagogy are to have meaning. For me, teaching is based on an understanding of oneself and others (it is not unlike the tact of teaching described by van Manen, 1991), hence the heart and soul of teaching begins with relationships. Teaching is a relationship. Without building relationships the purpose of teaching is diminished. Other principles of pedagogy are enhanced through relationships; therefore, not surprisingly, although I do not view my list of principles of pedagogy as a checklist to be considered in rank order, the first principle (relationships) is foremost.

Relationships

The ability to mould one's teaching so that it most closely aligns with students' learning needs is developed and enhanced through better understanding the participants in the teaching and learning environment. This understanding is based on developing relationships with students on a personal basis both as individuals and as a group. The personal aspect of knowing one's students is obviously something which is fundamental to helping each individual strive to learn for understanding. However, the importance of group relationships is sometimes overlooked in teaching. Yet the way individuals relate to one another and to their teachers is different in different situations, hence the need to be able to relate to learners as a group. This entails a need to know individuals and the ways they interact and develop within their group because, as the group develops, so relationships within the group develop, and these relationships are far from static, they are continually evolving.

Building relationships begins with a genuine concern to listen, to be aware of the changing nature of the classroom context, and to be interested in, and responsive to, the needs of students. For me, the development of relationships is fundamental to teaching and learning because relationships are built and enhanced through increasing the elements of trust which are so important if learning is to be more than knowing and if teaching is to be more than telling. Trust is a two-way process. It is equally important from the teacher's and learners' perspective.

Trust

Mitchell (1992) found through his work in the PEEL project, as he attempted to encourage school students to be more metacognitive, that trust was important in shaping students' changes in their approach to learning. So, too, trust is an important element of teaching in teaching about teaching. As a teacher educator I need to be confident that my learners will see my pedagogy as a starting point for engaging them: it needs to be an impetus for learning. There is a continual need, therefore, for me to believe that the learners will want to grasp the major concepts and ideas under consideration and grapple with them in ways that are not solely dependent on me as their teacher for *absolute* direction, definition and understanding. Hence I need to be able to trust that, in the teaching–learning environment, regardless of the participants' previous learning experiences, they might genuinely be able to be encouraged to approach learning as a collaborative venture. However, this requires an acceptance of shared responsibilities in learning and therefore necessitates a joint trust from both the teacher's and learners' perspective.

From a learner's perspective, trust involves knowing and believing that individuals' ideas, thoughts and views can be offered and explored in challenging ways such that the challenge is professional not personal. Concerns that participants' suggestions, ideas and input might in some way be ridiculed or devalued by others need therefore to consistently be addressed. This is then a trust in the care for others as persons, and it has as its basis a need to maintain and develop one's self-esteem throughout the exploration of the content or issues being addressed. The learner therefore has a need to trust that the teaching and learning environment is a 'safe' place to raise and pursue issues, concerns and the development of understanding. This calls for a genuine commitment to the notion that 'challenge' is not a personal attack but a search for clarification and understanding.

There is also a trust whereby problems, concerns or issues which are raised in the teaching–learning environment will not superficially be dealt with but will be addressed in a manner which demonstrates a genuine attempt to resolve the concern. This trust is not really possible in an environment where the teacher educator assumes a role of 'expert' in total control of the direction of inquiry, and perhaps loses sight of, or does not acknowledge, the individual's needs. For students to be able to genuinely raise issues or concerns, they must be able to trust that in so doing their queries will be fairly addressed. Without such a trust, there is little incentive to take the risk to speak up.

Independence

Relationships within the teaching–learning environment are also influenced by the extent to which independence is acknowledged and respected. Despite the teaching concern to achieve desired learning outcomes (notwithstanding the fact that learners, too, have learning expectations), there is still a need to recognize that good teaching inevitably leads to a diversity of learning outcomes. Therefore, individuals' independence is important in shaping the extent to which they choose to take up the opportunities possible through their interactions. It is not possible to make real choices if there is not a sense of independence. I believe that a lack of independence encourages convergence of learning rather than a breadth of understanding.

A crucial factor associated with the development of independence is the teacher's ability to withhold judgment. Learners are not likely to pursue their own understanding or to reconsider others' views if they have a sense of being judged, or if they are trying to 'guess what is in the teacher's head'. The need to withhold judgment, to be conscious of one's own wait-time and to *want to hear* from others is a key to building relationships that enhance a diversity of learning outcomes.

Purpose

Teaching needs to be purposeful and this is important from both the teacher's and the learners' perspective. Teaching is more than an array of strategies and skills to be called upon or changed from lesson to lesson or day to day. Teaching is the use of appropriate methods designed to encourage learning. Pedagogy should not be something that is changed or selected in order to 'break-up' the normal routine. Teaching strategies should be carefully selected for the learning they can provide for the content being studied. Just as Shulman (1986) described pedagogical content knowledge, so there is a pedagogical content knowledge which teacher educators possess and develop whereby ways of best probing the content are enhanced through the appropriate use of pedagogy. It is therefore clear that teacher educators need to have this sense of purpose foremost in their minds as they construct their teaching episodes.

In a similar vein, this sense of purpose also extends to the learners. They need to know and understand why particular pedagogy is employed and to be able to question their involvement in the learning process. If there is to be a common understanding of the 'expectations' of learning, there needs to be a clear purpose and it needs to be clearly articulated. However, this does not mean that the purpose should be a restriction on teaching and learning but, more so, a starting point for exploration, a touchstone (Walker and Evers, 1984) or reference point, a signal of the expectations of engagement for learning.

Engagement/Challenge

Learning about teaching involves an extensive and complex array of skills and knowledge which are called upon in different ways in different situations, but it is not really possible to describe this learning as linear, nor to consider that a particular end point might be reached. The accumulated wisdom through reflection on experience is an important aspect of teaching which continues to shape one's practice. Therefore, in a teaching–learning environment, something is missing if the participants (teacher and learners) are not engaged or challenged by the experience.

Learners clearly need to be challenged through the pedagogy if they are to do more than absorb information. They need to reconsider their existing knowledge in light of the experiences being created with them. There is also a need for them to process information and ideas and to synthesize these in new ways if their learning is to be active and purposeful. Similarly, processing and synthesizing are enhanced through metacognition, yet these skills and attributes are restricted if learning is not engaging and challenging. Therefore, an important element of pedagogical purpose is to encourage engagement and challenge in learning so that there is a likelihood that an active and persistent commitment to understanding subject matter is possible.

Just as learners need to be challenged by their understanding of subject matter, so to it should be that pedagogy has an impact on the teacher. The array of students' responses, the influx of new and challenging ideas and the experience of cognitive dissonance when alternative conceptions are explored should also engage the teacher as a learner. Hence, even though a thorough understanding of certain aspects of particular subject matter knowledge and pedagogical knowledge may reside within a teacher, when the two are combined within an interactive teaching–learning environment, understanding continues to be developed. For me, it is important to demonstrate this engagement in teaching about teaching. This demonstration of engagement/challenge in one's own teaching comprises modelling and can give student-teachers real access to the thoughts, skills and knowledge of experienced teachers in ways that allow them to make their own decisions about pedagogy (Loughran, 1996).

Modelling

As I have outlined above, I believe that teaching needs to be interactive and challenging as learning does not occur just by listening, it occurs by reconsidering one's understanding through deeds, thoughts and actions. It therefore follows that if student-teachers' learning about teaching is to be meaningful, they need to be adequately challenged and motivated to take the necessary steps to make new meaning from the teaching and learning episodes in which they are involved. Hence, for me, teaching student-teachers about teaching hinges on a need for teacher educators to 'practice what they preach'. For example, a lecture on role-plays or group work might well convey the information about the procedures involved but would certainly not encourage participants to be engaged in such a way as to better understand how the teaching strategy affects their learning. If student-teachers are to understand a particular teaching strategy, they need to experience it as learners and as teachers, not just hear about it.

Modelling teaching in ways that demonstrate this commitment to better understanding through experience is important to me. However, this does not mean that a model for how to teach is to be placed before student-teachers to mimic; rather it means offering them the opportunity to better understand the pedagogical purpose, to experience some of the likely learning outcomes as a result of the experience (both cognitive and affective), and to allow them to make their own decisions about how they might incorporate that into their own practice. In a similar fashion, it is also important to me to highlight the different 'ways of knowing' that arise in teaching and learning situations so that they can see the possibilities created through the appropriate use of teaching strategies. To do this, I try to help my student-teachers recognize what it is they need to know and why and, then, how to apply their knowledge in different problem situations to further develop their understanding. This is what I describe as modelling. It is modelling the processes, thoughts and knowledge of an experienced teacher in a way that demonstrates the 'why' or the purpose of teaching; it is not creating a template of teaching for unending duplication.

As teaching strategies are both content- and context-dependent, being able to respond to changes in the teaching and learning environment is vital. Modelling offers the ability to genuinely demonstrate that knowing how to use a strategy is one facet of teaching, but knowing why to use it is another. The need to adapt and change, to be responsive to the teaching and learning environment, is a critical attribute for teaching; modelling this is crucial if student-teachers are to understand the pedagogical reasoning which they, too, need to experiment with and develop. Knowing 'why' must be linked to knowing 'how' if student-teachers' pedagogical knowledge is to be more than a list of propositions. They therefore need to see this in their teacher educators' practice and to similarly experience it in their learning about teaching experiences.

Reflection

Teaching is inextricably linked to learning; therefore, teaching is a two-way process. Teaching about teaching should extend teachers' and students' views of teaching and learning, and this extension is dependent upon reflection on both the teaching and the learning that occurs; it follows that reconsidering one's actions, reframing (Schön, 1983) problematic situations, mulling over the flow of suggestions, and reasoning through the implications of alternative views and testing hypotheses (Dewey, 1933) are the cornerstones of reflection. Again, if reflection is to be better understood by student-teachers, it needs to be explicitly modelled in practice in order to encourage them to consider approaching their teaching in ways that might be based on a similar basis or foundation.

My thinking aloud about my pedagogy (see Loughran, 1996 for more detail) is an attempt to give students immediate access to the thoughts, ideas and concerns which shape my teaching.

It would not be uncommon for me to preface my teaching at the start of a class with the reasons for the structure about to be employed. In so doing I would attempt to demonstrate my thinking about previous lessons, my intentions for the upcoming lesson, and what I anticipated for the following lessons, and that these are all linked in a holistic manner. Therefore, my reaction to what I perceived to be the learning as a result of a teaching experience is an important starting point for my thinking about the lesson to be taught. In essence, I would be giving my students access to the pedagogical reasoning which underpins my thinking as I attempt to develop the 'purpose' for, and approach to, a teaching and learning experience . . . Teaching and learning are interconnected through a dynamic system in which one continually influences the other. To appreciate this interplay 'in action' is difficult as the ideas, perceptions, reactions and recognition of anticipated and unanticipated learning outcomes ebb and flow in response to the stimuli which prompt the thinking. It is fundamental to my view of modelling that this thinking during teaching be overtly demonstrated for my students if they are to fully appreciate the complex nature of learning about teaching; even more so if they are to seriously consider their own practice in relation to my modelling . . . Although I have described my thinking about teaching within three distinct periods (pre [anticipatory reflection], post [retrospective reflection] and during [contemporaneous reflection] a pedagogical experience), clearly all three are linked and related in a complex web of thoughts and actions which are very much context-dependent. (Loughran, 1996, pp. 28–9)

This thinking aloud is designed to give my student-teachers access to my reflection on practice. For me this is a most important aspect of learning about teaching. Student-teachers cannot be told about reflection then be expected to simply incorporate it into their practice. They need to see and understand its use and development in the 'action setting' so that their understanding might be enhanced. However, I also believe that reflection facilitates risk-taking; therefore, if learning about teaching is to help student-teachers learn through risk-taking, then teacher educators themselves need to model this risk for their student-teachers. They need to be willing to expose their own vulnerability as a learner in teaching in ways similar to those which they would hope to encourage in their student-teachers. Of course little of this applies if learning about teaching is conceived of as being told how to teach, or simply knowing about a list of interesting teaching strategies. Clearly for me, learning through risk-taking is an important principle of learning about teaching.

Risk-taking

Learning about teaching requires a pushing of the 'boundaries of practice' in order to encourage seeing and understanding from a variety of vantage points. By attempting to implement the use of teaching strategies which challenge one's 'comfort level', new ways of seeing and understanding become possible through experiencing the discomfort of being less certain about the unfolding events within a teaching–learning episode. I would argue that this discomfort is an important attribute for learning and helps to heighten the senses so that the active reframing possible through such risk-taking substantially broadens one's understanding of both the teaching and learning (cognitive and affective) through the experience.

An important aspect of risk-taking is the need to recognize and acknowledge the individual nature of such activities. What may be a risk for one person may pose little risk for another, hence the extension of pedagogical knowledge and understanding possible by challenging practice and reasoning at the margins of normal practice will be different for different individuals. However, the powerful learning about practice as a result of actively choosing to extend one's repertoire of teaching approaches, to use familiar strategies in unfamiliar situations, or unfamiliar strategies in familiar situations, is the essence of personal professional development. As individuals learn in different ways, it is important for teachers to use pedagogy that is appropriate to the variety of learning approaches within their classes; therefore, it may well be that particular approaches to teaching which are uncomfortable for individual teachers are important to a range of students' learning. Risk-taking involves pursuing the implementation of such strategies as appropriate to cater for the diversity of learning needs within the teaching–learning environment.

To me, this is as equally important in teacher education as it is in school teaching generally. However, if teacher educators do not take risks in their own practice, if they do not overtly model the need to extend the margins of understanding and experience for their own pedagogy, it makes it difficult for student-teachers to believe that the value of taking risks will be worth the discomfort they will experience in practice. In many ways encouraging risk-taking involves a stepping out in faith, a faith which is based on a trust in believing that, through taking the risk of experiencing both the trials and errors of learning by experimenting with pedagogy in a range of situations, circumstances, subject-content and contexts, an understanding will emerge. I believe that this is an aspect of learning about teaching that many student-teachers are more than prepared to consider; however, they need to see that their teacher educators will positively support them.

The principles of practice which I have outlined above, for me, are the essence of teaching about teaching. They create the conditions which offer student-teachers opportunities to develop their teaching, and are the foundations of ongoing reflection throughout practice.

Creating a Context for Teaching about Teaching

Shulman (1986) described a perspective on teacher knowledge which encompassed content knowledge, pedagogical content knowledge and curricular knowledge. Just as these are important elements of teacher knowledge, so they should equally apply to learning about teaching. However, I would argue that, for student-teachers to better understand these aspects of teaching, they need to be continually reinforced through the learning experiences created within teacher education programs. Fundamental, therefore, to my view of learning about teaching is that student-teachers continually be placed in situations whereby they learn through being in a learning position, learning through the experience by being in the experience. If they are to understand how a teaching strategy influences learning, they need to experience the teaching strategy as a learner. Similarly, to understand the intricacies and subtleties of a teaching strategy they need to experience using it, unpacking it and reconstructing their practice through the experience. This learning through being a teacher and a learner is then what I would describe as the context for teaching about teaching. It is an important way of helping student-teachers come to see, feel and reflect on the complex nature of teaching and learning. It also highlights the diversity of learning outcomes associated with teaching–learning episodes and genuinely places student-teachers in situations whereby through discussion and de-briefing a range of attitudes, views and practices can be purposefully explored.

I recently taught a lesson on the Van De Graaf generator with the student-teachers in my Science Method class. As a biologist I find this topic challenging, particularly as my understanding of the content knowledge is sorely tested — 'I am not sure that Mr Van De Graaf himself really understood precisely the finer points of their operation' (Hodson, 1993, p. 27). I started the class by placing the Van De Graaf generator on a table in the middle of the room and asking if anyone could tell us a little about it. An hour and a half later, together as a group of learners, we had traversed a great deal from the workings of the Van De Graaf generator through to why it sparks, the important distinction between voltage and current, the principle of an earth, why touching the dome makes one's hair stand on end, and a host of other issues associated with the concept of static electricity.

In this class, it was important to me that I modelled the value of learning through questioning, developing and testing hypotheses, and working with colleagues to fully develop, articulate, test and reconsider one's own 'knowing' in order to lead to a better understanding of the content under consideration. At the end of the class we briefly discussed aspects of the session that we thought influenced the way the class had learnt and been taught. This placing student-teachers in a genuine learning about teaching and learning context is how the principles (outlined earlier) which underpin my practice are played out in my teaching with prospective teachers. It is something that I learn more about the more I use my own learning about a concept to drive my approach to teaching about teaching — as I actively consider (and reconsider) how I learn and come to understand content knowledge — so that it directly influences the way I teach about that content knowledge. This is what I describe as creating a context for teaching about teaching. The content under consideration is a vehicle for highlighting approaches to learning about learning, and learning about teaching. Appropriate use of context offers insights into pedagogical reasoning, intent and purpose as well as into learners' needs, processes and practices.

After this class, I asked my student-teachers to write a brief paragraph about, 'The things that help you learn about teaching.' Their responses included:

Student 1 I learn best by doing what the students will be doing in the classroom. Being taken through ideas for teaching as if I am the student so I can get an idea of how they would be feeling about it as well as taking note of what the teacher is actually doing and how to get things going. Getting a chance to practice taking classes is also important.

Student 2 A secure comfortable environment is necessary for most effective learning . . . debriefing after a lesson is an activity I find I learn a great deal from.

Student 3 Learning by doing — both the teaching part, and also being put in a student's position, and actually taking part in activities etc. That we will be getting kids to do, to see the problems etc. that they may have with concepts etc. Becoming more confident in myself, and my knowledge, not necessarily that it's right, but that it's acceptable to others [for me to develop this in our classes], no matter how convoluted it may be.

Student 4 At first, have a healthy rapport with the classroom environment . . . a good groundwork to start so everyone is comfortable. Most importantly the ideas, attitudes and knowledge expressed by other people in the class — this is a huge resource. Talking and discussing real life problems and the real life solutions of 'what would happen' in the classroom, e.g., What problem would arise if. . . . Bringing everything into classroom situations acknowledges the different knowledge and strengths of people. Discussion of case examples of what has happened [is helpful too].

Student 5 Firstly, to learn from experience: trying different things out in different ways (because one particular way is not going to suit every class, year level, student, etc.). A lot of this comes from trial and error because I learn both from things that go well and from things that don't work. Also looking at things from different viewpoints i.e., class discussion like what we did today to pool everyone's ideas. Not to be *told* things, but to learn things and discover things myself.

Student 6 I suppose one of the key things that helps me to learn to teach is trial and error. I feel it is important to try things out and then see how they go i.e., learn from experience. Also, if this was the case I'm sure it assumes that as I go along I should go from bad to better. This is not the case as I suppose it comes down to many factors e.g., Time of day, the students themselves etc. Also, I really feel that by putting myself in their shoes and trying to take it from a different perspective helps too. If I can imagine how they thought a lesson went (which is not always possible) then I may get an understanding of my teaching. The most important thing for me is not to be told *what* to teach, but to be given chances to learn how I may go about it. . . . Also, talking about experiences with each other helps me to figure out a lot of other people's ideas and to work from them.

Student 7 I think some of what we learn about teaching we learn almost unconsciously by the way we are taught ourselves by the teachers this year. Other things we consciously think about e.g., I like this, I don't like that, that was interesting, that was boring, that made me want to know more, this challenged me. We learn from making mistakes and our supervisors' suggestions. We learn a lot from each other — seeing how someone else approached something, different perspectives. We learn by reflecting on how we ourselves were taught by teachers in the past. Then we try to link all of this practical stuff with the theory (this is hard) and try to come up with a concept [of practice] that works.

Student 8 I think it's been good how we were taught to do a lot of question asking during the class. I was not very good at this during my first teaching round because I got frustrated and just gave the kids the answers, but in my second teaching round, I practised this and found that it works. They do get a lot more out of it [the teaching] if they think for themselves — with the guidance of the teacher.

Student 9   Being put in risk taking situations helps me to learn. It helps me to understand what it is like to be a student again. As a result, I enjoy activities which make me take risks. I find open class discussion very valuable. I value an environment in which everyone has a chance to contribute, not just those with the loudest voices or all the knowledge. Learning to teach is a very vulnerable experience and I think it is very important that we are in an environment which has trust — both teacher–student and student–student. I think a high interaction with your peers is very important in Dip. Ed. This interaction keeps us 'on track' and makes us realize that we all have similar problems.

It is not often that in the rush to teach about teaching we take the time to ask our students what they think they need to know, or how they would like to learn, but it is interesting to consider the responses above and to use these ideas as shaping factors for our approach to helping our student-teachers learn about teaching in ways that are congruent with their needs, expectations and concerns. What we do *with* our student-teachers is much more important than what we do *to* them.

Conclusion

Many years ago, Fuller (Fuller, 1969; Fuller and Bown, 1975) described the shifts in student-teachers' concerns as they progressed through their teacher education programs. I believe that teaching about teaching needs to occur in a context in which these shifts are constantly being recognized and responded to by the teachers of teachers so that learning about teaching is a dynamic, challenging and interactive process which encourages individuals to learn to reflect on their experiences and to pursue their pedagogical development in ways that are thoughtful and meaningful.

For this to be the case, we as their teachers must not lose sight of the challenge of learning ourselves and the importance of its relationship with teaching; otherwise, teaching about teaching might (sadly) too easily become just a way of trying to tell beginning teachers what we think they should know, bypassing the important learning experiences which are so crucial in shaping views of, and practice in, teaching. Through my experience in teaching pre-service teacher education students, I have come to believe that learning through the experience is highly valued by student-teachers and that they are more than prepared to take the risks and face the challenges associated with so doing. In this way their learning about teaching is significantly enhanced. Clearly, this is severely diminished if teaching is simply equated with telling, and understanding is not seen as a fundamental outcome of learning. Pre-service teacher education programs are the first place of contact between beginning teachers and their prospective profession. If they are to value the pedagogical knowledge that is continually being developed, refined and articulated within their profession, if they are to understand the complex nature of teaching and learning, and if they are to be 'teachers' not 'tellers', 'trainers' or 'programmers', then this first contact through pre-service programs is crucial. The pedagogy involved in teaching teachers is very important.

References

DEWEY, J. (1933) *How We Think*, New York, Heath and Co.

FULLER, F.F. (1969) 'Concerns of teachers: A developmental conceptualization', *American Educational Research Journal*, **6**, 2, pp. 207–26.

FULLER, F.F. and BOWN, O.H. (1975) 'Becoming a teacher', in RYAN, K. (Ed) *Teacher Education: the 74th Yearbook of the National Society for the Study of Education*, Part 11, Chicago, University of Chicago Press.

HODSON, B.L. (1993) 'Technical update: Power Supplies', *Lab Talk*, **37**, 4, pp. 27–9.

LOUGHRAN, J.J. (1996) *Developing Reflective Practice: Learning about Teaching and Learning through Modelling*, London, Falmer Press.

MITCHELL, I.J. (1992) 'The class level', in BAIRD, J.R. and NORTHFIELD, J.R. (Eds) *Learning from the PEEL Experience*, Melbourne, Monash University Printing Service.

MUNBY, H. and RUSSELL, T.L. (1994) 'The authority of experience in learning to teach: Messages from a physics methods course', *Journal of Teacher Education*, **45**, 2, pp. 86–95.

SCHÖN, D.A. (1983) *The Reflective Practitioner: How Professionals Think in Action*, New York, Basic Books.

SHULMAN, L.S. (1986) 'Those who understand: Knowledge growth in teaching', *Educational Research*, **15**, 2, pp. 4–14.

VAN MANEN, M. (1991) *The Tact of Teaching: The Meaning of Pedagogical Thoughtfulness*, Albany, New York, State University of New York Press.

WALKER, J. and EVERS, C. (1984) 'Towards a materialist pragmatist philosophy of education', *Education Research and Perspectives*, **11**, 1, pp. 23–33.

WHITE, R.T. and GUNSTONE, R.F. (1992) *Probing Understanding*, London, Falmer Press.

Challenges in Teaching and Learning about Teaching

6 Teaching Teachers for the Challenge of Change

Anna E. Richert

Introduction

To say these times are harrowing seems true enough. Change is happening so quickly that it is hard to keep track of what's what, who's who, and what matters. At least that is how it feels to me when I think about my work of teaching teachers to teach school in urban America. In school, change is the only thing we can predict with certainty. Yet change makes the work of teaching school difficult. It makes teaching teachers hard work as well. That is what this chapter is about — the hard work of teaching teachers to meet the challenge of change. I will begin by exploring the issue of change in school settings in order to lay out the challenge of change for teaching and teacher education and then I will provide examples from my own practice of my attempts to meet this challenge. Thirdly I will explore the results of those efforts. I will present the analysis of an example from my teaching as means for considering how my students think about their work in schools, and their preparation for doing it. As might be predicted, these results raise new questions. These new questions, and the persistence of *always* facing new questions, explains, perhaps, the most challenging part of dealing with change in the first place — its unending, enduring nature. Deliberating the challenge of change in school settings is where we will begin our consideration of what teachers need to know and be able to do to meet it. From there, we can look at the subsequent challenge of preparing them for that daunting task.

Change and Teaching School

An interesting paradox presents itself when one begins to consider the significance of change to the workings of school. On the one hand, change, more than anything else, characterizes the reality of school life. Everything about school changes all the time: the children change, the communities they come from change, the subject matters change, the teachers change, the purposes of school change, the sources of support for schools change as does the demands for support resources. On the other hand, in spite of these obvious and generally accepted changing conditions of school life, schools themselves appear to be relatively stable. Life in school goes along as it always has; teachers still do most of the talking and children most of the listening. Bells ring at predictable hours. Subject matters are still considered separately rather than interconnected as they would be if they were presented to describe the real 'stuff' of children's lives. Biology is taught separately from chemistry, for example, and chemistry separately from math. English is separate from history, and separate from mathematics as well. Algebra is taught before geometry, and American History before Government but after World. School leadership remains similarly stable in American schools with most schools having principals who lead them, and most principals continuing to be men. It is indeed curious to notice that, while the world changes, schools remain virtually the same. Why is this so?

The answers to this question, of course, are numerous, complex and beyond the scope of this chapter. We are perched to explore one set of them, however, the teachers who teach in schools — who they are, what they know and are able to do, how they understand the purpose of schooling in the first place, how they think about and deal with change, how they are prepared. It is the last of these — teacher preparation — that I address in this chapter.

Rather than confronting the issue of necessary change, it is more likely that teachers who teach in schools as we know them teach as they were taught; teacher education does little to challenge the systems of schools as they are. Nor does the reward system of schools (salaries, advancement, special assignments, and so forth) direct teachers to examine the purposes of their work in the first place, and/or explore alternative conceptions of what is and what might be to accomplish different ends. For better or for worse, schools are persistently stable places. Deborah Meier (1995) hints of this factor of persistence and its systemic and pervasive nature when she says in her recent work on school reform, 'The thing that is wrong with prescriptive teaching is not that it does not work — it's that it does' (p. 604). Teachers learn what school and teaching are first as students, and perpetuate through deed and action these conceptions in their new role as teachers. Interestingly, the problem we face in education and the urgency with which it confronts us at this time results as these two factors about school change intersect — the inevitability of change on the one hand, and the resistance to change on the other.

Those of us working in urban settings know, even without needing to explore very deeply, that while change is ever-present in school settings, undirected change does not work in the best interest of many of our school children. Nor does it work in the best interests of the teachers who teach them. We know, also, that schools are predictably less successful in reaching certain groups of students — the poor and the foreign-born, for example. Similarly, they work predictably less well for the teachers of those same children. But even for other children, including children who score high on standardized tests, and/or children from homes of affluent means, school does not work particularly well. It does nothing to teach these children of the problematic nature of schooling, or tests, or the mechanisms that sort them into their privileged positions. In fact, as it currently exists, school functions to muffle rather than sharpen consciousness about the social inequities it serves to perpetuate.

The challenge for teacher education, then, begins with the challenge of how to question the status quo of schools, and raise consciousness about the need to examine the conditions of school life. The process must begin with determining what our students know and believe about teaching and about schooling. It is commonly accepted practice in teaching children that one begins by determining what those children already know. Were we to follow that common practice in the teaching of teachers, we would learn what preconceptions our novice teachers hold about teaching and school, and begin there to prepare them for work that is new. In this way the task of preparing teachers becomes linked with that of reconceiving schools to better meet the needs of the people they serve.

Though there is a constant effort on the part of teacher education to do what it does better, the question guiding teacher education reform seldom takes us to the place of questioning the fundamental questions of schooling in the first place. This brings us to the importance of linking teacher education reform with school reform. To do this teacher educators must step back again to examine the core questions of what school is for, and what teachers need to know and be able to do to help schools accomplish those goals. Rather than accepting the factors of school as 'given', we must learn to cast them as 'problematic'. If we were able to do it, such casting would allow us to consider anew what and how we teach in relationship to who and why we teach. We would also be one step further in meeting the urgent challenge of change.

Where Should We Begin?

How, then, might we go about preparing teachers to both survive the system of school as it currently exists and contribute to reforming it at the same time? We might begin by asking ourselves what we believe teachers need to know and be able to do to function in changing schools. We must also examine where this learning might best occur (in the university or the school, for example) and when in the teacher's career. I begin by exploring the question of what teachers need to know.

Recent research on teacher knowledge suggests that beginning teachers need to know about all kinds of things: students, learning, subject matter, how to teach subject matter, context, curriculum, teaching (Grossman, 1990; Wilson, Shulman and Richert, 1987; Shulman, 1986). The list does not end there either. Policy-makers interested in extending the teacher's role to include participating in school reform, and managing the school's academic agenda, add to the knowledge-requirements list issues of school governance, conflict resolution, community building, etc. (Darling-Hammond, 1993; Grossman and Richert, 1996; Murray, 1994; Lieberman, 1995; Fullan, 1993; Sarason, 1993). While knowledge in each of these domains is essential for teacher success, the critical issue for beginning teachers, it seems to me, is how teachers learn to think about the source and role of that knowledge for their own school practice. Acquiring new knowledge is an important part of the process of learning to teach, to be sure. However, given the uncertain and changing context where that knowledge will be used, an approach to knowledge acquisition which accommodates uncertainty and change is needed. Learning to accept and deal with the inherent uncertainty of teaching is an important early step in preparing teachers to deal with change. Given this uncertainty, it is important, also, for teachers to recognize their professional role in determining how they will act in school — what they will do in their interactions with children, what principles will guide the decisions they make, how they will conduct themselves as colleagues, and so forth. The work of teaching is not predetermined; therefore, recognizing the moral component of the work is also central to meeting the challenge of change in schools. Let us push these ideas a little further before considering the form our programs might take to prepare teachers for this complex challenge.

Dealing with Teaching's Uncertainty

Learning about uncertainty needs to be one piece of the teacher education curriculum. From the start, preparing teachers to embrace uncertainty is an uphill climb. Students enter the profession having experienced literally thousands of hours of classroom life. They know a lot about school when they arrive, and about teaching, about kids, and even about curriculum. To make matters even more difficult for teacher education, the schools they will encounter within the teacher education context will do little to convince them that what they already know is not enough for smart teaching practice. As has already been discussed, schools are very stable places. They look pretty much like they always have — chairs, rows, desks, bells, blackboards, tests, teacher talk, detention, homework, points, grades. The systemics that characterize school life seem to endure in spite of the changing world that encircles them.

While schools look the same, however, the truth is that they are not the same. All of us involved in education must learn to look more closely at schools, and learn how to understand differently what we see. As familiar as school processes and procedures appear, we have learned that each teaching/learning situation is actually quite different (Brown, Collins and Duguid, 1989). Knowing how to ask questions of every particular situation is therefore critical knowledge for teaching. *Knowing how* to ask questions and *knowing what* to ask presuppose *knowing to ask* questions in the first place. All three are parts of reflective teaching that must be part of a teacher's professional preparation. A look at the changing demographics in this country underscores how critically important it is that teachers develop this reflective approach towards teaching. The population served by American schools in 1996 is much broader than the one they served at the time public schooling was initiated in this country; the world is different from the time when most of the school practices now in place were created.

For this reason, I think what teachers need to learn first in their professional preparation is to acknowledge change and uncertainty, and cast all aspects of school as 'problematic' rather than 'given'. Novice teachers must become aware that, while there is a lot about school that we *do* know, there is at least as much about school that we *do not* know. In confronting what we do not know honestly, and searching together to learn what we need to know, we can acquire the knowledge and skill to not only survive school as it is but to transform it in ways that better serve its clientele. This is the challenge of our work: how to deal with that uncertainty and use what we do know in service of what we do not know.

Considering Teaching's Moral Imperative

The uncertainty of teaching places teachers in the position of making moral decisions as a regular and routine part of their work. The changing world of which schools are a part renders both the ends and means of teaching uncertain. For this reason, the teacher must learn to examine both the purposes and consequences of his or her actions — a daunting challenge indeed. It involves questioning *why* do what we do, and constantly examining both what we teach and how we choose to teach it. For example, it is one thing to know algebra, or even how to teach algebra. It is quite something else to have considered why algebra is important to know in the first place. As part of the formulation of this chapter I gathered materials from my current teacher education students in order to explore their emergent skills for dealing with both the uncertainty and morality of teaching. I came upon several examples of my students examining what and how they were teaching, in relation to the purposes for which they saw themselves being there in the first place. Matt was a fifth-year credential candidate preparing to teach secondary mathematics who struggled with the question of 'Why algebra?'. His ruminations on a curriculum project, which I will describe more fully later in the chapter, reveal part of his journey to construct and/or articulate his purpose for teaching mathematics. His comments suggest an emerging sense of connection with a purpose that contributes to a greater good for his students — greater in that it takes them (and him) beyond the mechanics of doing math well.

In the context of the Curriculum Project Matt was put to the test of articulating his purpose by his student teaching partners who wanted to know 'Why math?'. Why teach mathematics as part of the K-12 curriculum? Matt found that he needed to question much of what he had taken for granted as a successful undergraduate math major in a competitive East Coast university. He said in his post-assignment reflection, 'I found myself wondering at times why the hell I'm teaching something which often lacks any obvious influence on students' emotional/personal lives' (MR, *Curriculum Reflection* 5/96). And continued later in that same document:

> As I struggled more and more . . . some very subtle but important realisations came up. I began to realise the important role math played in my own personal life, and not just in my intellectual growth. I began to look at math as a very pure and simplified medium to understand and practice important life themes. The beauty of math is that packed within those tiny equations are profound observations of nature's patterns, and tucked in all those models and proofs are helpful approaches to problem solving of all kinds. (MR, *Curriculum Reflection* 5/96)

Interestingly, Matt's examination of the discipline he intends to teach in terms of its potential for generating meaning-making possibilities for his students led him to a realization or position similar to my own: We both have identified uncertainty as significant in life, and consequently, important to teach in school. He continued:

> I am still fascinated that whenever one draws a circle and measures the diameter and circumference, they will be related by a factor of pi (3.14). Why is this always true? Who or what made nature have this relationship and why? Packed in the simplest relationships are some of the most profound questions, ones that we have no answers to. Math is another lens to dissect why things are the way they are, and to realise that we have a very limited understanding of existence in general . . . Math is important to do taxes and understand statistics, but it becomes relevant to students' personal lives (social, emotional, etc.) in that it is a powerful and safe place to face problems and cope with uncertainty. (MR, *Curriculum Reflection* 5/96)

Shoshana, a colleague of Matt's who is preparing to be an elementary school teacher, found herself grappling with the coupled questions of *why* teach history to fourth graders, and then *how to do it*, as she worked on the same curriculum project as Matt. Shoshana's process also began with a self-interrogation. After much searching through her own preconceptions about what school is for and how history as a content area within the structure of the school curriculum contributes to the aforementioned purposes, she decided to help her students situate themselves in time and space. She and her curriculum colleagues chose the concept of 'identity' which Shoshana conceptualized as foundational to understanding history. The process of interrogating herself and others about what she would teach and why led her slowly to new understandings about what history might be for fourth graders, and how she might approach it in her classroom. The choice of 'identity' as a focusing concept came about with effort that involved, among other things, extensive conversations with her curriculum partners, other teachers, and her college faculty. Rather than accept without question the concept of 'identity' to teach as part of a history curriculum, Shoshana framed the interrogation of identity as a concept to teach in terms of what she hoped to accomplish in her classroom and why. About this challenging journey to understanding which allowed her to move forward in her curriculum planning, she said:

> It was then, and only then, that I truly understood the value of children learning who they are, who their families are, and where they come from. By using one's identity as a foundation for studying history, then everything to follow has personal significance. (SB, *Curriculum Reflection* 3/96)

Teaching is fundamentally a moral endeavor made more complex by the uncertainty that surrounds it, and the need for teachers to examine, with each action, their purposes and the possible consequences. How to recognize teaching's moral content and work responsibly towards its moral imperative must also figure heavily in the pre-service education of teachers. As the examples of Shoshana and Matt exemplify, the exact substance of the teacher's moral reasoning will be as diverse as the people engaged in the reasoning process and the dilemmas they confront. So, too, will the outcomes of those deliberations be different. What must remain as consistent and centrally important are the processes of questioning purposes and consequences, reasoning through decisions about actions relative to those purposes and consequences, and acting with intent in one's work as a teacher.

Not unlike the inherent uncertainty that necessarily frames teachers' work in schools, the moral component of teaching can be invisible to the unconscious eye. Part of what teachers need to learn at the outset of their careers, therefore, is to *recognize* the uncertain and moral components of their work, and to operate in schools with those as given. Interestingly, part of what renders teaching uncertain is the unresolved morality that frames every aspect of the work. Part of learning to deal with uncertainty is learning how to resolve moral dilemmas and take moral action. Teacher education needs to set the stage for this work by establishing the existence of the conditions of morality and uncertainty, and preparing novice practitioners for a wholehearted engagement with meeting the challenges they present.

Agency, Reflection, and Learning to Teach

The ability to take moral action requires that teachers learn to act with intent. This means that teachers need to locate expertise inside, rather than outside, themselves. What I am suggesting here is that teachers learn to see themselves not as 'received knowers', (Belenkey, *et al.*, 1986), but as agents of their own school practice. The agenda for knowledge acquisition in teacher education must have two parallel strands: in one, the novices learn what knowledge the field has to offer about children, subject matter, teaching, curriculum, and the like; in the second they learn to construct new knowledge, to recognize themselves as experts, and to acknowledge the significance of their own knowledge construction in determining their practice. In this model, expertise is located both inside and outside the teacher-knower. The teachers are seen not only as users and dispensers of knowledge, but as creators of knowledge as well. Part of the work of teaching is constructing new knowledge in a vitally dynamic system of change. The process requires asking powerful questions and searching for equally powerful answers.

Asking questions and searching for answers is no small challenge in a culture that associates certainty with truth, truth with knowledge, and knowledge with power. It is no wonder that schools strive to be certain places where life is under control and outcomes are predictable and steady. Unfortunately, (or fortunately) real life in school is necessarily uncertain. Everything changes all the time. This is a hard lesson for novice teachers to learn; it is especially hard if they have no support in examining that truth as they encounter it in the daily world of school life.

The process of learning to teach needs to provide novices with both an experience in school, and an opportunity to think about that experience and make sense of it in new ways. They need to learn to look back and examine all-too-well known and comfortable 'certainties' about schooling, teaching, and learning. The imperative for teacher education is to offer novices that opportunity: it is our responsibility to prepare teachers with the knowledge and skills of reflective practice so that they can act with intent in morally responsible ways. Teachers need to know how to examine what *is* in school, and how to determine or imagine what *could be* or *might be* as well. They must learn to confront the uncertainty of their work, deliberate the moral questions that underlie their actions, and act with intent as both learners and teachers in the setting of school.

Program Form and the Challenge of Change

How might teacher education be structured to prepare teachers to accomplish these goals? In the following pages I will suggest several overarching principles that could guide the construction of such a program. I will follow this with an example from my own teaching that was designed to embody those principles. Included with the example is an analysis of my students' reflections on it. I have drawn on the work of the credential class which has most recently graduated. Their words provide insight as to whether or not, and how, these teacher education activities prepared them to embrace the inherent uncertainty of teaching, and to examine the moral content of their work. They also provide access to the connection between uncertainty, morality, and the possibility of change.

Problem Solving and Inquiry

A core feature of a teacher education program that is oriented towards change is that the program is inquiry based and geared towards the definition and exploration of problems/dilemmas rather than towards the acquisition of prescriptive teaching strategies and techniques. Such a problem-exploration approach to teaching and teacher education underscores the idea that 'things-as-they-are' in school settings is not necessarily the same as 'things-as-they-*might*-be', or 'things-as-they-*ought*-to-be'. Each situation involves different people, different subject matters, different purposes and so forth. Teachers need to be prepared to analyze the factors that define the different situations that confront them. From there they must learn to determine which of these factors is most important to guide action towards the purposes they define. The reflective process of inquiry that this examination entails is learned. It involves coming to hold the knowledge, skills, and commitments necessary to ask powerful questions and search for equally powerful answers about what they believe, what they see, what they know, what they do, and ultimately, what they have done. In developing the knowledge and skills of inquiry novice teachers will have the opportunity to draw on the substantial research literature in education. In this way they will learn to use that which we *do* know, in service of what we *do not know*.

Problems That Are Real and/or Problems That Cause Us to Stretch

The type of problems around which such a teacher education program might be constructed serves to define the second principle I will suggest for developing a teacher education curriculum. Donald Schön (1983) in his work on reflective professional practice cautions us to recognize that the most challenging part of problem-solving is problem definition. The problems or dilemmas that form the 'text' of a teacher education curriculum need to meet at least two overlapping criteria:

1   They need to be *real*, that is tied to real circumstances in local schools that are recognizable to both the university and school practitioners who are engaged in exploring them.
2   They need to be defined or constructed to challenge existing school structures and systems.

Let us think for a moment about these two criteria. Real problems are not difficult to find in the workings of school. However, they are difficult to capture in forms that are useful for teacher education. Part of the challenge of constructing an inquiry-based teacher education curriculum is finding a mechanism for capturing the 'real stuff' of school life and presenting it in a form that will generate a meaningful, extensive, rigorous, examination by the teacher education community (novice professionals, and their more experienced school- and university-based colleagues). Determining what is 'real', furthermore, is rendered problematic by the complexity of life in school, and the powerful role of perception in defining what matters. It is important that the problems that serve as text for teacher education be determined by the variety of people trying to understand them. Teacher-written cases of practice, video representations of work in school, curriculum representations of a variety of forms, aggregations of students' performances, etc. all hold potential for creating a text that is real.

The second criterion is that the problems open a conversation that pushes its participants beyond the status quo. The issue I raise here concerns both the learning context that frames the problem exploration and the problem itself. Certain problems or dilemmas lend themselves better to examining existing practices than others, and examining them in the good company of colleagues. Similarly, how we frame those problems suggests different kinds of conversations as well. Several examples can be drawn directly from the school reform agenda that has captured the attention of American educators: for instance, the question of how to get parents more involved in the education of their children, a common dilemma faced by many interested in school reform (Fine, 1993). The question that might guide the exploration of this issue could be framed in a number of different ways each one of which would suggest a different level of engagement with the issue of parent involvement. 'How can we get more parents involved in our school and our classrooms?', for example, suggests a different conversation from 'What role should parents have in the workings of our school?' Similarly, asking 'How might we implement the state's suggested science curriculum for K-1 classrooms?', is different from asking

'What science knowledge and skills do we want first graders to know by the time they head off to second grade?' Pushing ourselves and our students to consider a deeper or more fundamental set of questions about how life in school ought to proceed helps us create a meaningful conversation that promotes learning and challenges the status quo at the same time. We must be vigilant about asking ourselves 'Why?' 'Why is this important, why is this so, why am I doing this?' and so forth. Asking *why* allows us to define as uncertain that which may be perceived as given; it opens up the more fundamental questions which allows us to challenge things as they are.

Colleagues and Collaboration

The third guiding principle for teacher education that promotes and supports an agenda of change is that the program be designed to develop the knowledge, skills, and dispositions needed for collaborative work in school settings. Asking ourselves why, and exploring anew the practices, structures, complexities of school life, requires the presence of others. The work of teaching is far too complex for teachers to manage it alone — the problems are too numerous and complex, the uncertainties too ubiquitous, the challenges too great. Teachers need one another just as they need participation and support of their school administrators, the district personnel, the parents and other community members whose children they serve. Alone, teachers are limited in their ability to define the issues and dilemmas adequately, and limited in defining the best course of action for different situations — different students, different intended outcomes, and so forth. Shulman and Cary (1987) argued almost ten years ago that teachers are bounded in their ability to function rationally, and this has been exacerbated as the populations and purposes they serve have become increasingly diverse.

Given the norm of isolation in schools, the importance of developing the skills of collegiality in teacher education cannot be emphasized enough. The culture of teaching as work, and the culture of school which separates people — by grade, by age, by subject area, by role, etc. — does little to promote meaningful collaboration among school colleagues. Yet meaningful collaboration is essential if we are to expand our school agenda to help teachers teach all children important content in rigorous and challenging ways. Teachers need to learn the value of collaboration and develop the knowledge and skills that will allow them to do collaborative work successfully.

Teacher Education for Change

Perhaps the longest persistent challenge of teacher education is how to teach theory and practice together in ways which promote the use of theory to illuminate practice, and the use of practice to challenge and extend theory. These coupled practices are the mainstay of reflective teaching and, therefore, the core of inquiry-based teacher education as I've been describing it in this chapter. Existing theory helps teachers both frame and explore problems by helping them to ask pertinent questions, to know which questions to ask, to examine data that will help them answer their questions, and so forth. In a similar way, everyday practice challenges teachers to examine theory by looking for confirming and disconfirming evidence, and to construct new theory as a result of their reflective work. By definition, teachers who approach their work in this reflective and inquiring way necessarily embrace the uncertainty of the work of teaching because they do not take as *given* but as *problematic* the conditions of school. They see their work as guided by a process of coming to understand more fully what is, in order to determine what needs to be as the work proceeds. Understanding what is in relation to what might be requires these teachers to examine the purposes of the work of school in the first place. In the process, they necessarily engage the moral questions of their work.

In structuring teacher education to promote these capabilities in novice teachers it is important to consider all aspects of the program. Not only do the experiences that the student teachers have in their fieldwork placements need to be guided by norms of reflective practice, but the work in their university classes also needs to be guided by the same set of ideals. Teacher educators need to be reflective practitioners themselves, and the work that they require of students needs to consistently convey a reflective and inquiring stance towards teaching and the work of schools. This reflective stance necessarily brings together theory and practice in teaching; as the novice professionals engage in their work in schools, and as their faculty engage in the work of teaching them, both groups (the student teachers and their university faculty) will be simultaneously engaged in the complex processes of making sense of what they are doing and why. Each group alone and in collaboration will necessarily consider the purposes of their decisions and actions, as well as the consequences of what they do.

An Example

One place to examine how this might look in a teacher education setting is in the experiences student teachers have in their professional education programs. An experience my students have in their program occurs within the context of my course entitled 'Introduction to the Profession of Teaching Diverse Learners'. There are several structural features of the course that I designed to embrace the principles just described. First, all of the student teachers in the program take this year-long class. Elementary and secondary teachers are together in conversation with one another throughout the year as are subject matter specialists from all of the different secondary disciplines. First grade teachers work with high school teachers of mathematics. English teachers work with physics teachers, and kindergarten teachers work with both.

Second, I have conceptualized the 'text' for the class as having two sides that we examine simultaneously. On side one, the students do substantial reading of the education research literature; side two is a text they create by bringing to class various representations of the work they are doing in their classrooms. The dialogue among the class colleagues is one which consistently traverses the theory and practice divide. A goal of this course is that by its completion the students will see theory and practice as not separate but as parts of an elastic continuum that pulls and stretches at each end in an interplay that causes both ends to grow.

All of the assignments in this course, as well as the course meetings themselves, are designed to accomplish the goals I have outlined in this chapter. The second semester Curriculum Project serves here as a case example. For the Curriculum Project, I organize the group of sixty students into groups of three or four. In each group there is at least one elementary school student teacher, a second from the middle school and a third from the high school grades. The cross-grade-level and interdisciplinary design is meant to challenge the discipline and grade-level boundaries of most K-12 curriculum planning. Using Bruner's (1977) idea of the spiral curriculum as a guide, the student teachers work together in these mixed groups over a four-week period to plan the teaching of a concept they have chosen within the subject area and grade levels they teach. The four weeks end with a Curriculum Symposium where each group presents its work in the form of a poster presentation. The assignment requires that the posters convey the concept the teacher groups have chosen together with the justification they have created that will support their choice (in the paragraphs below I describe this piece of the assignment more fully). They must capture the essence of how the concept will be taught at the different grade levels represented in the group and the manner in which the team has considered the spiralling factor that Bruner suggests.

The concepts the students teach come from a list I provide, or from others that the students choose. Independent of its source, the assignment requires the students to justify the concept as to its importance in the K-12 curriculum. 'Interdependence' was one concept students chose this year, as were 'change', 'scarcity', and 'point of view'. The assignment requires the students to justify their choice of concept by answering the question: *Why teach this concept?* — what makes this concept so important that it needs to be taught (as Bruner would suggest) numerous times, with increasing complexity, over the twelve years students are in school? Rather than take as given the content of one's teaching, the students are asked to examine their purposes and justify their choices. In this instance, they are also asked to do this reasoning in collaboration with colleagues, further challenging the status quo of schooling which isolates teachers from one another. The groups prepare a joint justification statement which they either include or otherwise represent on the posters they create.

Once the group has chosen and justified its concept, each member is responsible for leading a discussion of how that concept might be taught at the level he or she is currently teaching. The assignment suggests that the teachers visit one another's classrooms so that the ensuing conversations are more fully grounded in the reality the teachers face. With the help of his or her colleagues, then, each teacher prepares either a lesson, a series of lessons, or a unit that is aimed at teaching the concept. Though those lessons are not necessarily presented in full on the poster, they are represented symbolically in some way, and are written up and available for distribution at the Curriculum Symposium. Critical to the lesson planning piece of this assignment — and significant in terms of the impact of this assignment on students according to the data collected during and at its completion — is the requirement that the plan reveals the pedagogical reasoning or justification for why the teacher aims to teach the concept indicated therein. If the teacher plans to use poetry to teach 'point of view', for example, she needs to explain why she has made these coupled choices — why point of view, and why poetry to teach it? If the elementary teacher chooses to situate her lesson on 'identity' in the context of history (as Shoshana did in the example presented earlier) she needs to explain why she has made this decision as well. Furthermore, the students are also asked to explain and justify their methodology. If the social studies teacher plans to randomly assign students to groups for an opening exercise on land acquisition in the United States, he needs to explain why groups?, why random assignment?, etc. In the development of their lesson plans, the students were asked to draw on what they had learned in this class and others, what they had learned from their work in the field, and what they believed to be the purpose of their work in the first place. The assignment brought them face-to-face with the reality that each decision a teacher makes represents what he or she knows and believes about teaching, learning, and the purpose of school. The work of school is not neutral; this assignment is particularly powerful in driving that point home.

The concluding activity of the Curriculum Project is the Curriculum Symposium, a two-hour event where the teachers publicly present their work. The Education Department teaching and supervising faculty are invited to attend the event, but the primary participants are the class members themselves. Organized to approximate poster sessions in professional settings, the Symposium consists of the teachers presenting their posters to one another in an open arena where colleagues meet somewhat informally to discuss their work. The requirement is that one person stays with the poster to explain it, distribute lesson plans, etc. while the others are free to visit other poster stations. Presenting their work in a coherent and compelling form that represents the group's joint perceptions, on the one hand, and the individual's special contributions on the other, is a challenge that many students mentioned as important to their growing identities as teachers and professional colleagues.

The final step of the Curriculum assignment is for the students to write a brief reflective essay on their learning in the context of this work. Using David Hawkins (1974) essay 'I, Thou, and It' as another guide for the curriculum work we do in this class, I generate feedback about the process at several points during the four weeks. The reflective essay at the end is the culmination of this data-gathering effort. Hawkins suggests that part of the teacher's role as curriculum developer is to be a diagnostician. As the student engages with the subject matter, Hawkins argues, the teacher (who is also engaged with the subject matter) needs to attend to what the student is doing, what the student knows, what the student needs to know, the direction of the student's work, and so forth. As the teacher watches the students engage with the work, she diagnoses their progress and feedback of that information to the students they teach. Teachers who have many students (such as I did in this class) need to create ways to acquire the information they need to accomplish this diagnostician role. Throughout the Curriculum Project I collected various forms of information (including an analysis of the first drafts of their lesson plans, for example, and the first drafts of their concept justifications). I analyzed during the process the data I was receiving from students, and fed that information back to the group as a means of modelling both Hawkins' idea, and the idea of reflective practice more generally. This system of data collection, analysis, and feedback is an ongoing process throughout the class. I make explicit my pedagogical reasoning which I base on my continuous assessment of purpose in relationship to the students I have and what I learn about their purposes and their reactions to and success with the work of the class.

A Look at Results

What did I learn about how this assignment works to promote reflective practice of the kind that will help novice teachers meet the challenge of change? Was there anything in the data that might help us understand what parts of the assignment the teachers perceived as particularly helpful with regard to their professional growth? In reviewing the data (including my viewing the process itself and the Symposium event at the end) I learned that several particular structures of the assignment were most powerful for accomplishing the change-agent goals outlined in this chapter. The first of these was the requirement of the assignment that the teachers work as colleagues in cross-grade level and interdisciplinary teams. While collegiality is a central goal of the program more broadly, what distinguished this experience from some of the others they had had working with colleague groups at other times was the composition of the groups, the focus on curriculum, and requirement for a final product that they perceived as having meaning for the profession more broadly. The second structure of the project that teachers reported as significant was the requirement that they justify their pedagogical choices to a professional audience (their curriculum partners first, and the broader professional community second). I will discuss what I learned from my students about both of these factors, and illustrate in my analysis how each of them contributed to the preparation of these novice professionals for their impending work as change agents in the setting of school. Their words provide access into some of the processes of conceptual change that are part of learning to teach in a reflective way which promotes and supports change. It appears that a careful examination of things as they are, in the company of others who are similarly engaged, is a first step in prompting novices to imagine things that could be new and different for schools.

Collegiality

In spite of what the teachers said about believing in collegiality before they began this assignment, and the program emphasis on collaborative work, the requirement that this assignment be completed in cross-grade-level, interdisciplinary teams was met with enormous resistance at the outset. The objections to their working in mixed groups was similar to the objection teachers in school settings have working together: it is too difficult to coordinate and there is too little in common to share even if the coordination difficulties were overcome. Most made manifest in their reflection essays their changes of heart over the four-week period. Still, the beginning was rough going. 'This curriculum project was a taxing task', one reported. 'Crowded schedules, differences of geography, style, and focus, and almost separate philosophies created a complex situation for collegiality to flourish' (MFD, *Curriculum Reflection* 5/96). Another corroborated, 'My first thought was "There is no way that we're going to be able to come up with something we can all relate to, let alone represent on a poster!"' (HR, *Curriculum Reflection* 5/96). A third began her essay:

> Asking four dynamic people with strong personalities, values and vision to create a piece of curriculum together is ambitious. To ask that same group of four people to create a fantastic, cumulative, continuous, structure-focused curriculum is nothing short of admitting that you believe in fate. From the start, this assignment seemed disaster-bound. (IK, *Curriculum Reflection* 5/96)

Ilana, the third of these teachers continued her essay by saying, 'Contrary to my original anticipation regarding the sanity of this assignment, I found that the project provided for a wonderful opportunity. . . .' The opportunity she went on to describe included working with colleagues from different grade levels and subject areas. Genevieve shared a similar reaction:

> Although we have been told that collaboration between teachers of all grade levels was crucial to our personal efficacy as teachers, I did not realise how fruitful an interaction it could be until we began our work on the Curriculum Project. We had in our group three teachers who taught the full spectrum of students: kindergarten-second graders, fourth graders, and twelfth graders. At first the task seemed rather daunting *because* of the differences in ages of the students that we had; how could we define a slippery and amorphous concept such as power and make it recognisable to 6 year-olds as well as students who are entering college in a few short months? (GH *Curriculum Reflection*, 5/96)

Most of them, as they moved through the steps of the assignment, eventually accepted the challenge, and came to experience, first hand, the value of collaboration. They also came to understand the particular power of working with colleagues whose perspective, responsibility and, consequently, insights are different. Genevieve continued in her reflective essay,

> Interestingly enough, the wide range of our teaching experiences and knowledge of students rendered this daunting task much easier to accomplish.

Drawing from each other's knowledge, we were able to scaffold our definition of power and its relationship to gender. (GH *Curriculum Reflection*, 5/96)

Drawing on each other's knowledge, learning from each other's perspective, meeting the challenge of speaking one's emerging professional truth, became factors of the Project that the teachers came to recognize as essential for meeting the extraordinary demands of their work. They also began to recognize their own resistance, and some located its origin in the structure of school. Ilana reflected, for example:

There is a hierarchy in place that divides teachers on a variety of different planes. Teachers are stratified according to grade level, academic discipline and institutional prestige. While there is a current separation that flows through many communities of teachers, there is dire need for a forum to be provided that not only encourages teachers to communicate with one another, but a forum that challenges teachers to look critically at curriculum and how that curriculum is being communicated to students. In the context of this collective Curriculum Project, I have been given not so much a taste, but an experience that demonstrates how teachers who are confronting challenges like their differences, can organise their thoughts, feelings, and expertise, to create an exceptional product. (IK, *Curriculum Reflection*, 5/96)

An exceptional product, yes, but more significantly perhaps, a sense of community, a shared sense of purpose, and ultimately a sense of hope:

In building bridges between teachers of different grade levels in order to create meaningful curriculum coherence, the concomitant creation is something which seems to be lacking in many of our schools, and in many of our individual teachers and students: a sense of hope. (GH, *Curriculum Reflection*, 5/96)

The sense of hope that Genevieve suggests here seems to come from several sources that warrant mentioning in the context of this argument about preparing teachers for the challenge of change. One is the feeling of purposefulness that the conversation about *curriculum* raised for the teachers. Their reflections on the process point towards a clearer idea about the substantive connections that could or might exist across the K-12 experience. Mary, who is preparing to teach secondary physics, said, for example, 'I learned first-hand how important it is for teachers to cross curricular lines and to cross those invisible boundaries of grade level of school group (elementary, middle, and high schools) . . . it focused the task of collaboration on curriculum where I believe it belongs' (MFD, *Curriculum Reflection*, 5/96). The power of crossing curricular lines and grade levels allows teachers to see the connections they have with their colleagues, and the connections that are essential in the development of knowledge and skills for their students. In this realization, there is hope for change. Genevieve captured this feeling that was shared by many of her colleagues when she said:

> I was fascinated by the idea that through curriculum development and teacher collaboration we stand a real chance of creating widespread change for our students, schools and communities. . . . This constant reinforcement of ideas which a spiral curriculum faithfully implemented at all grade levels brings to students, will, in my opinion, help to create a new generation of people who consciously seek to create for themselves, and for those less powerful, an equitable society. (GH, *Curriculum Reflection* 5/96)

The feeling of community that the project engendered, and the potential power of that community connection, was a second source of hope for the student teachers. People in community feel less isolated. For teachers this is critical given the complexity of the work and the inherent uncertainty that makes that work so arduous. One of the most difficult things to accept in teaching is the uncertainty of the task — a central point of this chapter. It is impossible to know with certainty that the choices you make as a teacher will help the children you are working with grow in the direction you hope they will. While this is hard to accept for all teachers, it is most difficult for novices who enter the profession with high ideals, and who have little evidence that they are making any progress towards reaching those ideals as they begin their work in the field. More experienced teachers are able to better predict student outcomes, at least a particular type of student outcome (those that can be observed, measured, quantified) with a modicum of success. Novice teachers are much less able to predict these outcomes (Jackson, 1986). Beyond that, outcomes that are not measurable in these ways — and outcomes that often capture the attention and imagination of beginning teachers such as equity and access for urban poor, raised confidence in marginalized children, raised consciousness regarding earth's resources — are problematic for novices in even more ways: They are not only hard to predict, but difficult to identify and articulate clearly in the first place.

From my student teacher colleagues I have learned that one mechanism to cope with these uncertainties is by working with colleagues. The Curriculum Project had an important impact on the students for this reason. The requirement to work with others in these mixed groups seemed to provide the occasion to experience the value of collaborative work especially as it functioned to result in a sense of shared responsibility. Sheryl wrote on a feedback form, for example, 'Being able to collaborate, struggle, and be unsure together was essential. We were not isolated and this was *good*' (Sheryl, 5/96). What was *good* about it was elaborated by Louise who said, 'I have learned that it is okay and educative *not* to know, and that there is so much to be learned through collaboration. I get to have the privilege and responsibility of not knowing which, when working on things with others, means I will always be learning more' (Louise, 5/96). Carol Margaret's reflection revealed the pain of coupling responsibility with uncertainty — a pain familiar to all teachers. She also described the relief that comes with learning to trust colleagues with whom you can share the load:

> As you know very well — the most problematic experiences for me are those over which I have no control yet feel entirely responsible: the lives of my students, the pressures/problems of society. If I can let go of my notion of having to do all things at all times, for all students, being always right and having to do it all on my own, then I think I'll really be able to be present, real, and make a difference in my own life as well as those of my students. (CM 5/96)

Reflecting on this further she says:

> The biggest lesson has been to *communicate* with others, not to shut down, isolate myself and pretend everything in my classroom is *just* my responsibility; I don't have that much control. . . . We are all in this together — amazing how we are trained and brainwashed to isolate ourselves when it is the connections with others that hold us, suspend us in the living, breathing world. (CM 5/96)

Articulating One's Beliefs: Pedagogical Justification

Genevieve closes her reflection by addressing this issue of collaboration and trust that the Curriculum Project seemed to engender:

> Through teacher collaboration, we not only strengthen our students' academic experience, but also foster a sense of trust between us as colleagues. In so doing, we can entrust each other with the care of our students, knowing that we share the same fundamental goal — to help our students live as powerfully as possible. (GH, *Curriculum Reflection* 5/96)

In order for teachers to come to trust one another, they need to talk about things that matter to them. Ironically, there is little opportunity in teaching for teachers to have such a conversation, and little opportunity to develop the knowledge and skills necessary to have it as well. There is considerable evidence in the data that the Curriculum Project offered the student teachers an opportunity to speak about what they believe, and to become clearer about what they believe through the process of these conversations. Though there were several points in the project where the teachers were challenged to justify their work, one frequently mentioned place was in the conversations they had with their colleagues about their plans. Louise described a learning opportunity like this:

> My thinking was more disciplined as a result of our collaborative efforts. I recognised that as a multiple subjects teacher, my thinking is frequently

too broad. I want to teach because I want to give children a certain sense of purposefulness, intention, and unique contribution. I seek to create ties between the individual, the classroom, the school community, the family, the neighbourhood, and the world. My colleagues forced me to ask, 'But what specifically are you teaching in this instance? What is sustainability a foundational idea to? How can you justify teaching this concept through Language Arts lessons?' . . . Certainly I recognise in a more practical way how my teaching is informed and made meaningful through a collaboration with primary and secondary teachers. (LM, *Curriculum Reflection*, 5/96)

For Louise, and for many of her colleagues, this challenge to clarify her beliefs and articulate them occurred in the collaborative planning meetings. In these planning sessions, which were mentioned by almost all of the students as particularly powerful in the learning opportunity they offered, the students worked diligently to explain to their partners how they planned to teach their concept, and why they planned to teach it in that way. They reported that at times this self-interrogation drove them to the depths of their beings in search of who they were and what motivation or belief guided their intended action. The experience also caused them to draw on sources of knowledge that were tacit — and in certain instances somewhat unconscious. Several reported that the challenge helped them recognize how much they knew; apparently, the process raised consciousness about how much they had learned on this journey of learning to teach. In her reflective essay Joanna exclaimed, for example, 'I realized I do have the rationale in me. It gave me confidence about my pedagogical choices' (JT, *Curriculum Reflection* 5/96).

The challenge of needing to justify their pedagogical choices was built into the assignment in a number of ways. In an indirect way the teachers were in constant conversation with their colleagues which, as the quotations above indicate, required them to justify their ideas, plans, and beliefs. Similarly, the culminating Curriculum Symposium made this conversation even more public and was seen by many as an additional opportunity for probing more deeply into the reasons for teaching. Throughout the assignment the students were asked to bring consciousness to their pedagogical choices, and therefore engage with the moral questions underlying their work. Joanna explained how she began to connect the challenge of constructing knowledge in collaboration with her partners and the concomitant revelation of beliefs and commitments. She began to see this process as part of the moral dimension of teaching:

From walking around at the symposium I . . . noticed I was getting in touch with others' moral reasoning. Something about this assignment brought us all to make some kind of public statement about why we teach — what is of worth in our curriculum plans. (JT, *Curriculum Reflection*, 5/96)

In addition to these ways in which the assignment positioned students to speak with colleagues and thus reveal their goals, it also required that they include a pedagogical rationale or justification for every step of their written plan. This requirement, incidentally, met with the same resistance initially to that of the mixed group collaboration. The students reported that the requirement that they justify what they intended to do was difficult (both in terms of what they decided to teach and how they intended to teach it). The process involved laborious conversations that required them to articulate their beliefs about what students need to know and why, what school is for, how they plan to teach children from backgrounds very different from their own, and so forth. Not only did the teachers need to consider these factors for themselves, the structure of the assignment placed them in the position of needing to articulate those beliefs to their colleagues. Given the multiple perspectives inherent in any group of teachers — especially one that is mixed by both grade level and subject area — conflicts arose. While I understood the challenge these conversations entail, I found their reaction surprising given the lateness in the term, and capability I knew the students had for accomplishing the task. Their resistance indicated to me that thinking about what they are doing in relationship to why they are doing it is not part of the typical discourse of the profession. 'I really struggled a lot with the lesson plan', one student reported, 'with thinking about *why* of everything' (Janan, *Curriculum Reflection* 5/96). In reflecting on the process further, this same student stepped back one layer more when she asked subsequently, 'Why was it hard for me?' Another reported, 'When I first received my rough draft with all of your "why"s and "what is the connection between"s, I felt somewhat overwhelmed' (Joanna, *Curriculum Reflection* 5/96). Overwhelmed and discouraged according to Virginia whose comments lend insight to the process:

> When I first got back my first draft of my lesson plan, I was a little discouraged — what are all these notes and questions, did I do it right? And then I really appreciated, though it was difficult to get started, the processes involved in *justifying* my lesson. I think oftentimes we have these notions of what we *must* teach according to standards, and what we think will be 'fun' and engaging. But we fail to really think about *why* we want it to be fun and engaging; or why it might be important that our lessons adhere to 'standards'. I often think a lot about the methods and not as often about the reasons. This seems to relate to our many discussions about knowing where we are going when we are teaching . . . what does it matter what they (my students) produce? But, in fact, it matters very much. And here, it also becomes a moral issue. Why do we want to teach about change, (for example) why should this concept spiral throughout the curriculum? I think the members of my group really believe in the moral imperative we have as teachers to teach children how to *identify* and understand change, to see their role as both observers and *participants* in change, and also to help them find the tools to enable them to be *agents* of change. (Virginia, *Curriculum Project*, 5/96)

Interestingly, Virginia's group selected the concept of 'change' around which to focus its curriculum work. My questions of her during the assignment began by probing for her pedagogical rationale about teaching the concept of change in the first place. I asked her what about change she intended to teach and why, and why she would teach it as her plan indicated she would. Given the culture of school where such questions are seldom asked, my queries indicated to Virginia that perhaps she was not doing the work 'right'. Like many of her student teaching colleagues, until she was in the position of responding either to me or to her curriculum partners about the purposes and consequences of her work, she did not recognize the importance of probing herself more deeply about the content she teaches, and the methods by which she chooses to do so. The coupled facts that this assignment occurred late in the Spring of a year-long credential program, and the students found both working with colleagues and justifying their work difficult, underscore the importance of this type of questioning in teacher education. I found that even in my own class, which was constructed to teach the value of reflective practice and eschew the notion of 'one right answer', the traditional standard of 'getting it right' prevailed. The Curriculum Project provided the students the opportunity to talk with colleagues about what they hoped to accomplish and why, as well as plan with them how they might go about accomplishing their goals. They were required to ask questions, search for answers, struggle with conflicting points of view, provide evidence from the field, and justify their work. Such opportunities are critical for undoing the culture of isolation in teaching, and building a culture that supports an agenda of change.

Concluding Thoughts

Learning to teach is an extraordinarily complex undertaking. These times of tremendous change make the challenge of learning to teach more complex still, and the challenge of teaching teachers one step beyond that. Teachers must be prepared with the knowledge, skills, and dispositions to be learners in the context of school. By learning this, novices can come to act with intent in their own classrooms and schools. In their multifaceted quest, they can learn to join with colleagues (other teachers, administrators, parents, etc.) to define and direct a larger school and change agenda as well. This challenge we face is two-fold: we must prepare teachers for excellent practice in schools as they *are* and, at the same time, we must also prepare them to engage in conversation and school practice as they believe it *ought to be*. This is today's challenge. It is for today's teachers and teacher educators, and for *tomorrow's* children.

References

BELENKEY, M., CLINCHY, B., GOLDBERGER, N. and TARULE, J. (1986) *Women's Ways of Knowing: The Development of Self, Voice and Mind*, New York, Basic Books.

BROWN, J.S., COLLINS, A. and DUGUID, P. (1989) 'Situated cognition and the culture of learning', *Educational Researcher*, **18**, 1, pp. 32–42.

BRUNER, J. (1977) *The Process of Education*, Cambridge, Harvard University Press.

DARLING-HAMMOND, L. (1993) 'Reframing the school reform agenda: Developing capacity for school transformation', *Phi Delta Kappan*, **74**, 10, pp. 753–61.

FINE, M. (1993) '(Ap)parent involvement: Reflections of parents, power, and urban public schools', *Teachers College Record*, **94**, 4, pp. 682–709.

FULLAN, M. (1993) *Change Forces*, New York, Falmer Press.

GROSSMAN, P.L. (1990) *The Making of a Teacher: Teacher Knowledge and Teacher Education*, New York, Teachers College Press.

GROSSMAN, P.L. and RICHERT, A.E. (1996) 'Building capacity and commitment for leadership in preservice teacher education', *Journal of School Leadership*, **6**, 2, pp. 202–10.

HAWKINS, D. (1974) 'I, thou, and it', *The Informed Vision*, New York, Agathon Press, pp. 49–62.

JACKSON, P.W. (1986) *The Practice of Teaching*, New York, Teachers College Press.

LIEBERMAN, A. (1995) 'Practices that support teacher development: Transforming conceptions of professional learning', *Phi Delta Kappan*, **76**, 8, pp. 591–6.

MEIER, D. (1995) *The Power of Their Ideas*, Boston, Beacon Press.

MURRAY, J. (1994) 'A response', *Teachers College Record*, **96**, 2, pp. 174–82.

SARASON, S.B. (1993) *The Case for Change: Rethinking the Preparation of Educators*, San Francisco, Jossey Bass.

SCHÖN, D.A. (1983) *The Reflective Practitioner*, New York, Basic Books.

SHULMAN, L.S. (1986) 'Those who understand: Knowledge growth in teaching', *Educational Researcher*, **15**, 2, pp. 4–14.

SHULMAN, L.S. and CARY, N.B. (1987) 'Psychology and the limitations of individual rationality: Implications for the study of reasoning and civility', *Review of Educational Research*, **54**, 4, pp. 501–24.

WILSON, S.M., SHULMAN, L.S. and RICHERT, A.E. (1987) '150 different ways of knowing: Representations of knowledge in teaching', in CALDERHEAD, J.E. *Exploring Teachers' Thinking*, London, Cassell Press, pp. 104–22.

7 Learning to Teach Prospective Teachers to Teach Mathematics: The Struggles of a Beginning Teacher Educator

Cynthia Nicol

Introduction

'I was kind of anxious but also excited about taking this course', said Kendra after the fifth class of our elementary mathematics methods course. 'But now I don't see how any of this relates to what we need to know — you're not listening to us!' she stated with contempt. Kendra, like many prospective teachers in my methods course, expected to learn what and how to teach mathematics. She entered the course assuming it would help her learn all the mathematics she needed to know as well as how she should go about teaching it to students. She was not prepared for, nor did she expect that learning to teach would involve investigating teaching. 'After all', she wrote in her journal, 'we as beginning teachers need to know about the math and how to teach it before we can start hypothesizing, exploring, and understanding students or teaching'.

Teacher educators in mathematics education face inherent dilemmas, tensions, and challenges in preparing teachers for life in classrooms as they are now and in preparing teachers for life in classrooms as they might be. Prospective teachers themselves are successful graduates of schools as they are now with mathematics classrooms that more often than not tend to focus on the learning and application of routine procedural skills. Visions for how mathematics classrooms might be, depicted in the various reform documents (National Council of Teachers of Mathematics (NCTM), 1989, 1991), portray teachers developing learning environments and activities which encourage their students' mathematical inquiry, understanding, and sense-making. Balancing the worlds of what is and what might be in teaching education is an activity fraught with difficulties and challenges.

The challenges of the teacher educator are further intensified by prospective teachers' desire and need to get through the course, have a 'successful' practicum, obtain a teaching position, and function in existing school cultures. Encouraging prospective teachers to view the teaching of mathematics differently from how they once learned it, from how their sponsor teacher may teach it, from how their students will most likely have learned it, and from how other teachers in their future school may teach it, is a tremendous challenge for teacher education in general, and for a beginning teacher educator in particular.

This is a story of my experience, the tensions, dilemmas, and challenges I face as I attempt to teach prospective teachers to teach mathematics for understanding. I work from the premise of teaching as inquiry in a mathematics methods course to future elementary teachers. Although I entered the university classroom with seven years of experience teaching mathematics from Grade 8 though Grade 12, I was not prepared for the challenges I met. Lampert (1985) and others (Katz and Raths, 1992; Ball, 1993; Cuban, 1992) suggest such tensions and dilemmas of teaching are more manageable than solvable. As teachers we hold conflicting purposes which tend to give rise to these pedagogical problems and, in attempting to work within these dilemmas, we are often not able to make choices but instead deliberate about alternatives. The idea of thinking of teaching as managing tensions and dilemmas provides me with a way of highlighting, discussing, and analyzing some of the issues and concerns that arise as I attempt to teach prospective elementary teachers to teach mathematics.

In this story I recount, reflect upon, and analyze my experience through three tensions or dilemmas: choosing and using worthwhile pedagogical tasks; listening for, listening to, and listening with; and researching teaching or teaching researching. These tensions emerged through my attempts to teach prospective teachers in ways which value inquiry — ways that might help my students make sense of things for themselves, help them gain the skill, knowledge, and confidence that they have the resources to investigate their own practice and that of others, and help them take the risk to share ideas and develop defensible reasons for particular standpoints in a public forum.

Teaching as Inquiry

I view teaching as both inquiry and learning. One of my goals is to provide opportunities for prospective teachers to see and feel teaching as a form of inquiry and as a continual learning experience. As teacher educators we, too, participate in that inquiry and in the continuous learning cycle. Instead of the teacher education model in which theoretical propositions, advice, and techniques are provided in a how-to, top–down manner, or as a 'bag of pedagogical tricks' (Wineburg, 1991, p. 277) I choose to take a stance similar to Jean McNiff's (1993) by encouraging prospective teachers 'to be critical of personal practice, and use [their] deepened insights to move forward' (p. 20). Following McNiff (1993), I felt teacher education should help to prepare prospective teachers to learn and inquire rather than help to prepare them to be taught. I wanted my prospective teachers to gain skill and confidence in investigating how their personal and professional conduct affects learners and how their own understanding of what it means to know, learn, and construct mathematical ideas influences who they are as teachers of mathematics.

My intent is for my pre-service teachers to become willing and able to reflect and inquire about the purposes and consequences of their actions as teachers, and to develop habits of mind that might be needed for personal growth and professional development. This means learning about and participating in an inquiry into their own understandings of mathematics and students' understanding of mathematics, as well as the discipline of mathematics and the teaching of mathematics.

Prospective teachers enter teacher education programs with a wealth of knowledge and beliefs about teaching and learning as experienced students in the schools they have attended. They have formed beliefs about schooling, teaching, learning, students, and mathematics. This 'apprenticeship of observation' (Lortie, 1975, p. 61) has led them to develop ideas and beliefs about teaching and learning that are generally consistent with the ways in which a subject is 'typically' taught. In a growing body of literature, researchers have described teachers' beliefs as lay theories (Knowles and Holt-Reynolds, 1991), images (Calderhead and Robson, 1991), webs (McDiarmid, 1990), and folkways (Buchmann, 1987). This research on beliefs about teaching learned through schooling and life experiences suggest that such beliefs are well-formed, powerful, and often resistant to change (Buchmann, 1991; Gore and Zeichner, 1991).

Communicating principles of professional practice to prospective teachers is therefore quite unlike that involved in most other professions (Feiman-Nemser and Buchmann, 1986). Prospective teachers enter teacher education with ideas and beliefs about what counts as 'good' or 'right' or 'poor' mathematics teaching. They come to their mathematics methods classes with clear images and preconceptions of teaching and learning mathematics.

As long-time students with a view of teaching from only the student's perspective, prospective teachers often consider teaching as a technical endeavor. As students they often do not see, nor become involved in, the conscious decision-making, deliberating, managing of dilemmas, and reflecting that is involved in preparing, enacting, and assessing teaching practices. 'They are not', as Lortie (1975) states, 'privy to the teacher's private intentions and personal reflections on classroom events . . . they are not pressed to place the teacher's actions in a pedagogically-oriented framework' (p. 62). As a result prospective teachers have developed powerful lay-theories (Holt-Reynolds, 1994), theories based on personal history which are often tacit and taken for granted, about mathematics, learners, schools, and pedagogical practices.

I have therefore sought to develop a pedagogy of teacher education that seriously attempts to address the prior beliefs that prospective teachers bring with them to the course by expanding teachers' visions of what is desirable and what might be possible in teaching mathematics. The pedagogical challenge for me then has been to develop instructional moves, activities, tasks, and problems which will encourage and open prospective teachers to asking questions, analyzing, taking new perspectives, and considering alternatives as well as developing defensible arguments for teaching practices that move beyond their personal experiences of studenting — that is, to develop a reflective stance, one of critique and inquiry. But the challenge is also for me to do this in a way which authentically represents the nature of teaching, its inherent uncertainty and complexity.

In attempts to address these challenges I teach from a perspective of teaching as inquiry. I attempt to construct and model a pedagogy of inquiry which parallels the pedagogy of mathematics instruction envisioned in reform documents. Just as the reform documents portray students investigating worthwhile mathematical problems in which they invent, conjecture, and reason about various mathematical concepts in a community of learners, I want my prospective teachers to be investigating genuine pedagogical problems through which they might develop reasoned arguments about the problems and dilemmas of practice. However, this is no simple task.

Emerging Struggles of a Beginning Teacher Educator

In researching my own practice and the developing thinking of prospective teachers, I video-tape all class sessions and record in a journal my own thinking and deliberations in preparing for, and in reflecting upon, my teaching. With permission, prospective teachers' journals and course work are photocopied, and prospective teachers are interviewed both informally throughout the course and more formally at the beginning and end of the course. This chapter draws on data from my teaching in 1995, in which I collaboratively taught the course with two colleagues.

Choosing and Using Worthwhile Pedagogical Tasks

The question of what might, or could, be considered worthwhile beginning activities for prospective teachers is a topic of continuing debate for me. My desire to develop, adapt, or select tasks that would be both mathematically and pedagogically rich is a challenge. I want tasks that provide opportunities for prospective teachers to re-visit and extend their previous understandings of mathematics and to consider new possibilities for teaching mathematics. But I want activities that are inviting rather than overwhelming, open-ended rather than closed, and ones that help me learn as much about the prospective teachers, in these beginning classes, as they help the prospective teachers learn about themselves. I want our tasks to be both the focus of our inquiry and the springboard for further inquiry. This is similar to what Lampert (1990) speaks about in choosing problems for her fifth-grade mathematics students. She writes, 'At the beginning of a unit, when we were switching to a new topic, the problem we started with was chosen for its potential to expose a wide range of students' thinking about a bit of mathematics, to make explicit and public what they could do and how they understand' (p. 39).

Such pedagogical reasoning for a teacher of mathematics requires some knowledge of mathematics, of students as learners, and of how students learn mathematics (Shulman, 1987). In writing of her experiences and pedagogical reasoning as a teacher of mathematics to Grade 3 students, Ball (1990a) suggests that teachers need to have a 'bifocal perspective — perceiving the mathematics through the mind of the learner while perceiving the mind of the learner through the mathematics' (p. 2). In a similar way I feel that I need multiple perspectives in thinking about the kinds of activities that might engage prospective teachers in mathematical and pedagogical inquiry. But rather than a dual perspective I often feel as though I am working through three or four perspectives. In deciding what tasks to select I need to consider both the mathematical and pedagogical aspects of a problem through both the minds of the prospective teachers and their prospective students.

I anticipate that many prospective teachers enter the class with somewhat limited understandings of the mathematics they may be expected to teach. I expect that, for some areas of the elementary mathematics curriculum, my students' under-standings will be procedurally strong but conceptually weak. I also anticipate that many experienced school mathematics in a traditional form of telling and doing rather than through inquiry.

The beginning classes I feel are extremely important. I want our beginning to be gentle, yet somewhat disturbing. I want to challenge my prospective teachers' ideas about what might be possible in teaching mathematics. I want to 'stir things up' but not so rapidly that they begin to fall apart. I want to, as Ball (1990b) notes, help our students reinterpret their past experiences and to use their experiences as trajectories for further learning. Hence, I need a rich problem. But what is a rich beginning problem for investigation?

To develop an activity that would engage the students in both mathematical and pedagogical investigation, that would pique the students' curiosity — again, no easy task. An excerpt from my journal provides some sense of the challenge and desire I felt in my deliberations in trying to select a good activity.

> It seems to be so difficult and frustrating to find good pedagogical prob-lems — or even construct good ones. I could go out and video-tape one of Karen's[1] classes again and gather her students' work — we could use that to initiate some discussion — but that will take time as usual. There are books and books of math problems that can be used as a resource for teachers — why don't we have books of students' responses to prob-lems and maybe teachers' interpretations of students' work that we could use as problems for beginning teachers to investigate? (Cynthia, journal, 10/02/94)

This excerpt from my journal depicts my early thoughts and deliberations and my frustration with the lack of resources offered to teacher educators. I continued to think about what to do for our second class.

> I want something interactive. Something that would set us up for some genuine pedagogical investigations — one where we could together, the pTs and *us*, explore, ask questions, inquire about, think deeply about some aspect of teaching math — or trying to get at a student's understanding of something. Using written work or video seems to still put us, as instruc-tors, in control — maybe it gives the impression that we've already had a chance to analyze it — since we've selected the piece. If we had an activity where we were all investigating it together — would that make it more genuine? More genuine for us, as instructors, in the sense that we

> would be exploring with our preservice teachers? And if we were explor-
> ing together — would that help to set an environment in the spirit of
> collaborative inquiry — where we could use each other's insight and know-
> ledge to help us make sense of something? (Cynthia, journal, 10/04/94)

The activity that I, in working with my colleagues, constructed and used was
an activity we called the Monster Problem. There are three parts to this activity
which span three consecutive classes. In the first part prospective teachers participate as learners of mathematics engaging in mathematical inquiry. In the second
part they observe and investigate myself and my colleagues as we work with a
small group of students on the same problem. In the third part of this activity
prospective teachers work individually with two Grade 6/7 students investigating
teaching and learning. Throughout the activity they are encouraged to write about
their thoughts, decisions, and feelings in their journals. In preparation for the first
part of the activity they are asked to work on the following problem:

The Monster Problem:[2]
Three tired and hungry monsters went to sleep with a bag of cookies. One
monster woke up, ate 1/3 of the cookies, then went back to sleep.

Later a second monster woke up and ate 1/3 of the remaining cookies,
then went back to sleep.

Finally, the third monster woke up and ate 1/3 of the remaining cookies.
When she was finished there were 8 cookies left.

How many cookies were in the bag originally?

Prospective teachers were asked to try the problem themselves, to consider
how students might solve the problem and what they might need to solve it, and
to think about how a teacher might engage students in a discussion through the
problem. At the beginning of the first class, our prospective teachers were asked
to share their own solutions to the Monster Problem with each other in a whole-
class setting. They were keen to be told whether or not they had done the problem correctly, and they were annoyed when I did not readily do so. I expect and
encourage them to explain and justify their solutions and some are frustrated with
my questions:

Why did you think that is the answer?
Why do you think that way of doing the problem is better than another
way?
Could you think of another way to try it?

Some become aware of their limited understanding of the problem and many find
it difficult to accept that there could be more than one acceptable way to solve it.

In solving the problem, the use of a particular formula or equation, or doing
the problem backwards by constructing an algebraic expression of the form $\frac{2}{3}x =$
8 is common. Many believe it to be too difficult for students to solve:

There is no way I think a Grade 5 student will be able to solve this problem; it took me almost half an hour to solve it myself. (Corrine)

I eventually solved it but it's not in a really mathematical way — I just guessed, did it by guessing and I'm still not sure why it works out. How could a student get it? (Kendra)

The second part of this activity moves prospective teachers into being observers and investigators of teaching and learning. After they have discussed their own solution strategies and solutions to the Monster Problem, four Grade 5 students are invited into the classroom. The Grade 5 students speak openly about what they like and dislike about math, what they find interesting and difficult, and how they most often work on math in their classroom. The prospective teachers sit in small groups observing, taking notes, and listening. They focus on the various kinds of questions asked by the students and the teacher, the ways in which the students interact with each other and the teacher, and the various ways in which the students approach the problem, their thinking, and what they are doing and saying. In about 45 minutes of work, the Grade 5 students are satisfied that the number of cookies in the bag originally was twenty-seven. The prospective teachers then ask their own questions of the students but some do not ask any questions at all because, 'If I were one of those students I would just die if someone asked me a question.'

During the next class we discuss and analyze the teaching and learning that occurred with the Grade 5 students. In this case, my colleague Andrea, as facilitator of the discussion with the Grade 5 students, shared her thinking, the decisions she made and why, and how she felt at certain times while working with the students. Andrea spoke about her decision to build the mathematical discussion around the students' ideas, to value their thinking and to get a sense of what the students were thinking. The strong views expressed by the prospective teachers in their journals as they reflected on the session with Grade 5 students were surprising.

What is the value of guessing? ... [it] wasn't productive and led to frustration [for the students] ... It is time to stop and reteach a concept or redefine the activity when the students resort to random guessing with no sense of meaning. (Kendra, journal, 01/06/95)

Although I think this method [trial and error] was useful, I think it is too time-consuming. The students should have been shown how to figure this problem out without guessing. Didn't you want the students to get the answer? (Janet, journal, 01/08/95)

The students should have been taken through the problem step-by-step. I don't think they got much out of if. (Kathy, journal, 01/06/95)

There is really only one way to solve the Monster Problem — going backwards. (Ken, journal, 01/06/95)

> Wasn't the problem too difficult? . . . The students didn't understand it . . . it took too long. (Jill, journal, 01/06/95)

> I was surprised that the students made it through the problem as far as they did. (Tanis, journal, 01/08/95)

> This problem was not within the students ZPD [Zone of Proximal Development]. We as teachers were wrong in presenting these students with a challenge which they could not meet. (Kendra, journal, 01/06/95)

As these comments were made in the journals, I responded to them by asking questions that I hoped would help them to develop defensible reasons for their claims: 'What did you see or hear that made you feel that the students were frustrated?' 'How do you know that students didn't "get anything out of the problem"?' 'What questions might you ask the students to help you learn more about what you think they learned?' But many viewed these questions as somewhat overwhelming and not very helpful. Many did not respond to the questions asked, either in class or in their journals.

The third part of the Monster Problem activity involves the prospective teachers as teachers. For the next class, our fourth class together, we meet at a local school and work with a class of Grade 6 and Grade 7 students using the Monster Problem as a context to investigate students' understanding of fractions. An excerpt from my journal retells the story.

> I welcomed the group of students and paired each student with one of the fourteen preservice teachers. Within seconds the room was filled with talk. I was pleased. Things seemed to be working. I moved around the room listening to bits of conversations. I noticed a number of people were beginning the interview with a set of warm-up questions. 'Do you like math?' I overheard Terrie ask the student she was working with. 'Honestly?' she asked again as if she didn't believe it when he had answered yes. 'What are you doing in math right now?' asked Tanis of her student. 'Fractions', replied the student. 'Oh, great' responded Tanis and then moved on to a question about the use of calculators in math class. 'Could you try to double 128?' I overheard Alissa ask her student. '256', said the student. 'Okay', said Alissa 'you've got that, we don't need to do any more of those'. And she moved on to try some fraction questions.

> I noticed that each preservice teacher and his/her student partner were engaged in conversation. From a distance things seemed to be moving smoothly. Yet, as I listened to bits of the various . . . they seemed to be asking questions of the students but not doing anything with their responses. . . .

> As I stood watching the activity, I wondered how I might respond to what I saw. If this were a mathematics class with pairs of students working on a math problem then I would not hesitate to enter a conversation with a pair — to pose questions and challenge ideas. But this was not a

math class, it was a group of preservice teachers working one-on-one with students. And it was their first meeting. How could I enter a conversation and not disturb the relationship that they were working to establish? There was nothing I could do but watch. I overheard pieces of student responses which offered possibilities or openings for investigation into student thinking only to be passed over, missed, or ignored. I longed to gently pose a question to a student as a way of helping a preservice teacher open a door to understanding more about her or his student's thinking. But I said nothing. (Cynthia, journal, 01/13/95)

The prospective teachers were quite pleased with their visit to the school and with the opportunity to work with, as one person put it 'real kids'. They spoke after the session about the difficulty they had in trying to listen to the students, 'to resist the temptation to tell the students the answer when they didn't understand'. They spoke about the range in ability and effort that they noticed between Grade 6 and Grade 7 students and between students in the same grade. Some were surprised when, in certain cases, a Grade 6 student was able to solve the Monster Problem while a Grade 7 student was not. They spoke about the struggle they felt in their roles as both teachers and investigators:

I'm not sure if I'm supposed to show these students a strategy? Am I more concerned about their discovery? I do feel, however, that once the students complete their discovery a strategy should be shown to them because often their discovery method can be a fluke if they get the correct answer. (Janet, 01/13/95)

Some wrote descriptions of their conversations, others wrote about their interpretations of the students' understandings, while others also included their developing ideas of students' sense-making and their own role in developing student understanding. Prospective teachers' overall reaction to the Monster Problem activity over the three classes was positive. They spoke about being able to discuss and share their interpretations with each other about doing the problem and about their findings in working with students. They spoke of a difference in knowing how to do a problem and understanding it in a way that helps someone else understand it. Some wondered when they might have suggested or told too much or told too little in working with the students. Overall the Monster Problem activity was a worthwhile task from the prospective teachers' perspective. The beginning classes were great, interesting, and exciting. As Lauren states:

It is neat to have the freedom of expression in a math class of all places. . . . This class is the least structured, most open, most cooperative we have. I was certainly expecting more 'sit down and do these problems' sort of atmosphere. (Lauren, journal, 01/13/95)

But I wonder how worthwhile this activity was? On the one hand the activity gave me insight into these prospective teachers' ideas, beliefs, and understandings

Lauren Journal 01/13/1995	**Cynthia's Written Response 01/16/95**

I found that I was able to pick up on things that the kids were saying and build upon them to find out what they were thinking. For example, Mia (Gr. 7) explained to me her perception of 1/4.

How did she explain to you that what she had drawn represented 1/4th? Is it 1/4th? Of what? What is the whole?

Two things tipped me off that something was not quite right. First, she wouldn't (or rather didn't want to) draw a pie as I'd asked; instead she asked if she could draw circles. Now, this is fine, but I wondered why. Next her explanation that one of four of something seemed vague.

I probed her by asking her if this was 1/4.

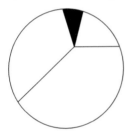

She said 'Yah, it is. It is less but still one fourth.'

Good, to see you explore her thinking. You've moved her to think about one-fourth from a discrete model to a region model. This is complex — it involves thinking about the denominators and the numerators and their relationship as well as what it is a fraction of. What did you ask her next? What does her comment 'it is less but still one-fourth' seem to indicate to you?
I wonder how she would respond to a question represented using the discrete model that had pieces which were not the same size. Like a group of four people who were different sizes. Would one person represent 1/4th of the number of people or would it depend on how big that person was? Or, I wonder how she would represent one-fourth of a group of eight people?
Is the Monster problem based on a discrete or region model of fractions?

The more I think about it the more what she said makes sense. It *is* one out of 4 things. Sure, that one thing is not the same size as the others. But it is still ONE OUT OF FOUR. I see now that I could have gone into $\frac{1}{4} + \frac{1}{4} + \frac{1}{4} + \frac{1}{4} = 1$ whole and Mia would have definitely responded as she seemed fixated on writing everything in equations.

When is 1/4 the same as one out of four things?

I'm interested in learning more about what you are thinking here. How do you think this would help Mia — or challenge her understanding of one-fourth — or be responsive to her thinking? Doesn't it really depend on one whole what? Would that equation also work for the four circles she drew?

Figure 7.1: Lauren's journal and Cynthia's response

of mathematics and mathematics teaching. The activity was designed to challenge prospective teachers' assumptions of what might be involved in knowing, doing, and teaching mathematics. For some the activity did this; for others, engagement in the problem seemed to strengthen their previous beliefs. For example, interactions with the Grade 6/7 students were described as 'frustrating' and 'unproductive'. In these situations the prospective teachers reported that the students were not able to solve the problem and they were not able to help them solve it. In thinking about how they would work with a different student 'next time', common strategies of making the problem easier, more clear, and presented in a more step-by-step manner were offered. These suggestions often contradicted their espoused beliefs that they would like to offer problems that would encourage student thinking and understanding.

> In the end I had to give him the solution because I didn't want him to leave without the answer . . . I tried to remain impartial and let students try the problems on their own — but it was frustrating for them and for me. I had to give encouragement and ideas or they would have simply given up . . . Next time I'll break the problem down into simpler steps and I'll re-word it. There is a great deal of improvement for me. (Ken, journal, 01/12/95)

How worthwhile is the activity if it seems to encourage prospective teachers to fall back on familiar routines or to substantiate old ideas and beliefs?

In addition, the activity challenged prospective teachers' ideas of mathematics and what mathematics might be needed to teach for understanding. But it also seemed to cause some to question their own confidence and ability to teach mathematics. Reconsidering their own beliefs about mathematics and about teaching and learning mathematics made some even less confident in their ability to teach math than when they first entered the course. Kendra wrote, 'It's hard to explain, but I am really worried that my own math skills are so weak that I won't know when a [student's] solution is rational or not' (Kendra, journal, 01/11/95). Then later, 'I'm feeling really frustrated with the course; we need to be spending more time on learning the mathematics if we are expected to be able to teach it differently!' (Kendra, journal, 01/18/95). Could an activity, such as the Monster Problem be considered as worthwhile if it promotes such disabling feelings for some prospective teachers? To challenge their underlying beliefs and ideas is risky if there is nothing offered in its place. How might I select or design tasks that both enable my students' confidence and their competence?

Listening for and Listening to

For our third class, one of the activities we worked on was the Horse Problem.

The Horse Problem:[3]
A man bought a horse for $50.

He sold it for $60.
Then he bought the horse for $70.
He sold it again for $80.
What was the financial outcome?

In previous years I have given this problem to both pre-service teachers and elementary school students. In most cases, the problem has generated a number of possible answers and stimulated some lively discussions. My plan was to use this problem as a way of modelling the kind of teaching we valued by having our pre-service teachers share their ideas and solution strategies in both small group and whole-class settings. I wanted the students, as future teachers, to participate in communicating their thinking to others while marshalling together sound justifications and, at the same time, participate in listening to others' solutions while trying to make sense of alternative points of view. I was hoping that this problem would provide further opportunities for our students to examine and assess their own assumptions about what and how mathematics could be taught. I retell pieces of the story here:[4]

I began by handing out a copy of the problem to everyone and asked that they try it first individually and then in their small groups.

I moved around the room as some groups quickly became loud as they argued about the answers. Some began to act out the problem, others were surprisingly quiet. One group near the wall agreed within a couple of minutes that 20 was the answer. I suggested they explore various possible solution strategies for an answer of 20 and then mentioned that they were welcome to move around the room to explore what other groups were thinking.

After about ten minutes, I interrupted the class. 'Um, how about we, uh,' I said 'share our answers right now and then we'll look at the possible solution strategies, or how we got them afterwards.'

A teaching colleague, Maggie, recorded the different answers on the white board at the back as the preservice teachers called them out:

$20 ahead
break even
up $10
$30 ahead

I was pleased that there were at least four solutions — there would be more room for debate with a range of possible solutions. Maggie had written down the responses in the order she had heard them. $20 ahead seemed to be one that a number of people accepted so I decided to begin the discussion from the bottom of the list.

Gary and Dan explained that, 'If you look at the intention of the problem' then $30 'would be potentially what he could have made'. There was a hum of talk as everyone considered what Gary and Dan were suggesting. There were a couple of questions, then Ann Martin offered her solution.

Beth spoke quietly; the room was still, 'Okay, a man bought a horse for $50, and he sells it for $60, so that's where he gets his $10 profit. But then he had to buy the horse for $70, so that $10 he has to add to that transaction cancels out the original profit of $10. Then he made $10 back when he sells it for $80.' She laughed nervously with this final statement.

Again there was a bit of talk among the prospective teachers as they considered Beth's solution. I heard someone quietly say 'That's interesting' and someone else say 'That doesn't make sense.' I looked around the room waiting for someone to respond. Alissa said 'But it didn't cost him anything to put $10 in — you're assuming the cost — like, I thought of that assumption as well, but if there were two different horses and he made his investment: $50 for the first one and $70 for the second one regardless.'

I asked if it made a difference whether or not there were two different horses or whether that should matter to the outcome of the problem.

Then Carole, a mature age student with a strong math background, spoke. I had noticed how other people in the class valued and sought her opinion when solving various math problems. 'I think, to counteract that line is, um, you have no money you go to the bank, you borrow $50, you take the $50, you buy the horse.' She spoke clearly and confidently using her hands to move imaginary money from one place on the table to another. Everyone listened. 'Then, you sell the horse, you get $60, you go back to the bank, you give them the $50, you have $10. Now you want to buy the horse again, it's going to cost you $70, you've only got $10, you go to the bank, you borrow $60, you take the $60, the $10, you give it to the person to get the horse. You get the horse, you go to sell it, you have $80, you go back to the bank, you give $60 and you're left with $20.'

A number of people applauded. But her response seemed so clear and easy to follow — so convincing that it made the consideration of any other possibility for an answer, other than $20, unlikely. No one was offering a counter argument to Carole's solution strategy. The group had certainly benefited from Carole's explanation but it now seemed as it closed down the conversation rather than open it up. We had just begun; it was too early to finish. I paused, wondering how to respond, hoping that someone might suggest an alternate solution. I decided to try to focus the discussion back on the other possible answers listed on the whiteboard.

'Are there any other ideas on how we could make $10?' There was no response. 'Okay, how about breaking even?'

A couple of students offered their solution strategy for breaking even. They spent some time answering questions from the group as people tried to understand how it might be possible to break even. But there was no passionate debate; it was as if people had accepted that 'making $20' was the solution and they were only entertaining other solutions out of politeness.

'I just have a question', asked Dan, moving the discussion toward thinking about how this problem could be used with students. 'My feeling is that — I know when I was a student, there were times when I felt really strongly that my answer was correct but it wasn't in the sense of what the actual — I mean — the way I came around to it made sense to me but it wasn't maybe the correct way. But then I remember having a really hard time believing the other way was the right way. And my way, maybe, wasn't right, but it wasn't, let's say the proper way of looking at the question. And what I'm asking is — if you have a student like that, how do you — how do you try to convince them?'

The question was wonderful. That was exactly the point of this problem, to help them think about how they might help someone else to reconsider their answer in a responsive and respectful manner. I wondered how to respond. I wanted to learn what others thought. How did they perceive the role of the teacher? What would they do in a similar situation?

Dan continued. 'Do you know what I mean? Like, maybe you're looking at in a fraction and the — kids are looking at the Monster cookie question. And you talk about — they came up with a thing and they really thought that's the way it works. But then we know the answer is 27. But if they came up with a way and they're really convinced that's, uh, what it is. You know what I mean it gets very difficult to explain to that student that perhaps it isn't that way and you should convince them that they shouldn't look at it in that sense? Do you know what I mean? I mean, I know myself the way I look at it might be one way. But if a student was looking at it and really felt strongly that that was the proper way, I think it would be really difficult to get them to think about the other way.'

I wanted, instead, to have us think about our own experience with this task and how that might help us address Dan's question of convincing. What are the difficulties, and challenges of teaching by being respectful of students' ideas, mathematics, and the prescribed curriculum? My reason for working with the Horse Problem was to provide opportunities for the prospective teachers to experience, and think about, how they might listen and respond to others who have alternative explanations. But the problem did not ignite much debate over the various solutions. It did not do what I had expected it would. I couldn't think of a way to address Dan's question through our class experience to help him answer his own question.

The Horse Problem has become an activity that is part of my teaching repertoire. I have worked with many different groups of people, including prospective teachers and elementary school students, and the problem has, in all cases, generated interesting and lively discussion. I have come to expect that within a group there will generally be a range of at least three or four different answers to the problem. In discussing the various answers people see, feel, and hear what it might be like to try to understand a solution strategy other than their own, a skill teachers need as they attempt to understand and make sense of their students' work. They also experience what it might be like to communicate a solution strategy to those who may not see the problem as they see it. Through the problem and its discussion, prospective teachers begin to accept that communicating their ideas involves more than just repeating their strategy over and over; they must also listen to others, to try to make sense of what it is that others do or do not see in their explanation. They begin to learn to question, listen, and respond.

Ironically, however, I think the Horse Problem did not generate the kind of discussion and debate I had anticipated this time with this group of prospective teachers because I was not listening, or rather I was listening differently. In spite of my desire to help prospective teachers learn to question, listen, and respond to each other during and through the Horse Problem, my listening *for* what I anticipated seemed to subvert any listening to what the prospective teachers were offering. I had left the class feeling discouraged and disappointed that the problem did not go as planned, feeling that there was little meaningful discussion or interesting ideas offered. I had interpreted the discussion on convincing, as raised by Dan's question, as evidence that the prospective teachers were not 'seeing' the value of the problem that I saw and the value that others who had worked on the problem had also seen.

However, instead of trying to understand what might be at the heart of the issue of Dan's question of convincing, I attempt to convince him that, had he and others experienced the problem the way I had hoped they would, he would be able to answer his own question. If the class was unable to experience the problem as I had hoped then perhaps telling them about how others experienced it might help. I then asked a series of questions which, I notice now, seem intent on leading the class to thinking of the value of the problem in the same way as I did.

> So what would be the point of giving this kind of problem to kids? Is it to lead them to, or direct them to an answer, that's 20? Or is there something else going on here that we would like to try to bring out? (Cynthia, class transcript, 01/11/95)

Hidden behind my statement and the questions that followed are my values and assumptions for how mathematics might be taught and why. But I do not make these explicit. The questions I ask do not invite others in the class to inquire into the basis of my statements or the worth of the problem. I do not pose these questions as a way to understand what others in the class may be thinking or to understand their interpretations. Instead, I seem to be intent on having them conclude what it is I want them to see. Perhaps Linda notices this in my comments and decides to take on the challenge with her strong remarks:

> I think that's [justifying] a good aspect. But the fact of the matter is when they hit Grade 12, and writing their Math 12 exam, the examiners aren't going to care whether or not they can justify their answer or not. If it's right they'll get the mark, if it's wrong they won't. So I think it's really

good for them to explain what they are doing but they also have to see if they did it wrong, why the right way worked, and why that's the right way. (Linda, class transcript, 01/11/95)

Here, Linda seems to accept the challenge to defend her ideas. She does not inquire into the basis underlying the comments and questions I ask. And I do not inquire more about her understanding of justify. But I did feel challenged and defensive. I took her statements, perhaps due to the tone in which they are asked, as an attack on my efforts and the ideas presented. I chose not to respond to her comments, and I did not make public my silent questions which focused on understanding the meaning behind her comments. Instead I sought to defend my position once again later in the discussion.

Carole addressed the class with a comment referring to a suggestion made by Clint[5], that students can act out the problem with play money to test the validity of their answers.

But using manipulatives, I thought, is not necessarily what convinces students. And I was confused over Carole's use of correct way of thinking and correct answer. There are some ways of thinking that are not correct. But I do not respond with an inquiry into what Carole is thinking or with the intent at unpacking her ideas. Instead once again I chose to defend and respond by telling.

I was contradicting myself, and I mentioned that convincing comes through discussion and debate, not with the teacher telling how it should be done, yet that is exactly what I did as I attempted to convince the members of the class to think about learning and teaching mathematics differently. I resorted to telling what they should do because I had no other resources. I attempted to defend the value of the Horse Problem both for elementary students and for our class. Therefore, rather than creating the collaborative learning environment that I had intended, I helped to establish a behavioral world (Schön, 1987) that locked us into defending our own ideas rather than exploring each other's ideas.

In her journal after this class (01/11/95) Carole wrote:

On leaving today's class I reflected on what I had learned during the preceding minutes. Two things stood out. The first was the comment by Clint that you always let the children role play their solutions so that they know the correct answer and if appropriate see that different strategies can lead to the correct solution. The second area that stands out were the general approaches to interacting with children outlined by Helen Kelly [a guest speaker]. What did we spend the majority of our time on? The Horse Problem. I then asked why? It was at this stage I began to have problems.

This course is a methods course in teaching math to elementary students. How does the horse problem help me become a better teacher? I don't think it did. The problem itself was too simple to promote any meaningful discussion on approaches and that could be used to solve it. Thus, no teaching techniques were developed. Similarly, for someone who may not feel comfortable with the content of the elementary math curriculum there was insufficient substance in this problem to improve their knowledge . . .

I'm interested in reading your comments on this and also what you expected our students to have learnt from the horse problem. My observation of your class composition is that you have the same range of abilities that exist in many elementary school classrooms: how are you going to meet the needs of your individual learners? How will we as teachers be able to translate what you do in this classroom to our own classrooms so that we meet the needs of all our learners?

Here begins an interesting learning bind (Schön, 1987) that Carole and I form. I would like to draw attention to the ways in which I responded to Carole and how such response continued to strengthen the bind I now see that we had formed. When I read Carole's journal for the first time I was struck by a couple of things.

I perceived her comments as a direct challenge to my competence and although I seemed somewhat concerned that I was not gaining the insight into Carole's experience my main concern seemed to be with the feelings that her journal entry brought forth for me. In a learning bind Schön (1987) states that the participants interact in a behavioral world of defensiveness and self-protection. Within this world each participant perceives the other person as the defensive agent whose goal it is to win.

In Carole's journal my responses to her comments sought to defend my own position and belief not only in the Horse Problem but also in the value of engaging students in mathematical discussion. I tried to impose my way of seeing on Carole rather than try to learn more about her ways of seeing. From the tone of her writing I inferred that her reactions were negative. Yet, I was quite dissatisfied with the discussion and outcome of the Horse Problem activity, just as she was.

Why did I feel the need to defend the problem and invite confrontation rather than respond in a way that might allow Carole entry into my own questions and frustrations with the problem? I could have reminded Carole that she was welcome to read my journal entry written after the Horse Problem class. I could have shared with her my concerns with the lack of discussion, my frustration at not knowing how to respond, and my surprise and disappointment that the activity didn't do what I had hoped or expected it would. But in so doing I would have made myself vulnerable, my mistakes exposed, my credibility questioned. We each suppressed feelings that might give the other an invitation to inquiry, an invitation that might allow for the exploration of ideas rather than the defending of positions. We had formed a learning bind that was to become stronger as the course progressed. And such a learning bind, notes Schön (1987), prevents any sort of reciprocal reflection-in-action between the participants; it is a 'process of systematic miscommunication' (p. 126).

Breaking out of this learning bind requires individuals to listen to each other rather than listening for the achievement of their own objectives and agendas. However, I do not think that listening for my own agenda is totally inappropriate. Listening for what we expect might happen provides us with a framework through which to interpret events. As a teacher with desired goals and intentions I listen for the various mathematical concepts and ideas that my students are required to know and understand. But at the same time I want to listen to and attend to students' experience. A focus only on listening *for* makes it difficult to listen *to* students' experiences, to focus on the meaning of the experience from the students' perspective, and to act upon events that are unanticipated. Listening *for* affects what the teacher finds as valuable information. A focus on only listening *to* may make it difficult to interpret students' experiences. Listening *to* means shedding preconceived agendas, being responsive and attending to what students say and do. Listening *for* involves listening for worthwhile subject-matter content within educational goals and intentions. The challenge remains for me as I struggle to remain suspended and attentive on a fine balance between accomplishing my own teaching goals and experiencing teaching from prospective teachers' eyes.

Researching Teaching and Teaching Researching

As a teacher educator learning to teach prospective teachers and to research my practice I would like prospective teachers to become researchers of their own practice. This means I need to think more about teaching researching, that is, I need to think more about the ways in which I might help prospective teachers research their practice. Researching my own practice is one way in which I might convey to students what the process might entail and what might be learned from engaging in the practice of researching. Researching my practice while helping prospective teachers research their own practice has raised a number of issues for me.

My decision to teach prospective teachers did not come easily. Although I have experience as a high school teacher I felt there was much I needed to know about teaching before I could possibly help others learn about it as well. And although I was considered a 'good' teacher by my students, my colleagues, and my district I did not feel that being a 'good' teacher would, or should, necessarily imply that I would be able to help others prepare for the world of teaching.

For me, teaching prospective teachers seemed to imply that I needed to be an expert — an expert in research on students' thinking and ways of making sense in all mathematics content areas, an expert in thinking about what mathematics students should be taught, an expert in the use and critique of various instructional strategies, and an expert in reflecting upon and thinking about teaching practice. As a practicing teacher I did not consider myself an expert in mathematics or in teaching mathematics. I considered myself one who was continually learning about mathematics, playing with mathematics, and sharing my uncertainties and puzzles with my students. Some of my mathematics students have said how much they have learned during those times when we would work together to solve a problem that was new to us all. But in teaching mathematics over years I had built up a rapport and trust with my students. I had many of the same students in Grade 12 as I had in Grade 8 and I often had the opportunity to teach all the siblings of one family. Students knew me and believed in me, if not by personal experience, by reputation. I was able to build trust in my students to engage in difficult challenging work; I was able to maintain credibility while at the same time establish some authenticity to what I did not know about mathematics and about teaching mathematics.

Teaching prospective teachers was different. The more I have studied, the more I have begun to understand and appreciate the complexity and uncertainty involved in teaching. I wondered then how I might establish a credible but authentic practice in teaching prospective teachers. What gives me the right or authority to teach a methods course? What might prepare me to teach prospective teachers? I see them for only two 1–1/2-hour sessions a week for ten short weeks. I have very large classes and the prospective teachers have very high expectations. They have claimed that they expect, among other things, to be taught by someone who is either a practicing teacher or a university professor, not by a graduate student who is officially between but in neither of these two worlds. Just being a graduate student reduced my credibility in prospective teachers' eyes. It was an indication that I was neither a 'real teacher' nor a 'real professor'.

Researching my practice as a teacher educator also weakened my credibility. Researching my teaching was an indication to some prospective teachers that I did not have the necessary expertise and knowledge needed to teach a methods course; I had not yet figured it out enough to be teaching it. The fact that this was the first time I had taught the course in this way and that I wanted to investigate the teaching and learning that occurred was evidence for some prospective teachers to doubt my ability to teach in this context. I had thought that researching my own practice provided opportunities for communicating teaching in an authentic manner, as a complex and uncertain endeavor. But researching my teaching was an indication for some prospective teachers that I did not know enough about teaching to be teaching about teaching. My striving to be authentic, to communicate teaching as a complex process in which there is much we do not know, reduced my credibility.

I had hoped that we would be able to use excerpts from either my teaching or the prospective teacher's teaching, as they worked with the Grade 6/7 students one hour a week, as springboards for the investigation of teaching. In this way I wanted to help prospective teachers learn more about investigating teaching and about investigating their own practice. I had envisioned a community of learners, exploring, inquiring and trying to make sense of various teaching episodes that occurred. I wanted collaboration in which prospective teachers and I could explore together problems, issues, and puzzles that arose from their experiences with their students and our experiences together as a class. I had hoped that such collaboration would help generate genuine pedagogical problems worthy of our investigation. And to some extent it did. When prospective teachers wrote about a pedagogical problem or something they found puzzling, I sometimes responded by investigating the strengths and weaknesses of the strategies being discussed in the context of the problem that arose. But for many prospective teachers this was unsettling.

There was an expectation from some that as a teacher educator I should focus the course on the best ideas and techniques for how to teach students to teach mathematics as defined by what works in the schools and by that in the research

literature. Some prospective teachers considered it to be my job to 'show us ...
what we [prospective teachers] are supposed to be teaching and how we should
teach ... we want to know what works' (Kendra, 01/18/95). 'You need to tell us,
from your experience what works ... what are some activities and ideas that work
in the classroom' (Carole, 05/16/95). I could understand their desires and concerns.
They had not yet had any field experience and they had practicums for which to
prepare. And I was in a position to offer them what I had learned from both my
teaching experience and my studies as a graduate teacher. But I wondered how I
might share with them my experiences, the knowledge and skills I have developed
about teaching, but at the same time work with them to investigate teaching. How
might I renegotiate prospective teachers' conception of expertise of myself as a
teacher and for themselves as future teachers? And how might I represent teaching
in a way that is authentic to the practice of teaching, to portray the messiness, the
unknown, the incompleteness, and the uncertainty of teaching, yet build and maintain credibility, authenticity, and collaboration within my practice?

The Challenge of Teaching about Teaching

As a beginning teacher educator I have faced difficult intellectual challenges. The
challenges I recount here have grown out of my attempts to help prospective
teachers create and re-create an inquiry mathematics tradition (Richards, 1991;
NCTM, 1989, 1991) in their future classrooms. I have struggled to select and use
worthwhile mathematical and pedagogical activities — tasks that help prospective
teachers reinterpret their previous experiences while both building their confidence
and competence. I have thought hard about both listening *for* my goals and intentions in prospective teachers' work and listening *to* the understandings and sense
prospective teachers are making of their experiences in the course. I have struggled
with establishing a credible yet authentic and collaborative practice.

Teaching prospective teachers by being both inside and outside practice and
research is difficult. I have sought to bring them both the inside and the outside of
mathematics and teaching practice. That is, I have sought to help them become
participants of mathematics within an inquiry community by participating in the
'doing' of mathematics while moving to the outside to reflect upon and analyze
their work as learners. I have also worked to bring prospective teachers both inside
and outside the practice of teaching by attempting to work with them to investigate
teaching.

But being both inside practice and research is messy, risky, complex, and
exhausting work that takes time, energy, and courage. It involves managing multiple tensions and dilemmas within a moral framework of trying to decide the
'right' course of action in a particular context, with a particular group of students,
at a particular moment in time. Sometimes these tensions can encourage the development of understanding, but sometimes they can become sources of anxiety and
uncertainty. However, they invariably involve making difficult choices which are
central to teaching practice (Ball and Wilson, 1996). Framing a practice around the

managing of tensions and dilemmas rather than the solving of problems can help reduce developing feelings of guilt and attributing difficulties to personal limitations. As Cuban (1992) notes 'reframing and managing dilemmas are art forms, filled with doubt but at least free of corrosive guilt' (p. 8). To know that as students of teaching we will encounter dilemmas that need to be managed, rather than problems that need to be solved, suggests a different context for our work, one that invites prospective teachers and teacher educators to both research and engage in practice in working toward figuring out better ways to manage difficult situations.

My purpose in sharing my story is to offer insights to others who might also be entering, or reconsidering their role, in teacher education.[6] As teacher educators we face problematic situations and dilemmas in the complex environment of the university classroom. Sharing our stories or narratives as cases of teaching and learning to teach prospective teachers provides us with opportunities to reflect upon and deepen our own understandings of teaching and learning, to grow and to change both personally and professionally. In this chapter I have shared my stories, inviting public scrutiny of my thoughts and actions, as a way of initiating discussion and broadening our understanding of what is involved in learning to teach prospective teachers.

Notes

1   All teacher, prospective teacher, and student names referred to in this paper are pseudonyms.
2   From Watson, J. (1988). Three hungry men and strategies for problem solving. *For the learning of mathematics*, **8**, 3, 20–26. The problem in this article was written with hungry men eating apples.
3   From Marilyn Burns (1987), *A Collection of Match Lessons: From Grades 3 through 5*, New Rochell, NY, Math Solution Publications.
4   This story is reconstructed from the video-tape of the class, transcriptions of that tape, my journal and prospective teachers' journals.
5   Clint is a mathematician in the university mathematics department who regularly visited our class.
6   Cynthia acknowledges the help and support to her research made possible through a Canadian National Research Grant (SSHRC).

References

BALL, D. (1990a) 'Halves, pieces, and twoths: Constructing representational contexts in teaching fractions', ERIC Document ED 324226.

BALL, D. (1990b) 'Breaking with experience in learning to teach mathematics: The role of a preservice methods course', *For the Learning of Mathematics*, **10**, 2, pp. 10–16.

BALL, D. (1993) 'With an eye on the mathematical horizon: Dilemmas of teaching elementary school mathematics', *Elementary School Journal*, **93**, 4, pp. 373–97.

BALL, D. and WILSON, S. (1996) 'Integrity in teaching: Recognizing the fusion of the moral and the intellectual', *American Education Research Journal*, **33**, 1, pp. 155–92.

BUCHMANN, M. (1987) 'Teaching knowledge: The lights that teachers live by', *Oxford Review of Education*, **13**, 2, pp. 151–64.

BUCHMANN, M. (1991) 'Making new or making do: An inconclusive argument about teaching', *American Journal of Education*, **99**, 3, pp. 279–97.

CALDERHEAD, J. and ROBSON, M. (1991) 'Images of teaching: Student teachers' early conceptions of classroom practice', *Teaching and Teacher Education*, **7**, 1, pp. 1–8.

CUBAN, L. (1992) 'Managing dilemmas while building professional communities', *Educational Research*, **21**, 1, pp. 4–11.

FEIMEN-NEMSER, S. and BUCHMANN, M. (1986) 'Pitfalls of experience in teacher preparation', in RATHS, J. and KATZ, L. (Eds) *Advances in Teacher Education*, Volume 2, Norwood, NJ, Ablex, pp. 61–74.

GORE, J. and ZEICHNER, K. (1991) 'Action research and reflective teaching in preservice teacher education: A case study from the United States', *Teaching and Teacher Education*, **7**, 2, pp. 119–36.

HOLT-REYNOLDS, D. (1994) 'Learning teaching, teaching teachers', Paper presented at the Annual Meeting of the American Educational Research Association in New Orleans, LA, April.

KATZ, L. and RATHS, J. (1992) 'Six dilemmas in teacher education', *Journal of Teacher Education*, **43**, 5, pp. 376–85.

KNOWLES, G. and HOLT-REYNOLDS, D. (1991) 'Shaping pedagogies through personal histories in preservice teacher education', *Teacher College Record*, **93**, 1, pp. 87–113.

LAMPERT, M. (1985) 'How do teachers manage to teach: Perspectives on problems in practice', *Harvard Educational Review*, **55**, 2, pp. 178–94.

LAMPERT, M. (1990) 'When the problem is not the question and the solution is not the answer: Mathematical knowing and teaching', *American Educational Research Journal*, **27**, 1, pp. 29–63.

LORTIE, D. (1975) *Schoolteacher: A Sociological Study*, Chicago, University of Chicago Press.

McDIARMID, W. (1990) 'Challenging prospective teachers' beliefs during an early field experience: A quixotic undertaking?', *Journal of Teacher Education*, **41**, 3, pp. 12–20.

McNIFF, J. (1993) *Teaching as Learning: An Action Research Approach*, London, Routledge.

NATIONAL COUNCIL OF TEACHERS OF MATHEMATICS (1989) *Curriculum and Evaluation Standards for School Mathematics*, Reston, VA.

NATIONAL COUNCIL OF TEACHERS OF MATHEMATICS (1991) *Professional Standards for Teaching Mathematics*, Reston, VA.

RICHARDS, J. (1991) 'Mathematical discussions', in VON GLASERSFELD, E. (Ed) *Radical Constructivism in Mathematics Education*, Dordrecht, The Netherlands, Kluwer, pp. 13–51.

SCHÖN, D. (1987) *Educating the Reflective Practitioner: Toward a New Design for Teaching and Learning in the Professions*, San Francisco, Jossey-Bass.

SHULMAN, L. (1987) 'Knowledge and teaching: Foundations of the new reform', *Harvard Educational Review*, **57**, 1, pp. 1–21.

WINEBURG, S. (1991) 'A case of pedagogical failure — My own', *Journal of Teacher Education*, **42**, 4, pp. 273–80.

8 Teaching and Learning in Teacher Education: Who is Carrying the Ball?

Peter Chin

Introduction

As teacher educators, we encourage our pre-service teachers to become more aware, and articulate of, their own professional knowledge so that they can better understand and improve their own teaching (Connelly and Clandinin, 1988; Schön, 1983). We should expect no less from ourselves. As such, this chapter describes how and why I 'practice what I preach' by focusing on elements of my own professional knowledge as a teacher educator. I begin by articulating some significant experiences that have informed my beliefs about teaching and learning within the teacher education context. Then I highlight certain ways that these beliefs are 'lived' within my work with pre-service teachers. Finally, I provide evidence that my teacher education practices make a difference to those I teach.

Knowing Ourselves

I begin the secondary science curriculum methods courses by explaining to my pre-service teachers that 'before we can understand others, we need to understand ourselves, and our views of teaching, learning, and science'. This is intended to initiate the process of coming to understand how one's philosophy of teaching has been informed by the deeply embedded images, models, and conceptions of teaching from one's own experiences as a learner (Brookfield, 1995). It also reinforces the important dialectical relationship between teaching and learning, where each component informs and is informed by the other. More specifically, understanding how one learns may help that person to understand why he or she holds certain perspectives about teaching. Conversely, understanding how one teaches helps that person to gain a better understanding of how such teaching impacts on students' learning. As a teacher and a learner, I constantly look for the powerful parallels between what I do in *my* classroom work with pre-service teachers, and what I encourage them to do in *their* classroom work with pupils. These parallels in teaching and learning are interwoven into the fabric of my work as a teacher educator, although one can catch glimpses of this thread as I share the sense that I have made of my immediate past.

Where do I begin to look at my own professional development as a beginning teacher educator? Where was the starting point? As a recent (three years) appointee to Queen's University, I am acutely aware of the fact that I have received little direct preparation for my new teaching responsibilities. As I reflect on my experiences as a science teacher and graduate student, it becomes obvious that these have played a major role in informing my practice as a teacher educator. It is within these settings that my perspective on teacher education has been articulated, critiqued, and practiced. Although what follows is somewhat chronological, I develop this section of the paper using Brookfield's (1995) four critically reflective lenses: autobiography, our students' eyes, our colleagues' experiences, and theoretical literature. Each lens casts a certain image about who I am as a teacher educator, and the composite of these multiple perspectives yields a product that has more clarity and depth than can be gained by one lens alone.

Autobiography

Within the context of learning about teacher education, my 'apprenticeship of observation' (Lortie, 1975) began as a pre-service teacher at the University of Calgary. The most memorable and significant course in the program was secondary science methods taught by Doug Roberts, my first mentor in science teacher education. The course focused on issues related to the nature of science and how we can understand our science teaching by critically analyzing transcripts of our lessons. Importantly, much of the course was discussion-based so that we were encouraged to voice our emerging understandings about science teaching. Unlike some of my frustrated classmates who were expecting a panacea to their pre-practicum worries about the unknown (i.e., a course that centred around 'practical' aspects of science teaching such as demonstrations and labs), I was comfortable with the focus on establishing frameworks for understanding science teaching. I saw these frameworks for understanding as useful for the long term, since I was confident that the practicum and my early years of teaching would more than make up for any lack of practical activities. Establishing frameworks for understanding and utilizing open discussions around issues of teaching and learning now plays a central role within my own science methods teaching. I also realized that the pre-practicum concerns of the class had to be addressed to some extent. Otherwise, as I had seen first-hand, people can become so distressed by the absence of the message they expect that they tune out the message being put forward. As discussed later, I see this as a balancing act of trying to address both immediate and long-term goals.

Understanding my own practice was a central theme during the early years of my teaching career, because of three salient and related experiences. First, while I was still student teaching, I agreed to be the 'subject' of a clinical supervision cycle being conducted by a graduate student. The research entailed a series of interviews centred around self-identifying issues that I found problematic in my teaching, and my subsequent attempts to make improvements in those areas (see Kilbourn, 1990).

From that study, I could see the value of recording, discussing, and analyzing my teaching in order to improve it. Throughout my five years of teaching high school science, I found value in occasionally audiotaping a lesson and doing a mental analysis of it.

Second, in the year I was hired as a teacher, the Alberta government was implementing an internship program (which was later dropped due to budget cuts). Although there was great variation in how interns were used in schools, my own experience consisted of being assigned to a high school science department and having a slightly reduced teaching load. As well, being in the internship program entailed a department commitment to support and monitor my progress and growth. By the end of the year, my teaching had been observed and debriefed by seven science teachers, one assistant principal, and two researchers from Alberta Education (who were assessing the program). By virtue of so many opportunities to discuss my teaching, continuous analysis of my own teaching was internalized as an integral part of being a teacher.

Third, during my second year of science teaching, I took a graduate course with Jean Clandinin. Here I was introduced to the value of 'storying' critical incidents that stood out in my teaching experiences and then weaving these stories into a broader personal narrative. I soon realized that the result of this process was something quite different from the kind of knowledge I had been exposed to in my pre-service program. My narrative centred around the metaphor of 'teacher as coach' and the end product represented my personal image of teaching and learning and captured the essence of my 'lived experience'. I still appreciate the importance of creating a setting for writing about one's views of teaching and learning and in developing the broader view that a personal narrative can convey. I also recognize that the depth and clarity of one's narrative can be enhanced by drawing data from other sources (such as students, colleagues, and the literature) rather than relying solely on personal critical incidents.

Our Students' Eyes

Improving my classroom practice was a primary focus during my five years in the high school classroom. In addition to analyzing my own teaching, I also had my students fill out informal course evaluations to find out from them what they did and did not like about my teaching. Much of their feedback confirmed my own dissatisfaction with the apparent content overload within several of the senior year courses. I recognized the need to cover the curriculum, especially when a government examination awaited the students at the end of the course, but there was too much emphasis on my telling, and their memorizing.

In order to create a setting where the students could take a more active role in their learning, I found it helpful to give out typed notes containing the material. Thus, instead of spending time copying notes, we used the class time to discuss the concepts and to enrich our understanding of the material. In order to make the handouts more consistent with active learning, I often left spaces where they were expected to answer synthesis questions about the subject matter or to write in their understanding of a topic that was discussed in class. In certain units, I would break up the class into groups where each group would focus on a particular topic and then share its work with the other groups. As well, many of the courses I taught contained one independent unit where the students used a study guide that encouraged them to work through the material on their own.

One result of this iterative process of improving my teaching through the feedback I was receiving from my students was that I was progressively doing less of the telling and they were becoming more active in their learning. Using the analogy of a ball, where the ball represents the 'mental work' of understanding the subject matter, my teaching was aimed at getting the students to carry the ball. Through the study guides that I developed for the independent units, emphasis was also placed on encouraging the students to monitor their own learning so they could better appreciate what and how they learned. This approach is similar to the development of students' metacognitive abilities as documented in an Australian initiative, the PEEL project, which aims to improve the quality of teaching and learning (Baird and Mitchell, 1987; Baird and Northfield, 1992).

Our Colleagues' Experiences

My first opportunity to work as a teacher educator was with a group of elementary pre-service teachers, and I was offered the opportunity to team teach two sections of the course with Dougal MacDonald, a doctoral student in the same department. Dougal and I spent countless hours in joint planning before each lesson as well as debriefing after each lesson. These activities served as powerful catalysts for reflecting on our views of teacher education and on the effectiveness of our classroom practice. Specifically, in the process of planning our lessons, each of us was forced to articulate rationales for wanting to do certain things. Through the process of negotiating a curriculum we examined our personal views of what constituted sound science education experiences for our pre-service teachers. The debriefing of lessons was also important because we were able to purposefully critique our sessions to improve our practice. It is not often that teachers or teacher educators have opportunities to have a 'critical friend' observe so many of one's lessons (Chin and MacDonald, 1994).

Early in our planning, Dougal recalled the adage that, 'If you give people fish, they can eat for a day, but if you teach them to fish, they can eat for a lifetime.' This statement has been a powerful beacon in my teaching because it signifies the balance that I continually try to achieve in my role as a teacher educator. For me, the adage captures the tension between the short-term and long-term needs of pre-service teachers. As a teacher educator I feel that I have an obligation to allay some of their pre-practicum concerns, but I also believe that I have a mandate to prepare them for long-term goals aimed at reflective professional growth. This is not a situation of 'either/or' — it must be both. I do want pre-service teachers to learn how to fish for themselves, but I also recognize that their more immediate concerns are for some fish of their own (practical strategies and materials they can use right away). When I cast the analogy onto my own pre-service program, I realize at once that one cannot engage fully in teaching pre-service teachers how to fish if they are preoccupied with the hunger pangs from their empty stomachs. Thus I see my own role as one in which I am endeavoring to teach people to fish, but also trying to give them enough fish so that in the interim they do not go hungry. The ongoing struggle becomes a constant search for ways of concomitantly achieving both goals.

Our fruitful efforts from team teaching have been helpful in my professional relationships at Queen's where, due to course scheduling arrangements, I work closely with my colleague Tom Russell. Within our consecutive program, both of us teach sections of the same course, and within our Queen's-Waterloo program we deliver a joint science program to a common group of pre-service teachers. By necessity, we need to keep each other informed about what we are doing in our individual courses. This arrangement serves as an ongoing context for supporting each other in articulating and critiquing our teacher education practices. Both the individual and collective senses that we have made of our practice serve as useful foci for the ongoing improvement of our own teaching (Chin and Russell, 1996; Featherstone, Chin and Russell, 1996). Our efforts were enhanced during the Fall of 1995 when John Loughran, while on sabbatical from Monash, was a participant observer in all the classes Tom and I taught.

I recognize these collegial relationships as opportunities through which I have come to better understand my own practice through shared experiences with colleagues. I believe that the most powerful kind of learning — both in the classroom with pupils, and in the staff room with colleagues — occurs when all participants are drawing from the same shared experiences. Within these collegial relationships, we have had many supportive and validating discussions centred around instances where we shared similar impressions about the particular class in which we both participated. Perhaps more valuable have been the discussions that focused on classroom instances in which our perceptions of the same events were quite different. These instances forced us to articulate our reasons for teaching the way we do, and demanded supporting evidence from the actions and reactions of the learners. In any case, forging opportunities to have shared teaching experiences as teacher educators creates both context and catalyst for better understanding our own practice.

Theoretical Literature

An important aspect of teaching about teaching is the knowledge of a broad range of theoretical literature that has implications for science teaching and teacher education. The two strongest and mutually informing influences on my teacher education practice have been constructivist views of learning and Donald Schön's (1983) work in reflective practice. Generally, constructivist views of learning assume that knowledge is personally constructed, socially mediated, and inherently situated.

The three premises of constructivism have resonated within my own view of teacher education. I recognize that pre-service teachers cannot merely be 'told' what I want them to learn. Rather, they must be provided with opportunities to 'experience' and make sense of what it is that I am trying to help them understand. I try to create a safe atmosphere so that they feel comfortable talking and writing about how they are making sense of the issues of teaching and learning in which we engage. In addition to the shared experiences of the science methods course, I also make attempts to draw upon their classroom experiences as teachers and learners, because understanding these experiences is pivotal to their personal professional development. Perhaps the most difficult time within the methods course is the first five weeks of classes prior to the pre-service teachers' first practicum round. As mentioned earlier, I try to attend to their pre-teaching concerns but their lack of recent experience of teaching always makes it frustrating. For example, when dealing with classroom management, I usually suggest to the class that the practice of having students raise their hands to answer a question (rather than allowing them to call out answers) is helpful in keeping classroom order. During the classroom visits that I make while they are on their practicum placements, I often have the feeling that my suggestion has fallen on deaf ears. When the issue of controlling the noise level of the class comes up during the debriefing session, I often repeat my suggestion to the pre-service teacher. In most instances the pre-service teacher is appreciative of the helpful suggestion and states that he or she will work on it. While I can never resist the opportunity to remind them that I had mentioned this prior to the practicum, I believe that the second instance is actually the first time that the point registers for them. For me, this example of the inherent situatedness of learning to teach is best captured by Schön's (1983) tenet that one cannot tell others what they need to know, and that new teachers will only recognize their needs when they are immersed within the practice of what it is they are trying to learn.

Schön's depiction of the importance of one's experiences within the action setting dovetails nicely into Posner, Strike, Hewson, and Gertzog's (1982) assertions specific to a particular approach to teaching from a constructivist perspective of learning. These authors contend that, within the context of conceptual change science teaching, instruction should be planned in such a way that students become dissatisfied with their existing conception of a phenomenon and then recognize that the scientific conception being taught is intelligible, plausible, and fruitful in a variety of new situations. In my work with pre-service teachers I have them participate in carefully designed in-class activities that draw upon their shared experiences as teachers and learners as a first step toward them articulating their own dissatisfactions with ways in which they experience teaching and learning. Even if pre-service teachers recognize the intelligibility, plausibility, and potential fruitfulness of the teaching approaches I advocate in the science methods course, my efforts are fruitless unless they are personally dissatisfied with some facets of their current conception of teaching. As a parallel to my own 'indirect' learning as a teacher educator, perhaps my role can best be described as providing pre-service teachers with experiences and opportunities as the professional development context in which their perspectives on teaching can be articulated, critiqued, and practiced.

The four critically reflective lenses outlined in this section are intended to convey some of the significant experiences within my life history that inform my current practice as a teacher educator. Using frameworks for understanding to reflect on and critique my own practice continues to be important in my own growth as a teacher. This is done by listening to my students and by working with critical friends. As a former high school teacher and now, as a teacher educator, I continue to look for ways in which class members can 'carry the ball' in order to meet both the short-term and long-term goals in their teaching and learning. I have come to believe that learning about teaching best occurs through shared experiences and critical discussions. In this way individuals can increase their awareness of their own growth as a teacher as they critique the views of teaching and learning they hope to put into practice in their own teaching settings.

How Beliefs Inform Practice

Although it is important for each of us to articulate our core beliefs about teaching and learning, Brookfield (1995) also suggests that we should explicitly communicate these to our classes through the course outline. What follows is my first attempt to articulate these core beliefs in a 'jargon-free' summary for my preservice teachers in the B.Ed. program in which I teach.

My core beliefs about teaching and learning:

- Learning to articulate, question, and understand our beliefs about teaching and learning is the first step to improving our practice.
- Personal understanding is enhanced through writing about and discussing our beliefs with others.
- Learning about teaching and learning occurs best when we are placed in a context where we are teachers and students. Experiencing something is far more helpful than being told.
- Monitoring and understanding how we teach and how we learn is important to our professional growth.
- Our teaching is improved by listening to ourselves, our colleagues, and our pupils.
- The classroom is better when students take a more active role in their learning.
- The instructor's role is to facilitate and guide these teaching and learning experiences.
- Teaching this class in a way that is consistent with the way I suggest that you teach your class is an important goal in my own teaching.

A session discussant's statement, at a recent conference, that 'teacher education is all about learning how to see' captures the essence of what I am trying to do in my curriculum methods classroom. I am attempting to help my pre-service teachers 'see' their own philosophy of teaching and learning, how they can learn through discussions and activities with their peers, how they can improve their teaching through self-analysis and by listening to their pupils, and how educational research can enhance their practice. This notion of 'seeing' relates well to the image of critically reflective lenses and again illustrates the importance of understanding the difference between telling and teaching.

It would be impossible to outline the specifics of how my core beliefs about teaching and learning are translated into all facets of my curriculum methods classroom practice. Thus, consistent with my core beliefs, I instead highlight four salient activities important in my teaching in the B.Ed. program. These are helping pre-service teachers to:

1 examine their views of teaching, learning, and science;
2 reflect on their teaching;
3 recognize the value of using teaching strategies for enhancing understanding; and
4 develop their skills in unit presentation and planning.

Examining Our Views

Early in the course we spend several lessons exploring our views of teaching, learning, and science. Drawing on an activity that I saw as a teaching assistant at the University of British Columbia, I distribute a sheet with several common metaphors of teaching and have the pre-service teachers write about the ones that resonate with them. Later, we discuss their chosen metaphors in small groups and then in a whole-class discussion. Within these discussions it becomes obvious that their views of teaching and learning are influenced by memorable images of certain teachers (good and bad) from their past. What we also quickly realize is that, although one metaphor is not appropriate for everyone, an understanding and acceptance of the rationale for choosing a particular metaphor emerges through listening to others. From this, they begin to compile a list of the features of good teaching and good learning, and throughout the year, we return to these lists to provide an opportunity to review, add to, and clarify them.

In our exploration of our views of teaching it is also important to examine our views of science because, as Wideen *et al.* (1992) argued, how we view science influences what and how we teach science in our schools. Using a series of statements about science (Bell, 1993) the pre-service teachers' views of science are challenged within both small-group and whole-class discussions. The energetic conversations progress through a series of teacher-led, open-ended science demonstrations as we reconcile and review our original ideas and thinking.

Reflecting on Their Teaching

Personal growth in one's teaching comes from improving one's skills at self-monitoring and self-analysis. My efforts to encourage self-monitoring centre around encouraging the pre-service teachers to articulate their concerns about their teaching and to monitor their learning and growth as a teacher. On the first day of class I have each person write down their three main concerns about teaching, and just before their first three-week practicum I ask them to tell me how these concerns have or have not been met. On their return from the first practicum I have them write down three things that they want to do better and three things that they want to understand better about their teaching. This serves as a focus for my teaching and their professional growth and, as in the case of examining their views, we return to their lists prior to the two subsequent practicum experiences in order to clarify the areas in which they want to improve. As well, after each practicum I ask them to reconsider their lists and to change them as necessary.

I encourage self-analysis through a lesson analysis assignment that requires them to audio-tape a lesson during one of the practicum experiences. The assignment, which is done while back on campus, entails transcribing a 30-minute portion of the lesson and then answering a series of questions that focus on the 'pedagogical moves' of the lesson and providing evidence about the success of the lesson. I make it clear that my purpose is to assist them in improving the quality of their analyzes and not to judge the quality of the lessons. An extension of this develops when they analyze their teaching through a critique of a video-tape of their in-class science demonstrations. Many pre-service teachers state that they intend to repeat this exercise during their teaching careers. It would certainly be interesting to investigate such analysis during their teaching careers.

Enhancing Student Understanding

The importance of getting students to carry the ball is something that I encourage my pre-service teachers to engage in with their pupils. The PEEL project's (Baird and Mitchell, 1987; Baird and Northfield, 1992) descriptions and explanations of its efforts to enhance student understanding are singularly helpful to me in achieving this, particularly through documentation of their teaching strategies. To get my pre-service teachers to carry the ball, we work with some of these teaching strategies through a jigsaw activity. The class is divided into groups of four, and each group is given a sheet that describes, in minimal detail, how a particular teaching strategy works. The group is then responsible for learning how the strategy works by determining the subject matter to employ as a content-based vehicle for teaching the strategy to the rest of us. This is an independent activity that extends over some time, and at the completion we debrief the activity and highlight significant issues in both the teaching and the learning for each teaching strategy.

This structured episode encompasses many of my core beliefs about teaching and learning. First, the pre-service teachers take a very active role in the teaching and the learning associated with the strategies. Second, the groups need to socially mediate their understanding of how the strategy works. Third, the jigsaw activity illustrates how we can learn from each other. Finally, the activity establishes a setting where at some point each class member is a teacher and a learner. In our debriefing session, I start by asking the teachers (i.e., the group that presented the strategy) to discuss the significant features that they considered in the planning and delivery of the strategy. This is followed by inviting the learners (i.e., those learning the strategy) to share the significant features of their learning through use of the strategy. Thus we expose some sense of the reasoning behind how the strategies were interpreted by teachers, the factors that affected what subject matter to select, and the rationale behind the pedagogical moves that each group used to teach the strategy to the rest of the class. In addition, we are also able to discuss the impact that each strategy and its delivery had on us as learners. The end result is that the quality of our learning as prospective science teachers is far superior to what could be achieved had I formally 'taught' the strategies to them. More importantly, the activity encourages us to monitor our own understanding of the strategy, our teaching, and students' learning throughout the process.

Unit Planning and Presenting

The unit planning and presentation course component involves pairs of pre-service teachers designing a curriculum unit and then presenting this to the class to engage them in some of the learning activities contained in the unit. It is up to each pair to discuss and negotiate both the substance of its curriculum unit and the structure of its class presentation. It is my intention that pairing the pre-service teachers creates a team-teaching situation where each person must articulate his or her rationales for the sequence of the topics and the selection of appropriate pupil learning activities.

The tangible products of this course component are obvious and are seen as valuable teaching resources that are helpful to any beginning teacher. The learning about teaching that can occur throughout the process of developing the units is less obvious. By preparing the units in pairs, groups must negotiate the curriculum and articulate their rationales for why they propose to teach the subject matter in that way. In most cases, groups also select some student activities that are specifically aimed at enhancing student understanding. Again, it is necessary for each group to provide their rationales for why they selected certain strategies rather than others, and they need to articulate the rationale for their approach to teaching the strategy. Although much of this explication is assumed to be occurring between the partners, there are instances where such explanations are explicitly requested during my monitoring of the unit development, and through class questioning during presentations. Next year, I hope to improve the monitoring of the learning and understanding during the process of unit planning by scheduling specific meeting times with each group, and by having a mid-point peer critique where each group will read and react to another group's unit.

Listening to Their Voices

How do I know that my particular stance to teacher education makes a difference? It would be ideal to revisit the pre-service teachers a few years down the road in their own classrooms, to determine what facets of their classroom practice were influenced by the approach taken in the curriculum methods course. The evidence that I can provide to illustrate that my classroom practices (and the beliefs that underpin them) have a positive influence on the pre-service teachers in my charge appears in their own words and actions. As mentioned earlier, I teach a science curriculum methods course both in our regular program, which involves two terms of instruction with nine weeks of practicum scattered throughout, and in our joint program with the University of Waterloo, in which the pre-service teachers attend one term of education courses immediately after a sixteen-week teaching placement. The impact of the recent and relevant classroom experience of the Queen's-Waterloo pre-service teachers greatly enhances what can be done in a science curriculum course (Chin and Russell, 1996). Because of the exceptional nature of that unique program I limit my evidence to data from those in my regular program course.

I have two sources of data in which the pre-service teachers' own words can speak for themselves. One source is the open-ended response section of our standard faculty teaching evaluation forms. The second source of data is provided by two Fall term writing activities where I ask the class members to write down statements about what they perceive to be the purpose of my teaching approach. To provide a structure for the selected comments that follow, I revisit my core beliefs about teaching and learning. Basically, these beliefs centre around the importance of:

- understanding our own beliefs about teaching and learning;
- writing and discussing;
- learning by doing; and
- monitoring our teaching and learning.

What follows is a series of selected pre-service teachers' comments under each of these categories.

Understanding Our Beliefs

- Thought-provoking stuff was great.
- A guided discovery of our own teaching strengths.
- Peter's approach leads to a lot of open class discussions which I appreciate. This forces us to really think about our views about how science should be taught.
- His approach seems to be to have us reflect on our own personal teaching style/teaching philosophy.

Writing and Discussing

- There was a lot of student input and a lot of sharing of knowledge between peers.

- The class was encouraged to carry discussions where we thought they needed to go, i.e., what we thought we needed to know.
- Many excellent group discussions.
- He has illustrated how effectively things can be learned/taught in informal class-led discussions.

Learning by Doing

- He is trying to guide and motivate us to finding the answer(s) and often the question(s) from the students themselves.
- I think Peter is trying to model everything he is trying to teach us. We also get to practice running the class and working on our own teaching styles through participation in the class. We are both learners and professionals in development at the same time.
- Peter tries not to get involved in too much of the teaching. I think he wants us to teach one another.
- The knowledge and skills gained in this class are from active participation.

Monitoring Our Teaching and Learning

- Material covered was geared to make us think about why we are doing it, as well as what we are doing.
- When activities are being done we can ask ourselves how we would do it if we were running the show.
- We are leading more and becoming more aware.
- I find that you guide or prompt the class more than you specifically instruct us.

The authors of these comments do seem to recognize what it is that I am trying to attain through my particular teaching approach. As well, several of the comments convey a normative sense that appears to be supportive of the direction taken in my science methods course. For others, the teaching approach was recognized but not necessarily fully appreciated, as illustrated by the following comments:

- Too often he asked the students what should be taught and I for one would consider myself arrogant to answer such a request.
- I think Peter did a wonderful job with the course as it was laid out but it certainly wasn't what I expected or maybe needed.

These comments suggest that, for some class members, the balance of fish and fishing that I offer still leaves them frustrated. Comments such as these continue to push me forward in search of ways to address their concerns without undermining or contradicting the core beliefs that I hold as a teacher educator.

To indicate how teacher candidates embrace the idea of 'carrying the ball', I highlight several instances where the actions of the various class members can be seen as confirming evidence that they are attempting to 'live' this approach to learning. Volunteers from my class participate in events such as National Chemistry Week activities and judging science fairs in local schools. The majority of my class also attends the conference of the Ontario Science Teachers Association. When one person started a class newsletter about secondary science teaching, several other class members contributed articles (ranging from teaching strategies and lab demonstrations to cartoons appropriate for use in the science classroom). Finally, all of the class members pooled their curriculum units with those developed by people in other courses and the entire collection was placed on the science teaching link of the faculty's world wide web home page (http://educ.queensu.ca).

Conclusion

As I reflect upon the core beliefs that I have about what I stand for as a teacher educator, it becomes clear that I advocate the importance of articulating, critiquing, and understanding one's beliefs about teaching and learning. These beliefs serve as the foundation that informs practice as a teacher designs curriculum for students. Finally, the importance of establishing frameworks for understanding so that one can monitor the effectiveness of one's teaching leads to an iterative process of professional development and the improvement of one's teaching. These same core beliefs about my role as a teacher educator are mirrored in this chapter as I apply these beliefs to my own role as a learner.

This chapter surfaces my own beliefs about teaching and learning, illustrates how these beliefs are conveyed within my practice, and assesses elements of the effectiveness of this teaching. The samples of the class members' written responses and the descriptive instances of their visible actions suggest that my approach to teacher education, which encourages the pre-service teachers to be reflective and active participants in their professional development, does indeed make a difference. The data suggest that most members of the class are comfortable with teaching that encourages them to carry the ball in their teaching and learning, and that is exactly what I think they need to learn to do if they are to enhance learning for understanding by their own students.

References

BAIRD, J.R. and MITCHELL, I. (1987) *Improving the Quality of Teaching and Learning: An Australian Case Study — The Peel Project*, Melbourne, Monash University Printery.

BAIRD, J.R. and NORTHFIELD, J.R. (1992) *Learning from the PEEL Experience*, Melbourne, Monash University Printery.

BELL, B. (1993) *Taking into Account Students' Thinking: A Teacher Development Guide*, Hamilton, NZ, Centre for Science and Mathematics Education Research.

BROOKFIELD, S. (1995) *Becoming a Critically Reflective Teacher*, San Francisco, Jossey-Bass Publishers.

CHIN, P. and MACDONALD, D. (1994) 'Team teaching elementary science methods: Potential payoffs and possible problems', *Educational Insights*, **2**, pp. 15–23.

CHIN, P. and RUSSELL, T. (1996) 'Reforming teacher education: Making sense of our past to inform our future', *Teacher Education Quarterly*, **23**, 3, pp. 55–68.

CONNELLY, M. and CLANDININ, J. (1988) *Teachers as Curriculum Planners: Narratives of Experience*, Toronto, OISE Press.

FEATHERSTONE, D., CHIN, P. and RUSSELL, T. (1996, April) 'Extending professional trialogue: Self-study across the teaching spectrum', Paper presented at the meeting of the American Educational Research Association, New York.

KILBOURN, B. (1990) *Constructive Feedback: Learning the Art*, Toronto, OISE Press.

LORTIE, D. (1975) *Schoolteacher: A Sociological Study*, Chicago, University of Chicago Press.

POSNER, G., STRIKE, K., HEWSON, P. and GERTZOG, W. (1982) 'Accommodation of a scientific conception: Toward a theory of conceptual change', *Science Education*, **66**, 2, pp. 211–27.

SCHÖN, D.A. (1983) *The Reflective Practitioner: How Professionals Think in Action*, New York, Basic Books.

WIDEEN, M., MACKINNON, A., O'SHEA, T., WILD, R., SHAPSON, S., DAY, E., PYE, I., MOON, B., CUSACK, S., CHIN, P. and PYE, K. (1992) *British Columbia Assessment of Science 1991 Technical Report IV: Context for Science Component*, Victoria, Ministry of Education, Multiculturalism and Human Rights of British Columbia.

Rethinking Teacher Educators' Roles and Practice

9 Learning about Learning in the Context of a Science Methods Course[1]

Garry Hoban

Introduction

Darling-Hammond (1995) contends that an 'understanding of learners and learning . . . is the most neglected aspect of teacher preparation in this country' (p. 13). Referring to the USA, she explains that teacher education emphasizes trainee teachers developing an understanding of subject matter and instructional strategies, but does not provide a sufficient grounding in student learning. The consequence is that teaching, especially in secondary schools, is often driven by a prescriptive curriculum which rarely takes into account students' prior knowledge and experiences. She argues that if teacher education places more emphasis on pre-service teachers developing an understanding of learning, then they will develop a 'greater command of both content and pedagogy in order to create and manage students' learning' (1995, p. 14).

So in what ways do pre-service teachers currently learn about learning? In many teacher education courses, research findings on student learning are presented to pre-service teachers in lectures or they are provided with educational literature to read as the basis for discussion in subsequent tutorials. There are, however, two limitations that restrict opportunities for pre-service teachers to develop a broad understanding of student learning if only research articles are used. The first limitation relates to assumptions that underpin the discipline upon which the research is based. For example, many studies on student learning over the last fifteen years support a constructivist perspective emphasizing the influence of an individual's prior understanding on the way meaning is constructed. This perspective is grounded in the discipline of psychology that is underpinned by the assumption that the individual is the unit of analysis (Cobb, 1994). Hence, studies on student learning often focus on the prior beliefs of individuals and how this personal understanding influences subsequent learning (Bell, 1981; Driver, 1983; Driver, Guesne, and Tiberghien, 1985; Driver and Oldham, 1986; Erickson, 1979; Faire and Cosgrove, 1988; Gunstone, 1990; Osborne and Wittrock, 1983; Osborne and Freyberg, 1985; von Glaserfield, 1989). This focus on the individual, however, ignores the influence of contextual factors such as the social and cultural conditions that support an individual's learning.

In contrast, other studies on learning are often based on a sociocultural perspective emphasizing the interdependence of the individual and the context (Rogoff,

1993). This perspective is grounded in the discipline of sociology that is under-pinned by the assumption that the unit of analysis is the individual-in-social-action (Cobb, 1994). This assumption suggests that learning by individuals cannot be separated from the context and emphasizes social and cultural interactions that influence learning (Lave and Wenger, 1991). The influence of context on learning has been demonstrated in many different settings such as apprentices learning to become tailors (Lave, 1988), children learning to cost and sell candy (Saxe, 1988), dairy workers learning to stack and count milk crates (Scribner, 1986), women learning to become midwives (Lave and Wenger, 1991), and bookmakers learning to formulate betting odds for horse races (Ceci and Liken, 1986). This type of learning in a real context is *purposeful* and *holistic*, such that the learner has some control over what and how they are learning. Hence, studies based on a sociocul-tural perspective focus on the social engagement of individuals as they participate in various activities, but often ignore the influence of an individual's prior know-ledge that is emphasized by a constructivist perspective.

An issue for teacher educators to consider is how and when to use research articles in pre-service teacher education courses. For instance, if an instructor relies only on articles based on a constructivist perspective, then pre-service teachers may acquire a narrow understanding of learning and not gain an appreciation of influ-ential social, political, and cultural factors. Conversely, if an instructor only uses research articles based on a sociocultural perspective, then pre-service teachers may not gain an understanding of personal influences such as prior knowledge on stu-dent learning. Hence, a possible consequence in exclusively using research articles supporting one perspective on learning, constructivist or sociocultural, is the com-plaint from some teachers that what is promoted in research articles does not match the complexity of a real classroom because opportunities for student learning are related to many different influences — individual, social, cultural, and political (Hoban, 1996). In comparing the differences between sociocultural and construct-ivist perspectives on learning, Cobb (1994) recently argued that both perspectives should be considered in discussions about learning and are complementary as 'one perspective constitutes the background against which the other comes to the fore' (p. 18). It should be noted, however, that some current research articles on student learning reflect a broader approach coupling both individual and social influences such as situated cognition (Brown, Collins, and Duguig, 1989; Hennessy, 1993), and social constructivism (Driver, Asoko, Leach, and Scott, 1995; Prawat, 1995; Prawat and Floden, 1994).

A second limitation in exclusively using research articles in teacher educa-tion courses, whether they are underpinned by a constructivist or sociocultural per-spective, is that they present decontextualized knowledge for pre-service teachers. In this respect, formal knowledge presented in a lecture or a research article has been generated by educational researchers using an extended process of reading relevant literature, gathering data from a setting, and finally analyzing as well as synthesiz-ing the data into a research article. Hence, providing pre-service teachers with edu-cational literature to read is expecting them to understand the product of a long term investigation without being involved in the process of generating the findings.

Furthermore, these articles use an academic genre for publication in research journals which assume prior knowledge of reference articles cited and often use educational jargon that pre-service teachers may not be familiar with. This method of instruction is similar to the way some secondary science teachers present isolated facts to school students when the students have not participated in the process of knowledge construction and so teachers expect them to 'arrive without having travelled' (Barnes, 1976, p. 118).

There is, however, another way for pre-service teachers to learn about learning — by studying their own experiences in their teacher education courses. Munby and Russell (1994) emphasize pre-service teachers' 'authority of experience' that highlights the importance of their reflection on their instruction in schools. Why not also encourage pre-service teachers to value and analyze their experiences as learners in teacher education classes? Methods courses are supposed to assist pre-service teachers to 'learn about teaching' so these experiences can be used as a context to generate an understanding of their own learning. The purpose of this chapter is to outline a teaching strategy that I explored to assist pre-service teachers to use their own experiences from their methods course as a context to reflect and analyze not only *what*, but also *how* they did or did not learn. Baird (1992) has argued that teachers need to be metacognitive and become more aware of their practice in classrooms to inform their pedagogical decisions. Pre-service teachers also should be encouraged to be metacognitive and become more aware of how they learn in teacher education courses with the intention of informing their decision-making as they construct their personal pedagogies.

Procedure

This chapter outlines how eighty-five pre-service elementary teachers monitored and analyzed their own learning on a weekly basis throughout a thirteen-week science methods course that I taught in 1994. The pre-service teachers were in the second year of a three-year Bachelor of Teaching degree at a university in Australia. They had three contact hours each week in the form of a fifty minute group lecture and a two hour hands-on practical session[2] with twenty-one pre-service teachers in each class. The weekly practical classes commenced with an activity to elicit students' prior knowledge/experiences about a topic followed by hands-on investigations focusing on a particular science concept. The class concluded with a discussion to clarify any concerns raised by the pre-service students that may have arisen during their investigations. The lectures in the subject mainly focused on content suitable to provide pre-service teachers with background knowledge for topics in elementary science classes.

The pre-service teachers used a journal to critique my teaching each week by recording and reflecting upon their positive and negative learning experiences during the practical class. They were asked to write about two aspects: to document *what* they learnt in terms of the content of the class instruction, as well as *how* they were learning to monitor and analyze the processes involved. To address the latter aspect, the pre-service teachers were asked to document factors that enhanced their learning by identifying 'ways that helped them to learn' as well as factors that inhibited their learning or 'ways that did not help them to learn'. Most of the pre-service teachers found this self-monitoring of learning to be a new experience, and so it was important to discuss these issues, using examples, in class. In addition, aspects about their own learning were regularly discussed throughout the course in the lectures and the practical classes. At the end of the course I evaluated the usefulness of this teaching strategy by asking the pre-service teachers to write a one page anonymous report to address the following questions:

> One of the aims of this course has been for you to develop a self-awareness about how you learn or do not learn.
> 1 Did you develop a self-awareness about ways that help you to learn or ways that do not help you to learn in this course? If you did can you describe these ways?
> 2 If you did develop this self-awareness, has this had any impact on the way you think you would teach science to elementary children?

In addition two pre-service teachers volunteered to participate in an informal conversational interview (Patton, 1990) to discuss their experiences in the course. The next part provides a pre-service teacher's view on this procedure of monitoring and analyzing her learning experiences from her science methods course.

Carolyn's View of Analyzing Her Learning in a Teacher Education Course

> As a student in the second year of a three year education degree in which one's academic ability and perception of a lecturer's point of view enables one to do well, the prospect of openly writing about my ideas appeared quite daunting. In fact, it took a good deal of time and effort on the behalf of our lecturer requesting honesty before I, and many of my colleagues, felt comfortable in doing so. Even so, there still remained the entrenched mistrust of the lecturer's true motives. For once rather than being taught what was accepted thinking, I was being encouraged to think for myself — what a novel approach! By not immediately launching into the documented literature of various theorists and so adapting my thoughts to their thinking (out of respect for their expertise in their field), I found that the weekly documentation of my positive and negative learning experiences provided me with a basis from which I was able to further develop original ideas about my own learning. This was different from some other educational classes in which lecturers informed us about documented educational theory which we were expected to learn.
> At first documenting my own learning was a different experience. This is not to say that until this moment in time I had never thought about

how I learn, but rather this work gave me an opportunity to monitor and analyze my learning in a systematic way. This resulted in giving me a better insight into the complexities of learning and an appreciation for the various learning styles of others. I found that the weekly documentation of my positive and negative learning experiences provided me with a basis for developing my personal ideas that were original and not contrived to address university assessment tasks. As a result, I have come to a deeper, more personal understanding of the role the individual plays in influencing their environment, and how the environment influences an individual's level of learning. This knowledge leads me to an understanding that learning is cyclic[al] having a spiralling effect from which prior knowledge is drawn, added to, and drawn again.

There were several strengths to this approach to learning being heightened self awareness, increased self-esteem, motivation, and the development of strategies which will assist me in a multitude of life situations, not just those connected with teaching science. Through this heightened self-awareness I am able to target those learning strategies that work best for me whilst also developing an adaptability to learning situations in which I do not learn as well. For example, by analyzing my learning I realized that I learn best when I have some prior knowledge about a topic while I find pure discovery learning difficult, particularly when my prior knowledge is limited. This ability to understand my metacognition has increased my self-esteem and motivation and has added some maturity to the teaching strategies that I would use in a classroom.

Although I developed a positive attitude and gained self-esteem as I analyzed my own learning, there are some disadvantages. I can see how there is a possibility of a less than positive appraisal of one's learning abilities. For example, if a student has a negative attitude and a poor self-esteem about his or her learning, then it is a real possibility that these negative feelings may be incorporated into other investigations. This may lead to reinforcement of their negative attitude and as such they may be left believing that their analysis has only proved just how incompetent they really are and so a state of learnt helplessness may become increasingly apparent. This would lead to lower self-esteem and motivation. Also the lack of life experiences for some may make the task of metacognition difficult in that their store of knowledge and understanding is limited by the extent of what they have previously experienced.

In summarizing, it has only been through the ongoing documentation and analysis of my own learning that I have come to more deeply appreciate the complexity of my own and other's learning. Analyzing my own learning in the science methods class has been extremely worthwhile and necessary for my ongoing development as a trainee teacher. As a future teacher it is my responsibility to be aware of and attuned to the ways in which my students learn best. Through this understanding of learning I will be better able to develop those strategies which will assist me in catering for each student's individuality while still allowing for social interaction within the classroom.

Results

The results of this investigation will be presented in two sections — a summary of the written data from the one page report completed by the eighty-five pre-service teachers will be presented first followed by interview data from two of the pre-service teachers.

Data from the Written Reports

Self-awareness about Ways That Help Learning

Eighty-one out of the eighty-five pre-service teachers wrote that they had developed a self-awareness about their own learning as a result of the methods course. Although I will not attempt to rank the importance of the twenty-two different 'ways' described, I believe that it is worthwhile to show the range of responses along with the number of students who mentioned them in their reports. In all, the pre-service teachers documented three sources of influences on their learning:

(1) personal influences;
(2) social influences; and
(3) influences related to the type of activities.

The variety of different responses is now described including the number of students who mentioned such influences. Several 'ways' related to personal influences on learning: experimenting with their own ideas (28), personal prior knowledge (19), personal confidence to 'have a go', personal feelings (1), and personal motivation (2). Other 'ways' related to social influences on their learning. Some of these related to my teaching: teacher enthusiasm (9), teacher explanations (3), modelling teaching techniques (4), and relationship with teacher (2). Other social influences related to interactions with other students: group work (26), class discussions (23), writing in journal (16), and watching other students (1). A third influence was the type of activity that the students had been involved in: theory in lectures (7), interesting topics (17), hands-on activities (18); friendly classroom environment (10), enjoyable activities (9), time to reflect (7), trial and error (13), follow-up readings (3), and variety of activities (3).

The range of student responses was quite broad which is not surprising, as they were asked to monitor any influence on their learning. To get a better sense of what the students described, I have included five comments from the written reports that show some insights into their own learning:

I have become more aware of the way I learn best and it will help when I begin to teach students. I realized that I can do science, that it is not all irrelevant formulas that don't relate to anything. I have furthered my thinking skills and have taken more risks in questioning and thinking. The fact that we could learn independently helped me the most and trial and error is always a great help.

I did develop ways or factors that helped me to learn. I learnt that learning should be interesting, motivated and pupil oriented. For the first time I realized that trial and error is a useful and appropriate method of discovery and should be more emphasized and encouraged to be useful when appropriate.

It helped me to discover that I do not learn very much when I am completely bored by a topic, do not understand the topic, or do not have any prior knowledge.

I think discussing the basic facts at the end of each lesson was a good idea because by then we had seen the need to know more and try to understand it better.

The experience of us teaching the class helped us to understand the ways we learn. By applying teaching strategies you are better able to understand the practicality of their use.

Self-awareness about Ways That Did Not Help Learning

Four of the eighty-five pre-service teachers wrote on their report that they did not develop a self-awareness about their learning in the course. Comments from these written reports are presented below. These comments show that this particular teaching strategy did not suit all the pre-service students:

No — my self-awareness of the learning process had already been raised by other subjects devoted to this topic namely psychology, English, and learning to read. I thought this subject was a waste of time.

I hate group work! Time and time again I heard of one or two students in a group of four get stuck with doing all the work. It is unfair and should be changed. There is not enough work for a group of four to cover and many parts of the work need or had to be done individually.

Sometimes I needed more structured guidance with hard topics like electricity.

No, I did not become more aware of my learning and I did not like being a guinea pig for your study.

Influence of Self-awareness on Views about Teaching Science and Technology

I was hoping that if the pre-service teachers did develop a self-awareness about their own learning, that this may effect their views about teaching to elementary children which was the reason for the second question on the written report. In all, seventy-nine of the eighty-five pre-service teachers wrote positive comments to address this question. However, six students did not respond to this question. There were no negative responses. A selection of comments from the reports is provided below. Several pre-service teachers commented on the value of reflecting on their experiences to develop an understanding about learning:

> Yes, I did develop an awareness of what helps me to learn including linking the topic to prior knowledge, the importance of hands-on experiences to see and test hypotheses ourselves, talking to fellow peers to help put something into context or foreign language into our language, trial and error and so forth. Doing the practicals helped me to understand this self-awareness. We may have been told about it in lectures but it went in one ear and out the other whereas having to assess each lesson ourselves and writing about factors helped me to understand what you were saying.

> Many ways of teaching have been shown. Thinking about it allows you to become aware of what the factors were that seemed to help the children the most. I've become aware that children need to discover things themselves, have time to finish activities and ask lots of questions. Without these factors I wouldn't have really known where to start to teach science.

> Yes, it helped me in developing a way I will teach science and technology. I will let children have a go and try to work out their own ideas. I definitely won't just tell them facts and expect them to remember them, or write notes on the board and get them to copy out masses of notes, as I know I don't learn this way and don't enjoy it. So I want them to enjoy it.

Furthermore, three pre-service teachers commented on their negative experiences whilst learning science in high school and how this methods course had changed their views about teaching the subject:

> Before doing this course I had a real phobia about science and a fear of teaching it because I was under the impression that I had to know everything. I have now come to realize that I don't have to be a super brain to teach science. It's better if the children learn with me and I with them. This way we can construct our own understandings in the topic and get more from it.

> At high school I thought 'science sucks'. I now enjoy science and feel challenged by new ideas, I realize that I am still not 100 per cent confident

in this area but who is? I don't plan to be an expert in science but I do plan to teach children to the best of my ability and let them experience science as it would be a shame to miss out as I did.

I had memories of teacher-oriented learning from high school and this is how I imagined university science to be, only worse . . . In relation to teaching science I have gained a new perspective on how and what to teach in the classroom. I realize that children have much the same learning experiences as I do and so when I teach I should ask myself, 'Would I like to learn this way? Would this be effective for me?' I also have more confidence about teaching science in the classroom.

Data from the written reports suggest that the majority of students believed that the teaching strategy that I was exploring was beneficial and resulted in a better understanding of their own learning. However, this belief, was not held by all students and several reported that they did not benefit from monitoring their positive and negative learning experiences.

Interview Data

At the end of the course I asked the pre-service teachers if any were willing to share any particular experiences regarding this teaching strategy. Two of the students volunteered and were interviewed individually using an informal conversational interview (Patton, 1990). Key aspects from the interviews are now presented.

Gloria: Understanding Her Teaching

Gloria was 44 years old and enrolled as a mature age elementary student-teacher. She had trained for two years (many years earlier) to be a secondary science teacher at a teachers' college and subsequently taught the subject for two years in a high school. She described her teaching style at that time as, 'I was the person at the front who gave science lessons to the kids and they'd all write down what I said, and then they'd write it, rehearse it and write it all back in the exams.' She stated that she taught science this way because it was the way she learnt science when she was at school. She claimed that her initial teacher training to be a secondary teacher did not change her view about science which had been based on how she was taught in her own schooling:

It was a bit piecemeal, it was bits here and bits there and it didn't seem to flow and we weren't challenged with much. It was a very rushed year, I didn't feel I was challenged to learn how to teach. We were just told, 'Right this is the topic we're going to teach and this is the content we have to teach.' I mean it's probably not the way they taught it but that's the way it appeared to me, cause that's the way I had learnt.

Gloria then had a long break from teaching and raised four children. Many years later she returned to teaching high school science and she taught the same way as she did at her first school. She did lots of practical work in her classes 'because it keeps the kids happy, they're doing things and they enjoy it'. However, she always made a point of making her students copy the right answer into their book at the end of a practical class, 'At the end of the prac[tical] I would say, "Right, this is what you should have had and if you didn't have it write this from the board."'

At age 44 she commenced her teacher training to be an elementary teacher and was given an exemption from the first year of the degree due to her previous teacher training. During the interview she discussed her experiences in my course and stated that she had developed a better understanding about learning. In particular, she stated that she began to appreciate learning by trial and error:

> What I've really enjoyed and really learnt is the value of making mistakes in learning. I know I've always understood that you've got to make mistakes in learning, but I've never realized until this class how important it is, to make a mistake and get something wrong and how much value there is and how much learning there is, in that.

She explained that the component of the science methods course which helped her to develop this understanding was analyzing her own learning:

> The most powerful thing I think was each week in the practicals we had to write down why did I learn in this class and why didn't I learn, if I was confused or if there was problem, why didn't I learn, what were the difficulties in that. I think that started me realizing that there were times when, umm, not learning was more powerful than learning because then you'd go away and you'd think about it and you'd talk about it with other people and you'd sort of listen to others, what others said in the prac[tical] and, umm. Like the last one we did with light there was, we came up with this really strange fog, we didn't understand how come sometimes when you mix colours they go black and sometimes they go white. There were the three of us over there, we were in real confusion. But because of that, now I understand it better because I've had to do a lot of reading and questioning and I'm talking and I've learnt now. I never realized before just how much value there is [in that].

Later in the interview she explained how monitoring her own learning influenced her views about teaching. Asked whether her view about teaching science had changed she replied:

> Oh a lot. Lots of practical work, lots of time for kids to investigate and play and to observe, times when they come together and each group shares what they've found and the teacher then would draw it all together. But I wouldn't be a teacher saying, 'This is what we're going to do today, this

is what I want you to learn, have a little play and I'll tell you what I've found'. I'd never do that again. I'd encourage kids to have a go, don't worry if you fail, don't worry if you make a mistake, don't worry if you don't make anything. But next time you can have another go and don't do it that way, do it a different way and find out, try and figure out how you could have improved it. [I would] make sure that as a teacher I went around to each group who were working and sort of give them helpful little questions to make them think about what they could do better so that they didn't reach that point where they were completely lost. But not be so worried if they didn't make anything if they came out at the other end and they hadn't learnt what I wanted them to learn because they probably learnt something different which was important to them, umm, yeah. Making sure that learning is fun, I think I would have done that anyway. But now I've got more idea of how that affects learning, I've got more of an idea of the value of practical work and of talking together and of working together in cooperative groups.

Data from the interview suggested that Gloria had gained a self-awareness about her own learning during the methods course and that this had influenced her views about teaching science. Moreover, I received feedback about my own teaching from her during the interview. Apart from positive feedback, Gloria suggested that there should be more emphasis in the course on discussing the role of science in society.

Sue: Clearing the Block

Sue was 21 years old and in her second year as a trainee elementary teacher. She hated science during her own high school education because it was 'boring' and mainly taught in a didactic way from a textbook. She referred to experiments that she did in high school in which she just followed the teacher's instructions as a 'transmission prac' and how she prefers to experience learning herself:

I think you can't have a transmission prac with that thing where you've got the teacher as the source of learning. I think that sucks because that's basically what we had at school. And I just don't know why they just didn't do more experiments because they're bored, they get frustrated with us, we're frustrated with learning because it's all from the book or from the board. And we didn't get to experience anything ourselves, so we saw it as the teachers were pretty pathetic as well. But you know it wasn't something you looked forward to, it was just a bludge.

She stated that her past experience with science classes in high school had influenced her to have 'a phobia, a fear type thing' towards the subject. At the beginning of my course she had a practical class that focused on the topic of electricity and this resulted in a negative learning experience for her. She had not actively participated in some of the activities and wrote about this after the class in her journal to address 'ways that did not help me to learn'. It was during her subsequent reflections concerning her lack of learning that she began to realize that she had a 'block' towards science:

> Remember we had that big talk after I had the electricity one that you did and I didn't do anything, I couldn't understand anything. And it wasn't until I got home and did the write up and I thought, 'Wait a minute, was I really having a go?' And I wasn't because I just thought straight away, cause, I like, with subjects like that I suppose I feel I need more guidance like, and sometimes you kind of take a back step and basically work through them ourselves. And most of the other people in the group in the class know what they're doing and I just couldn't understand, like I mean I know it's basic about the electricity and everything but just the fact that we're using terminology that I didn't feel comfortable with. I just, you know, I didn't want to get into it. And so I just told myself that science, this was awful and I was bored and I didn't want to do it and I couldn't do it. And so yeah, and when I got home I realized you know, I looked over my notes and I had a bit of a talk to Di cause she did chemistry and biology and she's, you know, she's still a bit the same as me with being confident in science and she's changed a bit. But she said, umm, you know she explained a bit to me and I thought, 'Gosh it's not really that hard', and if I didn't have this block, if I just got rid of this block in my mind, you know what I mean, like what I'm trying to say?

Later in the interview she stated that she had never taught a science lesson on her two previous practicum experiences because of her negative attitude towards the subject developed in high school. However, as a result of analyzing why she was not learning in my class, 'the block has gone and I feel more confident and I can't wait to go on my next prac[ticum] and take a science lesson'. Asked about the reason for this change she replied:

> I've become more aware about the way I learn and I've realized that the main thing is the way you feel about yourself and, um, not feeling that you have any blocks. You know because the blocks that you have in your mind stop you from learning. Because you know, once you've decided that's it, science sucks, it's boring, it's ridiculous, I don't get anything out of it so I'm not going to bother trying. And you don't, it's kind of hard to push that aside. And on past prac[ticum]s I have never ever taken a science lesson. I saw it as, well, I've never really seen a lot of science in the primary schools and I used to view it as something that should only be focused in the high school area. And now I just realize well, that's just such a waste. I mean there's so much kids can learn and this is something they will really enjoy, you know . . . There's so much, everything's hands-on and, and it's not just the teacher saying 'Okay we're going through this

work, we're going to do this much.' They actually can discover things themselves, 'Oh, look Miss, what I've found, you know. Look what happens when I do this' and you know and so on. And I won't feel that I have to know everything in science because obviously even the experts can't really be called experts because they don't know everything about everything.

During the interview Sue also gave me feedback about my teaching. Her initial impression of the course was that I was lazy because I was not giving her information and teaching science the way she expected it to be taught; like her high school science teachers. This continued until she realized that I did not see myself as simply giving her facts, but that I was hoping that she would become responsible for her own learning:

> You were slack, you weren't doing anything, you weren't giving us all the knowledge ... and then, I don't know I just felt that I wasn't learning enough, I wasn't being given enough information. But then I realized that I was, I was discovering things for myself and I was enjoying it a lot more than I would have if you sat there and just, you know.

The interview data suggest that Sue gained a better understanding of learning in the methods course and she also provided me with some feedback on my teaching. She told me that I should make my rationale clearer at the beginning of the course to specify why I wanted the pre-service teachers to monitor their learning and to take into account their prior perceptions about the subject from their secondary school experiences.

Overview

Teachers have been labelled as 'transmissive' when they attempt to deliver facts to students as passive learners in secondary school classrooms (Barnes and Shemilt, 1974). Yet how different is it when teacher educators attempt to deliver educational theory to trainee teachers as passive learners in teacher education courses? In both situations formal knowledge, which has been generated by professional researchers, is summarized for presentation by instructors and delivered to students for their intended learning. But often this knowledge is inert for the learners; with little personal meaning except to be repeated back to the instructor in an examination or an assignment. It is no wonder that Lortie's (1975) 'apprenticeship of observation' suggests that 'teachers teach as they are taught' persists in the 1990s (Sarason, 1990). The challenge for teacher educators, I believe, is to bring theory to life and engage pre-service teachers as reflective thinkers in the knowledge-generating process.

This study explains one way in which pre-service teachers can generate understandings about learning by using their methods course as a context for reflecting on their own learning experiences. The written reports showed that 95 per cent (81/85) of the pre-service teachers believed that they developed a self-awareness about their learning and 93 per cent (79/85) commented on how this self analysis informed their views about teaching elementary science. In these reports, the pre-service teachers described twenty-two different ways that helped them to learn in my course. These included four individual influences (prior knowledge, personal motivation, personal feelings, and personal confidence) and eight social influences — four from myself as the instructor (teacher explanations, modelling of instructional techniques, relationship with the teacher, and teacher enthusiasm) and four from other students (group work, class discussions, type of activities, watching other students).

The interviews with Sue and Gloria also demonstrated the usefulness of this teaching strategy. Sue's story about her 'mental block' towards science is not unusual among trainee elementary teachers. Most do not enter teacher training with a solid knowledge base about science and many have negative attitudes about the subject (Department of Employment, Education and Training, 1989). I believe that providing them with large amounts of science content in courses is not the way to address this difficulty. Instead, I believe that Sue's story is evidence that getting trainee teachers to develop an awareness of their beliefs is a useful procedure and this can be addressed by having the pre-service teachers monitor their own learning. Gloria's story provided another window into a teacher's beliefs. She described herself as a science teacher who concentrated on giving students the 'right answers' because this is the way she was taught at school (Lortie, 1975). Developing a self-awareness about her own learning helped her to understand her previous teaching practice, and subsequently, to change her view about herself as a teacher. I have also benefited from using the teaching strategy in the methods course. I learnt that this strategy does not suit all pre-service teachers and that not all students learn in the same way, but overall I was pleased with the general response and would certainly try it again. However, as Sue said, I need to be more explicit about my rationale for using this teaching strategy at the beginning of the course and invite pre-service teachers to regularly discuss my ways of teaching to inform their learning.

This self-analysis of learning provides a means for students to gain a better understanding of how they learn, but it is important to extend their understandings beyond what they have generated from reflecting on their own experiences. This, I believe, is where formal educational theory has an important role. First, class discussions about pre-service teachers' learning were held to enable them to share ideas and help me to realize that the way they learn is not the same for all students. Furthermore, at times I introduced educational theory on student learning but in context with the students' discussions based on their own experiences. This led to further discussions about the complexity of learning and the inappropriateness of 'recipe' teaching approaches. Consequently, having engaged in a continual process of reflecting on their own learning themselves, the trainee teachers had an entry point into theoretical discussions about learning. Although not a feature of this course, perhaps students could choose an area of interest about learning to conduct some extended reading using educational literature. Toward this purpose research articles on students learning can be used by pre-service teachers to compare their own understandings based on their sustained reflection in their teacher education course with findings about learning from research conducted in other contexts.

There is also another spin off to using this teaching strategy — you are getting a weekly evaluation of not only *what* you are teaching but also *how* you are teaching. This is risky business; you are exposing yourself to criticism from your own students. But how can you expect trainee teachers to take seriously your recommendations about being a reflective teacher when you do not do it yourself? Loughran (1996) has demonstrated the benefits to pre-service teachers of teacher educators modelling reflective practice; this should be extended with preservice teachers evaluating the instruction of their teacher educators in an ongoing way. I am not talking about end of course evaluations, but a weekly critique as the basis for sustained reflection by pre-service teachers. This process not only informs the learners about their learning and the teacher about teaching, but can create a forum encouraging debate concerning ideas about a real teaching–learning context — from their own methods class! But this teaching strategy depends on developing a level of trust within the class; you will know that this has been established when pre-service teachers are prepared to discuss their negative as well as their positive learning experiences in your course. Furthermore, many pre-service teachers commented throughout the course that seeking their views about my teaching demonstrated that I valued their opinion and that I was 'practicing what I was preaching'. I think it is important that we, as teacher educators, model procedures to establish a dialogue between teachers and students to engage in ongoing discussions about the quality of teaching and learning.

Notes

The author would like to thank Carolyn Buttriss who wrote the student's perspective on the procedure outlined in this chapter.
1   This chapter is based on a paper entitled 'Generating Practical Knowledge about Teaching and Learning' that was presented at the annual meeting of the American Educational Research Association, April 1995, San Francisco.
2   A practical session is a 'lab' that focuses on a hands-on investigation.

References

BAIRD, J.R. (1992) 'Collaborative reflection, systematic enquiry, better teaching', in RUSSELL, T. and MUNBY, H. (Eds) *Teachers and Teaching: From Classroom to Reflection*, London, Falmer Press, pp. 33–48.
BARNES, D. (1976) *From Communication to Curriculum*, Portsmouth, Heinemann.
BARNES, D. and SHEMILT, D. (1974) 'Transmission and interpretation', *Education Review*, **26**, 3, pp. 213–28.
BELL, B.F. (1981) 'When is an animal not an animal?', *Journal of Biological Education*, **15**, pp. 213–18.

BROWN, J.S., COLLINS, A. and DUGUID, P. (1989) 'Situated cognition and the culture of learning', *Educational Researcher*, **18**, 1, pp. 32–42.

CECI, S.J. and LIKEN, L.J. (1986) 'Academic and non academic intelligence: An experimental separation', in STERNBERG, R.J. and WAGNER, R.K. (Eds) *Practical Intelligence: Nature and Origins of Competence in the Everyday World*, Cambridge, Cambridge University Press, pp. 119–42.

COBB, P. (1994) 'Where is the mind?: Constructivist and sociocultural perspectives on mathematical development', *Educational Researcher*, **23**, 7, pp. 13–19.

DARLING-HAMMOND, L. (1995) 'Changing conceptions of teaching and teacher development', *Teacher Education Quarterly*, **22**, 4, pp. 9–26.

DEPARTMENT OF EMPLOYMENT, EDUCATION AND TRAINING (1989) *Discipline Review of Teacher Education in Mathematics and Science*, Canberra, Australian Government Publishing Service.

DRIVER, R. (1983) *The Pupil as a Scientist*, Philadelphia, PA, Open University Press.

DRIVER, R., ASOKO, H., LEACH, J. and SCOTT, P. (1995) 'Constructing scientific knowledge in the classroom: A theoretical perspective on pedagogy', Paper presented at the meeting of the American Educational Research Association Annual Meeting, April 1995, San Francisco, CA.

DRIVER, R., GUESNE, E. and TIBERGHIEN, A. (Eds) (1985) *Children's Ideas in Science*, Milton Keynes, Open University Press.

DRIVER, R. and OLDHAM, V. (1986) 'A constructivist approach to curriculum development in science', *Studies in Science Education*, **13**, pp. 105–22.

ERICKSON, G.L. (1979) 'Children's conceptions of heat and temperature', *Science Education*, **63**, 2, pp. 221–30.

FAIRE, J. and COSGROVE, M. (1988) *Teaching Primary Science*, Hamilton, New Zealand, Waikato Education Centre.

FRANCIS, R. and HILL, D. (1993) 'Developing conceptions of food and nutrition', *Research in Science Education*, **23**, pp. 77–84.

GUNSTONE, R.F. (1990) 'Children's science: A decade of developments in constructivist views of science teaching and learning', *The Australian Science Teachers Journal*, **36**, 4, pp. 9–19.

HENNESSY, S. (1993) 'Situated cognition and cognitive apprenticeship: Implications for classroom learning', *Studies in Science Education*, **22**, pp. 1–41.

HOBAN, G. (1996) 'A professional development model based on interrelated principles of teacher learning', Unpublished Ph.D. thesis, The University of British Columbia, Vancouver, Canada.

LAVE, J. (1988) *Cognition in Practice: Mind, Mathematics and Culture in Everyday Life*, Cambridge, Cambridge University Press.

LAVE, J. and WENGER, E. (1991) *Situated Learning: Legitimate Peripheral Participation*, Cambridge, Cambridge University Press.

LORTIE, D. (1975) *School-teacher: A Sociological Study*, Chicago, IL, University of Chicago Press.

LOUGHRAN, J.J. (1996) *Developing Reflective Practice: Learning about Teaching and Learning through Modelling*, London, Falmer Press.

MUNBY, H. and RUSSELL, T. (1994) 'The authority of experience in learning to teach: Messages from a Physics Methods Course', *Journal of Teacher Education*, **45**, 2, pp. 86–95.

OSBORNE, R. and FREYBERG, P. (1985) *Learning in Science: The Implications of Children's Science*, Auckland, Heinemann.

OSBORNE, R. and WITTROCK, M.C. (1983) 'Learning science: A generative process', *Science Education*, **67**, 4, pp. 489–508.

PATTON, M.Q. (1990) *Qualitative Evaluation and Research Method*, 2nd ed., Newbury Park, CA, SAGE.

PRAWAT, R.S. (1995) 'Misreading Dewey: Reform, projects, and the language game', *Educational Researcher*, **24**, 7, pp. 13–22.

PRAWAT, R.S. and FLODEN, R.E. (1994) 'Philosophical perspectives on constructivist views of learning', *Educational Psychology*, **29**, 1, pp. 37–48.

ROGOFF. B. (1993) 'Children's guided participation and participatory appropriation in socio-cultural activity', in WOZNIAK, R.H. and FISHER, K.W. (Eds) *Development in Context: Acting and Thinking in Specific Environments*, Hillsdale, NJ, Erlbaum.

SARASON, S. (1990) *The Predictable Failure of Educational Reform: Can We Change Course Before It Is Too Late?*, San Francisco, Jossey Bass.

SAXE, G.B. (1988) 'Candy selling and math learning', *Educational Researcher*, **17**, 6, pp. 14–20.

SCRIBNER, S. (1986) 'Thinking in action: Some characteristics of practical thought', in STERNBERG, R.J. and WAGNER, R.K. (Eds) *Practical Intelligence: Nature and Origins of Competence in the Everyday World*, Cambridge, Cambridge University Press, pp. 13–30.

VON GLASERFIELD, E. (1989) 'Constructivism in education', in HUSEN, T. and POSTLETH-WAITE, T.N. (Eds) *The International Encyclopedia of Education*, 1st ed., Supplementary Vol. 1., Oxford, Pergamon Press.

10 Teaching to Teach with Purpose and Passion: Pedagogy for Reflective Practice

Vicki Kubler LaBoskey

Introduction

This assignment was certainly an intense personal journey. As I began to look at who I am as a teacher, who I am as a person also came into consideration. My own personal psychotherapy. The most powerful revelation was the depth to which reflection plays a part in growing. I know that may seem like restating the obvious, but I can't describe how enlightened I feel. Maybe I wasn't listening before. It's just amazing how you can know something but still not fully understand all its subtleties. It certainly provides another lens for me as I consider how my students will learn. I know now that I must incorporate reflection into my teaching. Students need time to reflect on their own growth. Otherwise, will they really know?[1] (Carrie, former student)

Like Carrie, I worry about what my students know and whether or not they really know it. Also like Carrie, I believe that engaging my students in the process of reflection will make 'full understanding' more possible. But because my students are future teachers and because I conceptualize reflection in teaching in a very particular way, I would extend Carrie's argument even further. According to my definition, the reflective teacher is one who questions and examines, as much and as often as possible, the reasons behind and the implications of her knowledge, beliefs, and practices. She recognizes teaching as a moral and political act and, therefore, tries always to teach with 'tact' (Van Manen, 1991), to interpret events and ideas from multiple perspectives, particularly those of her students, to temper her judgments, and to aim her efforts toward the enhancement of social justice. Since I believe that reflection in teaching is not only a means for coming to know, but also a means for monitoring the moral and ethical ramifications of that knowledge, preparing my students to be reflective about their work is my primary purpose as a teacher educator.

In my research I have found that those student teachers who are more reflective than others tend to be guided by what I call 'passionate creeds' and are likely to ask more 'Why?' questions (LaBoskey, 1994). I have also found that it is difficult, though not impossible, to develop the skills and attitudes of reflective practice in those student teachers for whom they are largely missing (LaBoskey, 1991; 1994). Therefore, I design my program and my practice to be relentless in the modelling of, and requirement for, purpose and passion in teaching. I try to have all of my assignments and all of my activities provide opportunities for everyone, including me, to examine, from a variety of perspectives, our beliefs, attitudes, reasons, intentions, emotional reactions, and intellectual processing. We learn together how to appreciate the complexity and live with the uncertainty as we construct and reconstruct our belief systems.

In this chapter I describe the rationale behind my pedagogy. I also illustrate and examine how this is played out in my own reflective practice by describing and assessing one representative assignment — the portfolio and portfolio presentation that are central requirements of the student teaching practicum.

The Portfolio Assignment

'Context matters', we tell our students. All educational endeavors take place within a certain context that will influence and should, therefore, guide the choices teachers make and the actions they take. I, too, am a teacher; thus, I, too, need to take context into account when I design my curriculum and pedagogy. I have structured my portfolio assignment for a particular group of students in a particular institution. Consequently, in order for that assignment to be fully understood, I need to provide information about my context.

My elementary credential program is actually one half of a K-12 program we call Teachers for Tomorrow's Schools. The other half is for those seeking a credential in secondary Social Studies or English. We have two other credential programs at Mills, one for secondary Math and Science teachers and another for elementary credential candidates who wish to obtain an emphasis in early childhood education. Each of the four programs is run by a tenured or tenure-track faculty member. The four of us have virtually complete control over the design and operation of the programs, and this includes teaching almost all of the courses, advising all of the students, and supervising many of them. The four of us get along extremely well and are compatible in terms of our philosophical and political orientations, and thus it is relatively easy for us to create a cohesive program where most aspects reinforce one another.

All of our programs are small; each cohort has an average of fifteen students per year. The size allows us to develop personal relationships with all of our students. It is a graduate program, so all of my students have completed a Bachelor's degree, usually at an institution other than Mills. About half are recent graduates and the other half are moving into a second career. Many who choose Mills come because of its location in Oakland, one of the most diverse cities in the United States. They are interested in working with diverse populations and in making a difference in the lives of children. They are usually aware of, and attracted to, the program goals and principles.

The program lasts two years. By the end of the first academic year the students have completed all of the requirements for a clear elementary credential and are eligible to begin teaching. The second year is to occur within five years of completing the credential. It is an evening program so that students can also be full-time teachers. At the end of that year they receive a Masters in Education. During the entire credential year, that first year, the students teach in the local schools in the mornings and take courses at Mills in the afternoons. One of the courses they take throughout the year is called the Student Teaching Seminar. My supervisors and I meet with our students every week to discuss issues that arise from their student teaching experiences and to build rapport within the group. The meeting is usually fairly informal, though on occasion we have a more structured session on an area of general concern. The portfolios are an assignment for this seminar.

   The directions for the assignment are deceptively simple. I tell the students about it during one of the first few seminars in the fall. My introductory remarks go something like this:

> One of the requirements of this seminar is the production and sharing of a portfolio. At one of the last seminars in the second semester each of you will share her portfolio with the group. It will not be graded — the only requirement is that you do it. The purpose of the portfolio is to give you an opportunity to represent yourself as teacher — who you are and what you believe and value most at that point in your career. You may or may not wish to use it in the job interview process, but that is not the focus. At different points throughout the year we will talk more about it; at the beginning of the second semester I will bring in some sample portfolios of former students for you to see. One of the things you will notice then is that they are all very different. There is no set format and there are no particular requirements for content — those decisions are up to you. However, I will say what it should not be — it should not be just a collection of things you like. In your presentation you need to be able to justify every item; you need to be able to tell us why it is in there and the reason must be something other than 'I liked it' or 'It was special to me'. Each item ought to represent some belief about teaching that you have — some value or goal. Many of the former students have put a statement of philosophy up front which they then try to represent in the portfolio — though probably not everything. One suggestion I have is to choose three of your most important beliefs, values, or goals and try to represent those. It should also not be just a documentation of what you did this year in chronological order; it needs to be organized around ideas rather than time. As I said, we will speak more about it as we go; please ask questions at any time. One thing you do need to do right away is to begin to collect things that you may want to use — examples of student work, copies of papers you write for your courses, supervisor feedback sheets, journal entries, great quotes from readings or colleagues, lesson plans you write, notes you get from students or parents or your cooperating teachers. Try to take photos — of your kids, of the room, of projects you have your

students do that are too big to fit in the portfolio. You don't know at this point what is going to be important and you don't want to limit yourself to what you have available in the second semester, so start collecting. Now let's answer any questions you may have at the moment.

And we go on to talk about it a bit further. I do, as I said, bring portfolios up on different occasions throughout the year. Sometimes, just as a reminder to be collecting and thinking. Sometimes it is a question-and-answer session and sometimes we do a freewrite on 'my philosophy of education', which I tell them to save and begin applying to their portfolio development. Early in the second semester I do bring in samples of portfolios from previous students and I give them an opportunity to review and discuss the samples. The students sign up for a presentation time in one of two designated weeks in the last month of school. Each student takes about fifteen minutes to share her portfolio with us and then we have a chance to make comments and ask questions. It is a very warm, celebratory event where refreshments are served, hugs are abundant, and tears are common.

So why do I do it this way? What makes me think that using this particular portfolio design will help to foster and reveal reflection in my students? Why do I, for instance, leave decisions as to the form and content of the portfolios up to the students? Why do I tell them that each item in their portfolio must be justified on the basis of their educational beliefs and values? In other words, what principles and perceptions guide my practice? My reasons come from two sources — initially and continually — from my definition of reflection — what I mean by it and why I think it is important. Subsequently and continually, my reasons come from the students via the portfolios they actually produce and their reactions to the process.

Rationale

First, I need to clarify my definition. It is similar to that originally formulated by Dewey (1910) and modified by Zeichner and his colleagues (Gore and Zeichner, 1991; Zeichner and Tabachnick, 1991). In my words, reflective thinking is a constant and 'careful reconsideration of a teacher's beliefs and actions in light of information from current theory and practice, from feedback from the particular context, and from speculation as to the moral and ethical consequences of their results' (LaBoskey, 1994, p. 9). Using that definition, I have identified some criteria of reflective thinking which I use in the design and evaluation of assignments and activities:

1 the teacher struggles with issues; she raises questions and expresses uncertainty,
2 she exhibits a propensity to consider alternatives and reconsider preconceptions,
3 she takes more of a long-term than a short-term view,
4 she shows primary concern for the needs of students — her decisions are guided by student needs and interests,

5   she seems to be open to learning about both practical and theoretical ideas — she is growth-oriented,

6   she sees herself as a facilitator of learning rather than as a transmitter of knowledge,

7   she recognizes the complexity of the educational enterprise,

8   she demonstrates an awareness of the need for tentative conclusions and multiple sources of feedback,

9   she considers the moral and ethical implications of her ideas and actions with a particular focus on issues of justice and equity.

It is important to note that I do not feel that a person can be identified as either wholly reflective or unreflective. What can be said is that some teachers reflect more consistently about more issues within more situations than others. I have called those student teachers on the 'more' side, Alert Novices, and those on the 'lesser' side, Commonsense Thinkers. In my research I have discovered certain thought processes that seem to be characteristic of the Alert Novices (LaBoskey, 1994). First is the tendency to be guided by a strong belief, or what I call a 'passionate creed'. Alert Novices tend to have a certain mission to accomplish in their teaching. They may, for instance, be passionately committed to the development of student voices or to the reduction of oppression.[2] Alert Novices are inclined to see the process of reflection as asking 'Why?': 'Why am I teaching what I am teaching in the way that I am teaching it?' The question is directed to the roots of problems and the meanings of ideas and actions.

My aim is to create a portfolio design that will help to foster these ways of thinking, as I do with all other assignments and activities in the program — a factor which greatly influenced my choice. I make the portfolio assignment so open-ended in terms of both form and content in part because the portfolio is only one of many assignments designed to foster reflection, most of which are more controlled than this one, and because it is a culminating event the main purpose of which is to provide an opportunity for the students to practice and make explicit the reflective skills and attitudes they have been developing all year. In this way I can find out what shows up and in what way. I can see if some of these characteristics of reflective thinking which we have been working on throughout the year appear spontaneously.

But there is more. I ask the student teachers to have the process of portfolio construction be guided by their educational philosophy — their most important beliefs, values, and goals — because I want the exercise to help them in the development and articulation of their 'passionate creeds'. Furthermore, I have them focus on justification during the selection and presentation of their materials because I want them to attend to the 'Why?' questions with regard to their teaching.

Assessment

The initial design of my portfolio assignment was guided by my definition of reflection and my conceptualization of the thought processes of Alert Novices. It was also informed by my understanding of my institutional context — a context where reflection is a centerpiece of the entire program. My decision to continue with this design, with only minor adjustments, for four years now is due to the outcomes of the assignment both in terms of the portfolios actually produced and the reactions of the students to the process. All sets of portfolios my students have created and shared have, with a few individual exceptions, seemed to achieve my goals. They have exhibited many of the characteristics of reflective thinking I am looking for; they have seemed to represent 'passionate creeds'; and both their form and content have been well-justified.

For the first two years that conclusion was based only upon informal impressions. At that point I decided to undertake some 'formal' research that could confirm or disconfirm my reactions and help to document the process for a larger audience. My first step in this process was both rather unusual and rather risky — a participatory research presentation to the American Educational Research Association (AERA). Since my portfolio assignment was designed in part as a culminating activity wherein students might reveal the processes and attitudes of reflective thinking they had been working on all year, an analysis of the products could make an important contribution to program evaluation. I decided to explore the possibilities with the AERA audience at an experimental session wherein we would all be researchers together. My students came to the session on a voluntary basis (nine out of thirteen appeared) with their newly constructed portfolios, only two of which I had ever seen before, and dispersed themselves at various tables throughout the room. I opened the presentation with a description of the program and the assignment. Then my students presented their portfolios to the audience members at their tables in a way similar to that they would use in our seminar. Next we came together as a whole and audience members shared their impressions of what seemed to be important to these students — their values, goals, and beliefs about teaching. I then presented my newly constructed portfolio to everyone and the audience tried to discern from it my values, goals, and beliefs about teaching which we subsequently compared with the list we had already constructed from the student portfolios. To the audience there appeared to be a considerable match between the values, goals, and beliefs about teaching, including the meaning and importance of reflection, evident in the student teacher portfolios and those represented in mine — a result that supported my decision to continue with this particular portfolio design.

An additional benefit to the exercise, and one consistent with my beliefs about teacher education, was my participation in the doing of one of their central assignments. On one level my portfolio and portfolio construction process can serve as a model to both current and future students. I wish to note here that by 'model' I do not mean 'prototype', a dangerous confusion to be guarded against whenever a teacher provides an example. Therefore, when I do share it, I am very explicit about the challenges I faced in the development process and about the questions and dilemmas that remain for me. I also emphasize the point that the format utilized is only one of an infinite number of possibilities. Given the diversity of form and content that has continued to appear in the student portfolios, I believe the message has certainly been understood and 'taken up'.

On another and even more important level, my experiencing of the portfolio development process has allowed me to better understand, empathize with and, thus, facilitate the students' negotiation of the task. I think it does, and should, give me more credibility with them when I talk about the challenges they might face and give suggestions for ways they might try to manage such difficulties. I believe that as a constructivist teacher educator I need to do as much as I can to understand the world from my students' perspective. Direct participation in the tasks I assign them is one way to do that.

Having given some attention to an examination of the actual products, I wanted to gather information about the students' reactions to the process. I sent a questionnaire to all members of the two most recent graduating classes. The questions I asked were as follows:

1   Describe the process through which you went in developing your portfolio in as much detail as possible, e.g., time frame, strategy, choice of format (what and why), etc.
2   Have you used your portfolio at all outside of the seminar context? If so, how and what is your reaction to that use (was it useful, effective, etc.)?
3   What do you think the purpose of the portfolios was?
4   What, if anything, do you think you learned in the process of creating the portfolio? In what specific ways do you think it was helpful or not helpful to you in terms of your teaching and/or your thinking about your teaching? Do you feel differently about it now than you did at the time and, if so, how?

   Comment separately on your reactions to the sharing of your portfolio in the seminar. Consider both the sharing of your portfolio and the listening to others. How did you feel about it at the time, and how do you feel about it now? Do you think the sharing process added or subtracted anything in particular in terms of your learning from the experience? Please explain.
5   In many other programs that use portfolios there is both more specificity in terms of content and structure and more guidance in the creation process. Would you like to see more of either included in our program? If not, why not? And, if so, what suggestions for improvement might you make?
6   Do you think your experience of the portfolio would have been at all different if it had been graded or formally evaluated in some way? Please explain.
7   Any other thoughts or comments on the topic you would like to make that you haven't already had the opportunity to make, including just general reactions, please do so here.

Thirty per cent of the graduates returned the questionnaire. The overall reaction to the portfolio assignment was very positive. An analysis of their comments gave me insight into both how and whether reflection had been involved in the process. I was also able to ascertain which features of the assignment seemed to facilitate reflective thinking and in what ways. One category of responses that most surprised me had to do with the processes they went through in developing their portfolios. I had expected that most of them would write their philosophies, as we had done once or twice in seminars, and then choose artifacts to represent those ideas; that was the suggestion for the procedure I had given them. However, instead, several came from the opposite direction; they used the materials they had been collecting to help them formulate or at least articulate more clearly their beliefs about teaching, as one graduate's response to the first question exemplifies:

> I spent about four weeks actually putting my portfolio together. I spent about four months thinking about it. I decided I wanted my portfolio to look professional for interviews and, of course, to reflect my values and who I am as a teacher. I spent a long time reviewing reading material and text I highlighted throughout the year, . . . I put post-its on pages with quotes and ideas that really stuck out for me. Themes began to emerge. I chose a paper I wrote that I felt reflected my thinking process and growth, and fit into one of the themes. I looked at my photos from my classroom experiences over and over, and pulled out photos that fit into my themes. I asked people's advice in choosing between photos. I pulled out lesson plans, student work, etc. This all helped me to come up with 'my philosophies' that I wanted to run systematically through the portfolio.

In cases like these the portfolio served as a quintessential culminating experience. The students reviewed everything they had done over the course of the year to determine what they had learned and what it might mean for them as teachers. This same person, in response to the question about what she had learned, said, 'I learned that I really learned a lot during the year! The portfolio was a chance to reflect on what is important to me, as well as a chance to express who I am as a teacher. . . . The portfolio helped me to synthesize what is specifically important to me — although, of course, it does not contain everything that is. . . .'

Another graduate, when responding to question 3 about purpose, said, 'I have come to the conclusion that the portfolio is a tool for teachers to use to formulate a teaching philosophy.' To question 4 she then replied, 'I learned the importance of having a teaching philosophy. Walking into a classroom without a sense of your own goals and objectives is somehow like attempting to work as a carpenter with no blueprints or direction. Somehow a teaching philosophy allayed some of the fear in approaching a classroom of thirty or more students.' In a subsequent phone call to me she reconfirmed and expanded upon her belief in the value of the portfolio experience; she said that she had 'used it often' during her first few months of teaching to help her resolve problems and make curricular decisions.

This latter declaration is representative of another pleasant surprise in the data — the number of graduates who referred to an ongoing use of the portfolio for reflection both individually and with other teachers at their schools. I would like to quote one new teacher's responses to questions one and two here because they speak so well to both findings — the contribution of the process of portfolio construction to the development of a teaching philosophy or passionate creed *and* an ongoing engagement with the portfolio as a means of fostering reflection:

1 I started collecting writing samples, pictures and students' work as soon as we were asked to do so. At first I didn't know what it was all for, and I didn't think it was important to know. At that time I was very excited about seeing students' work and figuring out the way they learn. As a student teacher it all seemed so interesting and this was a fantastic way to get into the minds of sixth graders. During my second semester I was equally intrigued by first graders, and by collecting work from students I was able to see where they were in their development and thus adjust to this new age group.

I did not follow any specific guideline when collecting samples, I picked stuff because I liked it. I am still working on my portfolio so it was never quite finished. I was forced to give it some sort of shape due to graduation date, but I never really felt I was done. . . .

As far as the format was concerned, I selected four very broad areas which I thought were fundamental to a child's education and I placed them in a binder. This was the most difficult part, as I was having difficulty selecting things I thought important. At first I thought I could explain what was important based on the student teaching experience alone. Soon I found out that in order to explain my choices I needed to include my culture and my own beliefs. I became aware of the difficulties of separating myself from my profession and that was a profound discovery.

I placed everything in a binder because it is easy to add to it or subtract from it as I see fit. So far I have changed it twice — the first time after our AERA presentation, the second time after my first 'real' teaching experience last summer. So it has become a way of assessing my growth as a teacher. I don't know if that is what you had in mind when you assigned this project, but it has helped me in making my way through these past few months.

2 Yes, I have used it to talk to other teachers at my school. As a first year teacher there were occasions when I felt intimidated by more experienced teachers when discussing 'education' or children. The portfolio is a 'friendly' way to talk about ideas. So far I have only found two other teachers who have done this type of portfolio — some say it's too labor-intensive and that there is little time for reflection!!!

This set of findings suggests to me that the portfolio as I designed it contributed to the formulation and articulation of 'passionate creeds' not only during, but beyond the teacher education program. The portfolio structure may be particularly well-suited to serve as an ongoing reflective tool because its potential for fluidity is greater than a typical term paper, for instance.

But the portfolio did not work this well for all students. Ironically, a response from one of the new teachers for whom it did work provided me with a clue as to why it might not have for others. She answered question 3 about purpose this way, 'As I said in the first part, I don't know exactly what the intent of the portfolio was. I don't think it is important to know . . . or is it? For me it has become a way of assessing my own growth as a teacher, and a way to reflect on my teaching. Since my school doesn't have a forum in which teachers can come together to discuss our profession, this has become my way of doing it.' She thought that she didn't understand the purpose, (not that I advocate that as a good thing) but it worked well for her anyway because on an implicit level she not only understood it, she embraced it. One of the two respondents for whom the portfolio did not seem to work did not appear to understand the task and did not really do it right. The other, though she understood it, she never really, in her words, 'bought-in'. These two seem to be representative of the two types of Commonsense Thinkers I identified in my previous research — those who have trouble with the procedures of reflective thinking and those who can do it, but have an attitude or emotion that interferes with the execution (LaBoskey, 1994). Such outcomes imply that we need to consider having different interventions for different students. We can not expect one assignment or one form of an assignment to work for all. I had hoped the open-endedness would be enough to accommodate the differences, but for these two at least, this was not the case. Therefore, I may need to consider providing more individualized instruction and guidance to certain students, but only to some, because most considered the freedom of design to be a definite asset.

Eighty per cent of the respondents felt that there should not be more specificity with regard to content or structure as these replies to question number 5 illustrate: 'No! I thought the individuality was vital to the power of the process.'; 'I appreciated the "discovery" that resulted from having a less directed or structured portfolio. I was allowed to uncover what my specific needs were and thus transform them into the creation of my portfolio.'; 'I liked the openness of it — I think it led to a greater diversity of portfolios. I'd hate to see some sort of formula. I think when you leave it more open, it allows people to include what is the most important to them.' This favourable sentiment was even shared by some who felt they usually functioned better with more structure. The open-ended nature of the portfolio assignment did seem to offer most respondents the opportunity to further develop and express their passionate creeds.

Many of those using portfolios in the educational field today are using them as a form of evaluation (Bird, 1990; Shulman, 1988; Wolf, 1991). I made a deliberate decision not to grade or otherwise formally evaluate the portfolios in any way. I provide no written comments and few verbal, though I do sometimes ask why a certain item was included, if the student hasn't made it clear to me, or give specific feedback as to what a student did particularly well. Such statements usually make explicit one or more of the identifying features of reflective thinking. My main reason for not grading the portfolios was that I did not have to. If I had my way, I would not give any grades in the credential program; prospective teachers ought to do what they do because they are intrinsically motivated to be the best teachers they can be, not because they want an A. I did not evaluate in other ways due to the ambience of the activity; as a culminating, festive, and poignant event, I did not feel it appropriate to criticize at that moment. Though I had my reasons for using only informal evaluation, I wanted to find out how my students felt.

Again 80 per cent of my respondents would not have wanted their portfolios graded, mainly because they thought the anticipation of grades would have interfered with the process and restricted the product. One said in response to the question about grading, 'Formal evaluations definitely scare me. I don't think I would have included some personal things about myself if my portfolio was going to be evaluated in some way.' Another said, 'The portfolio is required, but it is for us. I don't think there is any way to grade or judge them — it would be disastrous to do so.'

There were two former students who felt that the portfolios should be graded, but not in their current form. They both felt the assignment would need to be more structured with regard to both process and product if grades were to be assigned. Specifications would need to be given for what to include and, most importantly, the evaluation criteria would need to be explicitly identified and made available from the outset — a position with which I tend to agree. But greater standardization would reduce the open-endedness of the project — the very feature that seemed to contribute so much to its reflective power. Thus, both the positive and negative attitudes toward grading seemed to support my decision against it, though for slightly different reasons.

One final set of issues raised by these questionnaires has to do with the potential role of this portfolio assignment in helping my students learn to ask 'Why?' questions. One teacher replied to the question about what she had learned from the process as follows: 'I was put in a position to re-examine my beliefs about teaching because I had to choose what to include and what not to. It made me think, "These lessons are close to my ideal and if they're good enough to put in my portfolio, then I should be working hard to make all my teaching that way." I feel differently now because I now see the real value of it. I'll be honest — two years ago, part of me was probably thinking, "Oh, another assignment. I bet I'll never look at this again"; but now I know that I'll continue to use it and learn from it and update it to see my growth as a teacher.' Another said this: 'In the process of creating a portfolio I learned to ask the important questions about becoming a teacher . . . for me . . . at this point in my career. Specifically, it helped me to clarify my beliefs about education. In my situation, the process of discarding and adding ideas strengthened my ability to be more explicit about what I wanted to say.' Her response to the question about specificity continued with this train of thought: 'I like the fact that there is not a lot of structure in the process of creating the portfolios. We had the freedom and responsibility to determine the things we felt were important. This process of "figuring out" the important things and questions is very similar to the process we have to go through each day as teachers. What are the important things in "X" and "Y" concepts? Why should I teach this now and not later? Constant questioning. . . . In creating our portfolios I think we were gently introduced to this kind of questioning. I'm grateful for the experience.'

These responses seemed to suggest, as I had hoped they would, that the students were attending to the process at least as much as they were to the product. Too often, I think, the focus of both those who create portfolios and those who view and perhaps judge them is on the superficial glitz and glamour of the object produced. But reflection is an ongoing process, not a final product. My portfolio design appears to encourage the reflective deliberation and justification I hope my students will continue to use throughout their teaching careers.

Conclusion

I have found that reflective teachers tend to be guided by 'passionate creeds'. My passionate creed is that educators need to be thoughtful about their work, which means that they must question assumptions, consider multiple perspectives, avoid judgments, recognize complexity, and be primarily concerned with the needs of their students. The central mission of my practice is to help student teachers develop the skills and attitudes of reflective thinking. I designed the portfolio assignment to maximize its potential for contributing to the achievement of this goal.

1 The open-endedness allows students to engage the material in a personal way and to construct their own knowledge in the process.
2 The focus on an expression of personal beliefs and values encourages the development and sharing of passionate creeds.
3 The requirement for an ideological and theoretical justification of every item obliges the students to ask and answer 'Why?' questions.
4 The relatively fluid nature of the portfolio structure and the emphasis on process over product helps students to understand reflection as an ongoing undertaking and gives them a mechanism for doing so.

My research also suggests that reflective teachers ask 'Why?' questions, such as 'Why am I teaching what I am teaching in the way that I am teaching it?' In order to answer such questions, teachers not only need to consider their theoretical perspectives, but they also need to examine carefully the feedback they get from the context. They must be able to answer the question, 'How do I know that what I am doing is making a difference — is accomplishing what I hoped it would?' Both the portfolios themselves and the questionnaire responses seem to suggest that many of my students are using the portfolios to both practice and display reflective thinking.

Finally, reflective teachers need to consider the moral and ethical implications of what they do. They are obliged to do so because education is about intervention in the lives of children for the purpose of giving each of them the chance to dwell in an equitable and just society. Maxine Greene (1978) is 'convinced that, if teachers are to initiate young people into an ethical existence, they themselves must attend more fully than they normally have to their own lives and its requirements; they have to break with the mechanical life, to overcome their own submergence in the habitual, even in what they conceive to be the virtuous, and ask the "Why?" with which learning and moral reasoning begin' (p. 46). The portfolio assignment, as I have designed it, seems to fit Greene's criteria for an experience with the potential of preparing teachers 'to initiate young people into an ethical existence' — at least for these student teachers at this time.

Because I have also found, as have others (Baratz-Snowden, 1995; Gore and Zeichner, 1991), that reflection is not easily acquired or practiced, I recognize that no single assignment, no matter how well-designed, will suffice. An accumulation of interventions guided by the same goals and principles is what matters and the turning point may come via different means for different students. For Carrie it came with an assignment she was responding to in the opening paragraph of this chapter — an assignment given over halfway through the credential program year. She acknowledges that she had learned about reflection before but had not fully understood it until then. She suggests that she may not have listened in the past, but I believe that her breakthrough is due to the fact that she was indeed listening and doing all along. The accumulation of her previous experiences, including multiple opportunities to engage in reflection in a variety of ways, is what made it possible for her to come to understand and use it on a more authentic level in that assignment.

I was once asked by a reviewer if reflectivity ought to be a goal for all teachers (LaBoskey, 1993). The presumption seemed to be that because it was so difficult for many to achieve, it might be an unreasonable educational aim. A colleague in a current in-service project asked me the same question just the other day. My response both then and now is 'Yes!', 'Yes!' and 'Absolutely, yes!' All students deserve teachers who are primarily guided by student needs and interests and who are both willing and able to construct and examine their practice in conscientious, principled, and judicious ways. I design my portfolio assignment and the rest of my curriculum and instruction as I do because I owe it to the children to try ... and try again.

Notes

1 This comment was made by a former student, Carrie (a pseudonym), in a freewrite response to one of her course assignments.
2 These examples summarize the passionate creeds of two of the Alert Novices in a previous study (LaBoskey, 1994).

References

BARATZ-SNOWEDEN, J. (1995) 'Towards a coherent vision of teacher development', Paper presented at the meeting of the American Educational Research Association, San Francisco, April, 1995.

BIRD, T. (1990) 'The schoolteacher's portfolio: An essay on possibilities', in MILLMAN, J. and DARLING-HAMMOND, L. (Eds) *The New Handbook of Teacher Evaluation: Assessing Elementary and Secondary School Teachers*, Newbury Park, CA, Sage, pp. 241–56.

DEWEY, J. (1910) *How We Think*, Boston, D.C. Heath and Co.

GORE, J.M. and ZEICHNER, K.M. (1991) 'Action research and reflective teaching in preservice teacher education: A case study from the United States', *Teaching and Teacher Education*, **7**, 2, pp. 119–36.

GREENE, M. (1978) *Landscapes of learning*, New York, Teachers College Press.

LABOSKEY, V.K. (1991) 'Case studies of two teachers in a reflective teacher education program: How do you know?', Paper presented at the meeting of the American Educational Research Association, Chicago. April, 1991.

LABOSKEY, V.K. (1993) 'Why reflection in teacher education?', *Teacher Education Quarterly*, **20**, 1, pp. 9–12.

LABOSKEY, V.K. (1994) *Development of Reflective Practice*, New York, Teachers College Press.

SHULMAN, L.S. (1988) 'A union of insufficiencies: Strategies for teacher assessment in a period of reform', *Educational Leadership*, **46**, 3, pp. 36–41.

VAN MANEN, M. (1991) *The Tact of Teaching: The Meaning of Pedagogical Thoughtfulness*, Albany, NY, State University of New York Press.

WOLF, K.P. (1991) 'The schoolteacher's portfolio: Issues in design, implementation, and evaluation', *Phi Delta Kappan*, **73**, 2, pp. 129–36.

ZEICHNER, K.M. and TABACHNICK, B.R. (1991) 'Reflections on reflective teaching', in TABACHNICK, B.R. and ZEICHNER, K.M. (Eds) *Issues and Practices in Inquiry-oriented Teacher Education*, London, Falmer Press, pp. 1–21.

11   Advisor as Coach

Anthony Clarke

Introduction

This chapter begins with two autobiographical accounts that set the stage for the ensuing discussion of the significance of the teacher educator as practicum advisor to a beginning teacher. The first account describes my own experiences as a student teacher, 'surviving' on my own with the benign neglect of my advisors. The second account describes my earliest experiences as a young teacher receiving new teachers into my own classroom. With these two accounts as background, the remainder of the chapter argues for the importance of a number of criteria related to advisors acting as coaches for the development of understandings of teaching.

Has Anyone Seen My Advisor?

The day of my first lesson on practicum arrived. A group of Grade 1 children were escorted out to the playground where I had neatly arranged various pieces of equipment I wanted to use during the lesson. I was a little surprised when it took five minutes to organize the children into a straight line. While I was doing this, I noticed that one child's shoelaces had come undone, and I quickly bent down to tie them. When I stood up, the straight line I had worked so hard to organize had all but disappeared as the children had begun to wander off and explore the equipment that I had laid out on the ground. Ten minutes later, after a quick warm-up activity, I moved to the main segment of my lesson: skipping. It was at this point my lesson completely fell apart. In the next few minutes I was to learn what I suspect most early childhood teachers already know: young children can't skip! I was quickly forced to abandon my elaborate lesson plan and, noticing that one child had started to make letters of the alphabet on the ground with her rope, instructed the other children to also see how many different letters of the alphabet they could form. We spent the remainder of the lesson practicing letters and spelling words like 'cat' and 'dog' with the ropes. So much for my skipping lesson! If somebody had checked my lesson plan, perhaps the inappropriateness of the activities that I had planned would have been pointed out to me.

Of the four student teachers assigned to South Creek Elementary,[1] I had quickly been identified as the physical education (PE) specialist and assigned to several PE classes. I was keen to share my lesson plans with the staff but, as I was regarded as the PE 'expert', most staff felt that they had very little to offer me. As a result, my lesson plans were rarely scrutinized by the school advisors.[2] Indeed, very few teachers actually saw me teach. It was winter in Melbourne and the teachers would bring their pupils out to the courtyard and then disappear back to the warmth of the staff room. My faculty advisor observed my teaching on only one occasion during the four-week practicum and noted that, due to the large number of student teachers he was required to supervise, he would be unable to visit me again.

My next practicum assignment was at Highton Grammar School, an exclusive and private grade 8–12 school for boys. I was required to go to the school one day a week throughout the year and to complete three three-week teaching practica, one at the end of each term. The school had two gymnasiums, a swimming pool, a weight room, several playing fields, tennis courts, a judo room, and a well-equipped sports storeroom, etc. Accordingly, the students seemed to have access to a range of sports equipment that I had not seen in other schools. For example, during a cricket unit in PE, a number of the students wore expensive spiked cricket boots of the type usually worn only by competitive cricketers in weekend matches. I also noticed that the boys were very outspoken and at times quite brazen during the PE classes. In one class, I noticed the boys deliberately puncturing the cricket bats with their spiked boots.

My school advisor for this practicum was a sheet metal worker with a one-year teaching certificate. He had been hired because the school hoped to improve its standing in the inter-school basketball competitions. This gentleman was a successful state league basketball player and had been given the responsibility for developing basketball within the school. To this day, I am not sure that my school advisor knew what a lesson plan was; I never saw him with one or even refer to one. He certainly did not ask me for one during the time I was at Highton Grammar. In fact, he rarely observed more than the first ten minutes of any class that I taught and knew little of what actually went on in those lessons. For example, one day I was teaching football during PE and asked the boys to form a semi-circle at one end of the field in readiness for my next instruction. The boys, who just wanted to kick the footballs backwards and forwards to each other rather than practice specific drills, refused to comply with my request. The situation deteriorated to the point where they decided to stage a protest and walked off the field and sat in the pavilion at the opposite end of the ground. I was fortunate in that the grounds-man, who was well known and liked by the boys, saw what was happening and persuaded the boys to return to my class before the bell went to signal the end of the lesson. My sponsor teacher saw none of this, although he did notice the large muddy football print on the back of my windcheater where one student had 'accidentally' punted the ball during the early part of the lesson!

My faculty advisor for this practicum visited the school on two occasions, each time unannounced. The first was a twenty-five-minute visit: fifteen minutes at the end of a lesson followed by a ten-minute conversation after the lesson. The second visit occurred on a rainy July day. The bad weather forced us to combine three concurrent PE classes for team games in the gymnasium. My faculty advisor appeared at the door for five minutes and left before I had a chance to talk to him.

My third teaching practicum was at Yarra Bridge Technical School. I arrived when the school was in the middle of a long and very messy industrial strike involving the ancillary and cleaning staff. The teachers were working-to-rule in support of the striking workers. The physical environment within the school was considered to be a health risk and therefore sections of the building were closed down and classes were transferred to the local community centre adjacent to the school. My school advisor was a political activist and was caught up in the strike action and associated meetings with union and school administration officials. Unfortunately, his activities cut considerably into the time available for us to discuss the mathematics classes I had been assigned to teach at Yarra Bridge.

My classroom in the community center was the exercise room. My Grade 10 students sat on small benches arranged between the various pieces of fitness equipment to enable the best possible view of the small portable chalkboard that was supported by two chairs and propped up against the only wall space free of equipment. Unfortunately, the space against which the chalkboard was leaning was covered in a dazzling array of sport posters depicting young men and women shooting baskets, scoring goals, paddling rapids, climbing mountains, throwing javelins, etc. An experienced teacher might have been able to take advantage of this unusual environment and use it to motivate the students to explore mathematical principles related to physical movement (i.e., a kinematics approach) but, for a student teacher with a limited repertoire of ideas and a less-than-stellar set of practicum experiences, this was an extremely challenging environment in which to 'learn how to teach'.

My faculty advisor visited on only one occasion early in the practicum, prior to the move to the community center, and apparently felt that my teaching was satisfactory and did not require further observation. She, like my school advisor, did not witness the chaos that occurred during several of my lessons in the exercise room as the students continually messed about on, and fiddled with, the exercise equipment rather than attending to my teaching of mathematics instruction. I received a passing grade, although upon what this was based was never made clear to me by either of my advisors.

If my practicum experiences were indicative of the contribution that advisors make to the process of 'learning to teach' then one might conclude that learning on practicum was by trial and error and something that occurred largely in the absence of an advisor. At the conclusion of my Yarra Bridge practicum, I decided that if I ever was to be a practicum advisor then I would attempt to facilitate my student teacher's professional development in more substantive ways than I had experienced during my own practica. But my decision on how to work with student teachers could easily have gone the other way. I might have decided to model my advisory practice on the practices of my own practicum advisors, therefore perpetuating the 'sink-or-swim' model that had been so much a part of my own 'learning to teach' experiences.

Asleep at the Switch

The year after my Yarra Bridge practicum I secured a full-time teaching position at Aramis Park High School, a new school that had just enrolled its grade 10 class and was to enrol its senior classes in the following years. Once again I found myself designated as the PE specialist. The school had no gymnasium, and the outdoor facilities included an oval and a large paddock. There was one other PE teacher at Aramis when I arrived and we both shared a staff room with the History/Geography teachers. They were a very friendly group, and were occasionally given to practical jokes, especially with first year teachers. For instance, I would often organize the equipment needed for a lesson, perhaps a couple of crates of volleyballs, and leave them sitting inside the staff room door while I went outside to meet my class and take attendance, only to find that when I returned, the crates would be upturned and the balls scattered throughout the room. Understandably, I didn't take much notice when my name went up on the board to volunteer as a practicum advisor. Just another joke! Needless to say I was a little surprised when, on the Wednesday before an introductory practicum for student teachers at Aramis High, a young man knocked on the History/Geography staff room door and asked to speak to 'Mr Clarke', his practicum advisor. This was my first year of teaching and here was my first student teacher.

As the practicum unfolded, my work with that student teacher was to be one of the most rewarding experiences of my teaching career. The student teacher and I planned, experimented, co-taught classes, and critiqued each other's practice throughout the practicum. I found myself not so much *reporting on* the work of the student teacher during our weekly meetings and conferences but *inquiring into* teaching practice with him. Indeed, so powerful was this experience that I chose to regularly sponsor student teachers on practicum.

The school system in which I was working had a three-term school year and the various universities sent their student teachers out in different terms. I sponsored two and sometimes three student teachers each year for practica ranging from three to nine weeks in length. Over an eleven-year period I worked with more than twenty students with teaching abilities ranging from those who were absolutely brilliant to those who had failed previous practica and were completing a supplementary practicum at my school. This posed many interesting challenges as an advisor and gave me an extraordinary opportunity to explore and experiment with a range of advisory styles.

Perhaps the most surprising aspect of my work as a practicum advisor was that I was never offered any formal or informal opportunity to examine the role I was playing in the practicum setting. When I consider that the students with whom I was working were to be the next generation of teachers in our school system, the absence of any professional development for school advisors borders on negligence by those responsible for the direction of teacher education in that jurisdiction. Certainly, I was given the various student-teaching handbooks from the universities, and the faculty advisors who did visit the school provided examples of a few different advisory styles, but essentially what I learned about advising was what I constructed by myself when I interacted with the student teachers after they arrived on practicum.

Equally astounding is that this situation was largely reflected in the university's recruiting process for faculty advisors when I was first appointed to that role.

The principal criterion was previous experience as a school advisor, although this was waived for some appointees. Further, although a professional development course was offered, a number of faculty advisors paid lip-service to this requirement and avoided the classes when possible. (In fact I know of some who attended only one class and then absented themselves from the remainder.) I had some sympathy with those who adopted this attitude, as the course was the single most disappointing class that I attended while in graduate school. The course provided a very technical and rational view of advising. Class members were presented with a list of tasks to be learned, focusing largely on the activities of the student teacher and only peripherally examining in any critical way the activities of advisors in practicum settings. As an experienced school advisor, I found the material and substance of this course to be virtually useless in terms of exploring and preparing advisors for the educative function that exemplary advisors regularly play in practicum settings. Taken together, my preparatory experiences for both school and faculty advising might lead one to believe that practicum advising:

- requires *very little preparation*, (i.e., it is a fairly straight forward task);
- is a task *that anyone can do*, (i.e., regardless of selection criteria or course preparation, any teacher can perform that task); and
- *requires no ongoing support*, (i.e., once you have worked with your first student teacher, then you know all that you need to know about the task).

Sadly, these common beliefs could not be further from the truth, particularly as more and more faculties of education are changing their field experience in pre-service teacher education to a single extended practicum placement in contrast to two or three shorter placements with different advisors. With the extended practicum format, if a student teacher is assigned to an ineffective or uninvolved advisor, then that student's professional development as a teacher can be severely handicapped. Given that our student teachers are going to be our future colleagues in the teaching profession, every attempt should be made to ensure that practicum advisors are not only the very best people available for that task but well prepared to undertake that task.

Practicum Advisor as Teacher Educator

A review of literature reveals that advisor preparation is beginning to be taken more seriously in some institutions, with professional development activities ranging from distributed workshops (Browne, 1992; McIntyre and Killian, 1987), to semester courses (Johnston, Galluzzo, and Kottkamp, 1986) and, in one or two instances, extended graduate work (Garland and Shippy, 1991; Wolfe, Schewel, and Bickham, 1989). Unfortunately, the literature also indicates that many programs focus primarily on the activities of the student teacher in the practicum setting as opposed to the activities of the advisor in those settings. One reason for this fixation is the way that the work of practicum advisors has been, and in many instances continues to be, conceptualized in teacher education. To illustrate this more fully, consider the continuum depicted in Figure 11.1.

Figure 11.1: *Alternative conceptions of the work of practicum advisors*

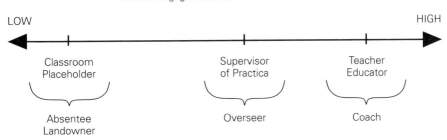

This continuum helps me understand my own experiences as a student teacher on practicum and suggests alternative possibilities for thinking about the work of practicum advisors. There are a variety of other points and, indeed, other ways to think about this continuum but I confine my comments to three points along the continuum and the notion of engagement between student teacher and advisor in the practicum setting.

Perhaps one of the oldest conceptions, and one more directly related to the work of school advisors, is *advisor as classroom placeholder*. An advisor who acts as a classroom placeholder is a teacher who gets a student teacher to take his or her place in the classroom and then exits to the staff room for the remainder of the practicum. I have certainly witnessed this approach to practicum advising and have had colleagues who believe this is the most appropriate form of field experience for student teachers. For some advisors, this is the way that they learned to teach on practicum, and they were simply 'teaching as they were taught'. The level of engagement with the student teacher is minimal when advisors hold this conception of their role in practicum settings. Fortunately, this 'absentee landowner' conception is quite rare but nonetheless is an indication of life at one end of the continuum.

I would like to move some distance along the continuum to what is perhaps the most common conception of the work of practicum advisors today, *advisor as supervisor of practica*. This conception is promoted in a number of universities and is often the way that practicum advisors view their work with student teachers. In short, their function is to 'oversee' the work of student teachers on practicum. Implicit in this supervisory role is an assumption that much of what the student needs to know about teaching is acquired prior to the practicum and that all the student teacher needs to do is to put that knowledge into practice under the supervision of an advisor. This particular conception has a strong connotation of a technical rational view of professional development: knowledge is in the academy, practice is in the field, and it is a one-way street from the first to the second. The level of engagement with the student teacher is considerably increased in this conception but unfortunately is quite uni-dimensional in nature: the role of the advisor is to observe, document, and report.

I would like to contrast these two conceptions with one that I believe is far more appropriate for the work that advisors do and, especially given the growing number of school/university partnerships that are being reported in the literature, the role advisors are increasingly expected to play in practicum settings: namely, *advisor as teacher educator*. In my work as a school and faculty advisor, the educative function has always been the most important element of that role. Practicum advisors are teacher educators. And to be a teacher educator in a practicum setting demands a level of engagement with a student teacher that far exceeds that demonstrated by other conceptions, for example, supervisors of practica. Advisor as teacher educator is not a task for the faint-hearted. It is not a job for those who want to have a rest from the classroom. It is not a job for those who want an easy term at the university. It is not a job for those who have a hundred and one other commitments in their professional lives. In short, this is not a job for everyone! If you elect or agree to be a practicum advisor, you are committing yourself to a level of engagement that demands all the skills of an educator, and then some. It is a role that requires advisors to be knowledgeable and conversant with the field of teacher education and the issues that pertain to that field.

I argue that practicum advisors are teacher educators in much the same way as many university faculty claim to be teacher educators. Obviously, this is an important point for me. The concept of practicum advisor as teacher educator should become the main referent for any discussion of the role that advisors play in practicum settings. This is even more important when we consider that it is practicum advisors who, by all accounts (Glickman and Bey, 1990; Guyton, 1989), have the most influence on the next generation of teachers in our schools.

Teacher Educator as Coach

Four years ago I was asked to teach a course for new school and faculty advisors. The course had been offered for a number of years at the University of British Columbia and was underpinned by a clinical supervision model of practicum advising. This is a very powerful model with much to offer new advisors. Unfortunately, clinical supervision tends to be interpreted in a variety of ways. For example, Hunter (1984) and Joyce and Showers (1982) have used it as a form of technological intervention specifically aimed at enhancing teacher effectiveness. In contrast, Kilbourn (1982) emphasizes autonomy, evidence, and continuity within a clinical supervision model to ensure reflection and understanding, a practice that is more faithful to Cogan (1973) and Goldhammer's (1969) original vision of clinical supervision. Still, Kilbourn's approach is more the exception than the rule, and in my experience many advisors tend to imbue clinical supervision with positivist notions of standardization, quality control and homogenization of pedagogy, the medical metaphor ' "clinical" connoting something in need of careful diagnosis and a prescribed course of action toward improved "health" ' (May and Zimpher, 1986, p. 88).

Figure 11.2: *A stereotypical view of coaching*

Further, as I have indicated earlier, the notion of 'supervision' does not capture for me the nature of the work that I believe good advisors engage in on a daily basis with student teachers on practicum. In searching for some way to capture the sense of what it is that school advisors do as teacher educators, I find the notion of coaching to be particularly useful.

First I wish to dispel a stereotypical image of coaching where the coach is the person who stands on the sidelines berating his or her players, arm thrust out, finger pointed at the player in error, calling the next play, etc. (Figure 11.2). This image of coaching is often portrayed in the media, but it is not how I conceive of coaching nor is it, in my experience, how many coaches perceive their work in coaching environments.

My notion of coaching draws on two sources: the work of Donald Schön (1983, 1987), and my own experiences as competitor and coach in Olympic gymnastics. Schön is well known for his work on reflective practice. Less known perhaps is his work on coaching with respect to introducing beginners to the world of professional practice. Schön's work coincides with the emphasis on engagement between 'coach' and 'learner' that I suggest is the essence of teacher educator as coach where 'the coach's legitimacy does not depend on his scholarly attainments or proficiency as a lecturer but on the artistry of his coaching practice' (Schön, 1987, p. 310). My own initial experience in coaching is Olympic gymnastics; the coaching takes place in the immediacy of the action setting in amongst the magnesium chalk and gymnastic equipment, working side-by-side with individual gymnasts exploring new options, experimenting with new repertoires, acting as a sounding board for alternative practices, bringing to bear resources not readily available to the gymnast, and so on.

This notion of coaching that I have begun to relate, and which stands in sharp contrast to the stereotypical view of coaching portrayed in the media, resonates in different ways for different people. For example, a woman with whom I was recently sharing this notion likened the intimate and interactive relationship between coach and gymnast/student teacher to her experiences with a labor coach during the preparation for, and delivery of, her children.

There are at least six ways in which my work as a coach of gymnasts and student teachers are linked:

- my work is set in *the immediacy of the action setting*;
- I work *side-by-side with the person being coached*, (not from afar);
- I am a *co-investigator in to the practice that is being learned* (and not given to the sink or swim method of learning a new competence);
- it is important that I *know when to watch, listen, speak, or act* and that I am able to distinguish between the value of these at different times for the person being coached;
- I am *an inquirer into my own practice* as a coach and actively seek opportunities to inform that practice; and
- in seeking to *analyze the particularities of practice*, I am attentive to detail and not given to a reliance on an approach that is often referred to as technical problem solving (if this is problem 'A', the solution always is 'A', if this is problem 'B' the solution is always 'B', etc.).

In short, good coaching practice is thoughtful, deliberate, and inquisitive. I recall watching an inexperienced coach working with a young gymnast in an attempt to improve her round-off (a cartwheel-like action that precedes a series of backward tumbling movements). The coach could see that something was wrong with the round-off and, in an attempt to help the gymnast improve the movement, encouraged the girl to reach up with her arms during the rebound phase at the end of the movement (one of the most common 'coaching tips' heard in gymnasiums in relation to this movement). Unfortunately, the problem lay in the hurdle step that the gymnast used to initiate the movement and not in the concluding phase of the movement. For twenty-five minutes the coach continued to instruct the gymnast to reach up with her arms at the end of the round-off with little or no improvement to her execution of that movement. The coach's inability to analyze the gymnast's practice was detrimental to the girl's performance of this particular activity. Ideally, the coach should have engaged the gymnast in a conversation about the particulars of the activity and the context in which the activity occurred (i.e., the movements that preceded and were to follow the activity). The conversation should also have been an opportunity for the coach to explore her own practice, to think critically about how this instance was similar to, and different from, past instances that she had encountered and its relationship to her own understanding of the particular activity and the gymnast who was performing it.

The links I suggest above between these two coaching contexts, student teaching and Olympic gymnastics, do not represent an exhaustive list of possible connections. Nor am I trying to suggest that there is an isomorphic relationship between coaching practices in the two settings: clearly the parallel between the coaching gymnasts and student teachers breaks down at some point. But the five aspects I have articulated above are central to my coaching practice, be it of student teachers or competitive gymnasts.

My concept of coaching as it pertains to teacher education differs from two earlier uses of that term in the teacher education literature. The first use is in the context of peer coaching (Joyce and Showers, 1982) where the outcomes of the process are deliberately reciprocal in nature and essentially technical in substance (Hargreaves and Dawe, 1990). In contrast, I argue that the concept of 'coaching' implies a level of expertise and experience on the part of the coach that is distinctly different to the person who is being coached. Further, I believe coaching to be a highly interactive and reflective activity, and not just a technical pursuit. The second use of coaching in the teacher education literature occurs in the context of cognitive coaching (Costa and Garmston, 1994), where a distinct line is drawn between thought (cognition) and action (practice). While there is much to recommend in this body of work, I find the distinction between thought and action to be quite artificial. Drawing on the work of Lave and Wenger (1991), among others, I believe that thought and action are mutually constitutive. Indeed, that thought is embedded in action, and that the separation of the two distorts the legitimacy and artistry that is the essence of good coaching practice.

Coaching is a highly interactive endeavor between advisor and student teacher and, in my experience, is one of the most taxing, exhausting, challenging activities I have ever undertaken. I never cease to be amazed by advisors at both the school and faculty level who tell me that they have taken on student teacher advising because they need time out from the hectic pace of their regular duties. Done properly, advising is a totally consuming activity. A recent experience with a student teacher named Mathew comes to mind.

Coaching Mathew

I was Mathew's faculty advisor, and in conjunction with his school advisor, had written two interim reports indicating that Mathew was 'at risk' in terms of successfully completing his thirteen-week practicum. Mathew needed to demonstrate significant improvement in specific areas within a designated period of time to avoid removal from the practicum and from the teacher education program in which he was enrolled. Grade 9 classes were the most problematic for Mathew. He was unable to establish any sort of presence as *the teacher* in the classroom at this grade level. As a result, leadership in the classroom came from three or four of the rowdier students who quickly co-opted several other students in what was fast becoming an all-out rebellion during Mathew's Grade 9 lessons. Even when I was present during these lessons, the student unrest showed no signs of abating.

Wednesday of the fifth week on practicum was particularly disastrous. One of the grade 9 classes had become so unruly that Mathew's school advisor, who had been sitting in a workroom adjacent to the classroom, had to intervene. He stopped the class, brought the pupils back to order, and taught the remainder of the lesson for Mathew. On days that I did not formally visit Mathew's classroom, I would drop by after school to see how things were going. This particular Wednesday was one such day. Mathew and I retreated to the grade 9 classroom to discuss the day's events. Unfortunately Mathew's advisor was unable to join us due to prior commitments at the school board office. I did not envy Mathew having to face the grade 9 students the next morning. I remember my own struggles with similar classes, both as a student teacher and as a practicing teacher; I often felt I was dangling over the edge of a cliff, holding on with just my fingertips, only to glance up and see the pupils standing at the cliff's edge about to stomp on my fingers!

What should I do as Mathew's advisor? I could provide him with a list of things to help with his classroom practice, for example: review his expectations with the students and be more rigorous in implementing the consequences for student failure to meet those expectations, move difficult students to separate parts of the room, introduce work contracts for the more intransigent students, reduce early 'off-task' behavior by having a daily question written on the board for the students to complete when they entered the room; increase student activity and reduce 'teacher talk' during lesson segments, provide clear instructions for students to follow during transitions between lesson segments, ensure that the bell at the end of the class is not the signal for dismissal, and so on. I was tempted to pursue this approach but as some of these issues had already been raised by Mathew's school advisor with little improvement in Mathew's classroom practice, an alternative approach was required.

As we pondered the day's activities, Mathew began to lay out the lesson content and topic area that he hoped to introduce the following day. I wanted to suggest that there were more significant issues to be addressed at this point but felt that it was important for him to approach the problem in his own way. There was no doubt in my mind that of all the topics in the year 9 curriculum, the one that Mathew hoped to introduce to the Grade 9 students the next morning was the most boring, dull, and uninteresting topic I could imagine at that level. I had visions of Mathew's school advisor once again having to intervene and take over the class. I wanted to suggest changing the topic altogether and selecting one that would potentially be of greater interest to the students (in the hope that pupil behavior might be moderated by their interest in the topic). Once again, I felt that it was important for Mathew to explore his own ideas in preparation for the next day rather than 'giving' him the lesson plan that I thought would work with the Grade 9 students. We spent the next hour and a half working and reworking the lesson plan. I regularly sought clarification and explanation from Mathew about his intended outcomes and how he felt these were going to be achieved with the plans he was suggesting. At times, we role-played some possible scenarios that might eventuate from the activities planned and listed the sorts of things that Mathew might draw upon in response to the students' reactions. Together we examined a number of different resources, with quick excursions to the library and the staff room for additional materials. As the lesson took shape, we examined the individual lesson elements both from Mathew's point of view and from what we thought would be the pupils'. Together we considered each element in terms of its intellectual level and associated pupil activity.

As the various elements of the lesson began to fall into place, Mathew explored more earnestly the nature of his relationship with the pupils. He had tried to be firm with the students early in the practicum but that had failed. He had tried to be friendly but that had also failed. Mathew wondered if at the outset of the lesson he should have an open conversation with the students about the difficulty he was facing with his Grade 9 classes, seeking suggestions from them about ways that he might improve his teaching practice. This was not an approach I would have suggested, nor was it an approach that I thought would work with these students (particularly given the events of that morning). As we explored the strengths and weaknesses of some alternative approaches, Mathew decided to opt for the open conversation approach; as he noted, 'things couldn't get much worse' and drastic measures were required if he was going to survive the practicum (at this point he wasn't worried about passing his practicum but just surviving with his pride intact). I wondered how much sleep Mathew was going to get that night.

I was feeling quite exhausted after working with Mathew that afternoon. As I reflected upon my interaction with him, it struck me that this was the first time that we had actually worked through a complete lesson plan together — a practice that as a faculty advisor had been increasingly absent from my work with student teachers (perhaps due to the pattern of weekly visits that are often tied to specific lesson observations, my interactions tended to focus on classroom practices as opposed to pedagogical decision-making during lesson preparation). We had worked in great detail through the design and content for the lesson. I realized that, through the series of questions we pursued and the judgments we made, I had in effect been modelling for Mathew the sort of pedagogical struggles that teachers engage in as they plan both for the management of pupils and for the management of the intellectual discourse in the classroom (Shulman, 1987).

We had spent over two hours planning and talking about Mathew's grade 9 classes for the next morning. While it would be impossible to spend this amount of time with all student teachers on a regular basis, my work with Mathew that afternoon reminded me that practicum advising is more than just supervising; it is more than just the clinical presentation of classroom observation data. Mathew and I had worked side-by-side, examining his, and in many ways my own, understanding of classroom practice: lesson content, theme objectives, unit plans, discourse patterns, management strategies, pedagogical approaches, pupil differences, and so on. Although sorely tempted, I avoided offering Mathew quick-fix technical solutions (or the 'the hands up at the end of the gymnastic movement' approach). Rather, together we sought to understand Mathew's teaching practice from his perspective, in much the same way that Mathew had begun to explore his pupils' learning from their perspective. In short, this session contained the key elements of coaching practice outlined earlier: working in the immediacy of the action setting;

working side-by-side; co-investigating the practice to be learned; knowing when to watch, listen, speak, or act; inquiring into my own practice; and seeking to analyze the particularities of practice.

Mathew invited me to the first of his two grade 9 classes the next morning (a brave move considering my position as evaluator of Mathew's teaching). To my surprise, Mathew's conversation with the grade 9 students was one of the most extraordinary events I have witnessed as a practicum advisor. The students were exceedingly blunt with Mathew about his teaching practice but the conversation never strayed from a respectful exchange between pupil and teacher. The tone established and set in the negotiations that occurred at the beginning of that class set the tone for an entirely different practicum experience for Mathew. Certainly, as the practicum progressed, there were days when he still struggled with the vagaries of teaching grade 9 students, but those struggles never approached the same crisis level he faced on the Wednesday of his fifth week of his practicum.[3] My work with Mathew on that day was an important lesson to me as an advisor — the value of attending to the student teacher's agenda — and underscored the value of the coaching approach in working with student teachers.

Advisor as coach plays itself out in different ways in different settings. For example, if pupils are at risk as a result of a student teacher's planned lesson (e.g., crossing a busy road during an orienteering exercise during a PE or Geography lesson) then the discourse practice that I have articulated in the instance of 'Coaching Mathew' might demand stronger intervention at the outset to ensure the safety of the pupils during the preparation and enactment of the lesson. Still, the skills and abilities demanded of coaching student teachers brings to bear a critical examination of the advisor role that is rarely considered in the professional development of advisors for practicum environments. In the course that I currently teach for school and faculty advisors, the notion of coaching is central to the exploration of the advisor role. This concept is explored in a self-directed coaching practicum that each participant undertakes during the course (see Clarke, 1995).

Three Steps: Professionally Ready, Carefully Selected, Continually Supported

Given the complexity and the demands of the practicum advisor role, and given that student teachers consistently report that the practicum is the most influential component of their teacher education programs (Blakey, Everett-Turner, Massing and Scott, 1988; Wideen, Holborn and Desrosiers, 1987), it is incumbent upon those responsible for the professional development of student teachers to ensure that all advisors are:

- *professionally ready*, that is, advisors wishing to work with student teachers are provided with professional development opportunities that prepare them for that role and clearly outline what is expected of them in that role;

- *carefully selected* from those who have completed the initial professional development program; and
- *continually supported* as they undertake their role as advisors (we should not abandon them once the student teacher arrives, or after they have had their first student teacher).

These three points are in direct contrast to my early observations of the way in which schools and universities seem to regard the work of practicum advisors. If practicum advisors are to be considered teacher educators and their work is to encompass the six elements of coaching outlined above, then these three steps are essential to ensuring exemplary advisory practice for teachers and faculty members working with student teachers in practicum settings. If we choose to ignore these steps, then we perpetuate the unevenness of advisor performance that I experienced as a student teacher and have witnessed on several occasions in my work with school and faculty advisors over the past twenty years.

Many problems stemming from the appointment of suitable advisors arise because the first two steps are reversed. This is akin to handing out a licence to drive a car before the recipient has attended any form of driver instruction. Worse still, in teacher education we often omit the first step altogether. If the first step is missing, we are then forced to work on the assumption that any teacher or faculty member will automatically be a good practicum advisor. Good gymnasts do not automatically make good gymnastic coaches. Good soccer players do not necessarily make good soccer coaches. It seems folly to me to assume that the same principle does not hold in teacher education. All the good will in the world and a willingness to volunteer one's time to the task of advising does not ensure that good or even adequate advising will take place. The mere fact that I might be proficient in a particular area does not necessarily ensure that I am able to coach someone else who is learning to become proficient in that area. In teacher education, are we prepared to allow 'professional readiness' to mean 'anyone who wants to volunteer' for the task of practicum advising? I believe the answer is 'No'. Rather, the role of advisor as coach demands that we thoroughly prepare teachers and faculty members for their work with student teachers. Having provided the opportunity for professional development as an advisor, we should then carefully select participants who we consider most suitable for the task (e.g., in the course I currently teach for advisors, the self-directed coaching practicum and the case study materials submitted as part of that process provide an indicator of the state of readiness of advisors for their work with student teachers in practicum settings).

The selection of practicum advisors is undoubtedly one of the most intractable issues in the area of pre-service teacher education. Recently, I was invited to a meeting of school advisors where it was brought to the attention of the group that one of the student teachers in that school had noted that the head of the department to which he was assigned commented that 'student teachers were more trouble than they were worth'. The student teacher's purpose in raising the issue was not to criticize the program but to find out what he and his fellow student teachers might do to be the least possible inconvenience to their advisors while on practicum.

Needless to say, the advisors at the meeting were quite surprised, especially as all advisors working with student teachers had volunteered for that task. The group of teachers (including a school administrator) noted that too often universities send a request to the school for names of those wishing to act as practicum advisors and the principal puts a blank sheet of paper on the staff room notice board calling for interested teachers. Staff members then add their names to the list and the principal sends the list back to the university. While this is not how advisor selection works in all settings, I have found this to be a very common practice in many settings, and volunteerism is often the easiest way to address the selection problem. Over the years there have been various attempts to address the selection issue, but given the conception of advisor as teacher educator and the attendant notion of coaching outlined in this chapter, a need for a review of the selection process for advisors at both the school and university level is clearly indicated.

I envision the possibility of advisors, both school and faculty, belonging to a designated group, for example a region-based 'College of Teacher Educators', and that group serving as the pool from which advisors are selected to work with student teachers. Membership in the group would require evidence of professional development commensurate with the work of teacher educators in practicum settings and of regular upgrading of one's knowledge to remain current with the literature in the field of teacher education.[4]

Turning briefly to the notion of upgrading or ongoing professional development for school advisors, I think that it can safely be said that this is virtually non-existent in most settings. In those jurisdictions where some ongoing professional development is available, it is often piecemeal and infrequent: a couple of half-day workshops at most. The briefer the time period provided for ongoing professional development, the more likely it is to be technical in nature (and in some jurisdictions with which I am familiar, completely administrative in nature with an emphasis on filling in and filing student teacher reports). This technical emphasis is often exemplified in many 'clinical supervision' workshops that abound today. Unfortunately, ongoing professional development support that focuses solely on supervisory exercises rarely asks advisors to scrutinize their own activities to the same extent as it asks advisors to scrutinize the work of their student teachers. It would be illuminating, for example, as part of an ongoing professional development program, to ask advisors to record, categorize, and analyze the types of questions they ask of their student teachers.

Conclusion

I believe we need to reconceptualize the way we think about the role of practicum advisors. I suggest that the notion of teacher educator is a far more appropriate conceptualization than those currently in use in teacher education. Further, the notion of coaching has much to offer in terms of capturing the level of engagement that we expect of advisors as they work with student teachers. The advisor as coach notion also provides a useful heuristic for explicating the relationship between advisor and student teacher in practicum settings. I have argued that there are certain principles that are common to exemplary coaching practice in site-based educational settings and that these are worthy of consideration in our work with student teachers. Finally, our *modus operandi* as we prepare sites for student teaching practica should be to ensure that advisors are professionally ready, carefully selected, and provided with ongoing support for their work with student teachers. Each of these points is important if the work of practicum advisors is to feature more significantly than is currently the case in our discussion of, and contribution to, pre-service teacher education.

For me, the role of practicum advisor is critical in complementing and extending the professional development opportunities that we provide for beginning teachers in practicum settings. Unfortunately, it is a role that is often overlooked and undervalued in conversations about pedagogical practices in teacher education. Writing this chapter has enabled me to articulate the strategies that I use in my work with student teachers. I look forward to continuing this conversation with other advisors and hope that the ideas presented here act as an impetus for both critique and further exploration of our work in practicum settings.

Notes

1 Pseudonyms are used for all schools, teachers, faculty members, and student teachers.
2 Throughout this paper the term 'school advisor' is used to refer to school teachers who work with student teachers in practicum settings. The term 'faculty advisor' is used to refer to university faculty who work with student teachers in practicum settings. When the term 'practicum advisor' is used it refers to both school and faculty advisors who work with student teachers in practicum settings.
3 Mathew has since gone on to full time employment in a school district as a specialist teacher for behaviorally difficult students. He conducts small classes with eight to ten students who voluntarily withdraw themselves from regular classrooms, and he works with them to develop strategies to enable gradual integration back into regular classroom environments.
4 Networks such as these exist already in regional mentorship programs (e.g., in the Richmond School District in British Columbia, Canada) and could serve as a model for practicum advisor networks.

References

BLAKEY, J., EVERETT-TURNER, L., MASSING, C. and SCOTT, N. (1988) 'The many faces of beginning teachers', Paper presented at the annual meeting of the Canadian Society for the Study of Education, Windsor, Ontario.
BROWNE, C. (1992) 'Classroom teacher as teacher educators', *Action in Teacher Education*, **14**, 2, pp. 30–7.
CLARKE, A. (1995) 'Becoming a teacher educator: A coaching practicum for co-operating teachers', Paper presented at the annual meeting of the American Education Research Association, San Francisco, CA, April, 1995.

COGAN, M. (1973) *Clinical Supervision*, Boston, Houghton Mifflin.

COSTA, A. and GARMSTON, R. (1994) *Cognitive Coaching: A Foundation for Renaissance Schools*, Norwood, MA, Christopher Gordon Publishers.

GARLAND, C. and SHIPPY, V. (1991) 'Improving the student teaching context: A research based program for school advisors', *Action in Teacher Education*, **13**, 1, pp. 37–41.

GLICKMAN, G. and BEY, T. (1990) 'Supervision', in Houston, R. (Ed) *Handbook of Research on Teacher Education*, New York, Macmillan, pp. 549–66.

GOLDHAMMER, R. (1969) *Clinical Supervision*, New York, Holt Reinhart and Winston.

GUYTON, E. (1989) 'Guidelines for developing educational programs for cooperating teachers', *Action in Teacher Education*, **11**, 3, pp. 54–8.

HARGREAVES, A. and DAWE, R. (1990) 'Paths of professional development: Contrived collegiality, collaborative culture, and the case of peer coaching', *Teaching and Teacher Education*, **6**, 3, pp. 227–41.

HUNTER, M. (1984) 'Knowing, teaching, and supervising', in HOSFORD, P. (Ed) *Using What We Know about Teaching*, Alexandria, Virginia, Association for Supervision and Curriculum Development.

JOHNSTON, C., GALLUZZO, G. and KOTTKAMP, R. (1986) 'The effects of training in transactional analysis on supervisory interpersonal communication', Paper presented at the American Educational Research Association, San Franscisco.

JOYCE, B. and SHOWERS, B. (1982) 'The coaching of teaching', *Educational Leadership*, **40**, 1, pp. 7–10.

KILBOURN, B. (1982) 'Linda: A case study in clinical supervision', *Canadian Journal of Education*, **7**, 3, pp. 1–24.

LAVE, J. and WENGER, E. (1991) *Situated Learning: Legitimate Peripheral Participation*, New York, Cambridge University Press.

MAY, W. and ZIMPHER, N. (1986) 'An examination of three theoretical perspectives on supervision', *Journal of Curriculum and Supervision*, **1**, 2, pp. 83–99.

MCINTYRE, D. and KILLIAN, J. (1987) 'The influence of supervisory training for school advisors on preservice teachers' development during early field experiences', *The Journal of Educational Research*, **80**, 5, pp. 277–82.

SCHÖN, D. (1983) *The Reflective Practitioner: How Professionals Think in Action*, New York, Basic Books.

SCHÖN, D. (1987) *Educating the Reflective Practitioner: Towards a New Design for Teaching and Learning in the Professions*, San Francisco, Jossey-Bass.

SHULMAN, L. (1987) 'Knowledge and teaching: Foundations of the new reform', *Harvard Educational Review*, **57**, 1, pp. 1–22.

WIDEEN, M., HOLBORN, P. and DESROSIERS, M. (1987) 'A critical review of a decade of Canadian research on teacher education', Paper presented at the annual meeting of the American Association of Educational Research, Washington, D.C. April, 1987.

WOLFE, D., SCHEWEL, R. and BICKHAM, E. (1989) 'A gateway to collaboration: Lynchburg's Clinical Faculty Program', *Action in Teacher Education*, **11**, 2, pp. 66–70.

Section 4

Conversations about Teacher Education

12 Obligations to Unseen Children

The Arizona Group: Karen Guilfoyle,
Mary Lynn Hamilton, and Stefinee Pinnegar

Introduction

This chapter reveals through dialogue our shared and divergent views about becoming teachers of teachers. These views have emerged as we have studied our experience in the various institutions where we have practiced as teacher educators. We usually represent our collaborative work with the moniker, the Arizona Group, and then list our names alphabetically. We call ourselves the Arizona Group because we began our formal education as teacher educators at the University of Arizona together during the mid-1980s, and have been close friends and colleagues ever since. Peg Placier is the fourth member of the Arizona Group, but time commitments precluded her official involvement in the writing of this chapter. Her voice is with us as we write.

We share many things as a group. First, we all began as teachers. In our teaching experience, we worked with a diversity of students. We found their academic records seldom reflected the intelligence, wit, or creativity we observed in our interactions with them. We struggled to teach ourselves how to teach these students. We think it was our desire to learn better or more about how to teach that led us to the College of Education at the University of Arizona. Second, we share an interest in the use of qualitative methodology in the study of education. Third, in our teaching of future teachers we are committed to model the kind of work we expect from them. Fourth, we constantly examine our own practices as teacher educators and the implications of our own teaching for our students' teaching.

Within this shared framework, we have different interests, and different themes emerge in our work. Karen Guilfoyle is centrally committed to creating university classrooms based in a whole language philosophy of teaching as a strategy for educating teachers whose classrooms will more clearly meet the needs of all learners. The learning journey including the processes of learning, the negotiation of multiple roles, and feminism are often themes in her work. Mary Lynn Hamilton is committed to creating teaching experiences that prompt students to recognize their own beliefs about teaching and learning and the negative and positive elements of those beliefs. She speaks of 'bringing them to the point of choice'. In her work, she frequently focuses on cultural models, the tacit messages of classroom environment and routine, and issues of equity and diversity. Stefinee Pinnegar is committed to creating classroom tasks that build upon the beliefs and tacit theories of students in settings that capture experience to enable future teachers to bring the theoretical to the practical from the beginning of their teacher education experience. She has an interest in tacit knowledge and the development of community.

We accept social constructivism as the most accurate representation of how learning occurs and we believe in the fundamental nature of a person's beliefs in shaping her or him as a teacher. We are concerned, therefore, about the connections of theory, experience, and practice for our students' development. We feel an obligation not just to our students but to the students our students will teach. Our chapter, then, presents an analytic representation of these themes through the e-mail conversations we shared as we discussed our views in an attempt to respond to the five issues suggested by John and Tom as a possible framework for this text. The issues were:

- why you teach teachers the way you do and how you know it makes a difference;
- the principles that underpin your practice;
- the purpose behind your teaching;
- the way(s) we model what we 'preach'; and
- our approaches to teaching about teaching.

When we completed our final conversations, Stefinee organized the messages and sorted them according to the themes. She then edited the messages and organized them to present a coherent and integrated representation of the e-mail conversation contained in the original messages. In her organization of the messages she attempted to capture our critique of each other's comments and to maintain the informality and 'flow' of the conversational tone. We saw this as a 'distanced' conversation which included not just e-mail, but telephone and fax as well. The e-mail dialogue attempts to capture and maintain the spirit of this distanced quality of our conversation.

We see this chapter as a representation of our analysis of ourselves as teacher educators: how we came to be the way we are, the principles that underlie our practice, our purposes in teaching our students and our obligations to the students of our students. Our dialogue has been edited around the following themes: social constructivism in the education of teachers; beliefs; resistance; development; relationships among theory, belief, practice, and experience; community; and obligations to unseen students. In the dialogue we include some of the extraneous details that we feel help to capture the quality of the distanced conversation as we experienced it. Although we did not provide official citations as we wrote, our reference list cites all works mentioned in our messages to each other.

Social Constructivism in the Education of Teachers

From: Kareng@uidaho.edu

Throughout all of our texts, our use of reflection and the role it plays in our teaching is mentioned again and again. I think it played a powerful role in our teaching ourselves to teach — it is central. I also see another important piece to that process. Along with reflection and self-study, my collaboration with you and others has pushed my teaching/learning. While collaborating with my students is helpful in extending my understanding, the insights I gain from sharing my inquiry with colleagues are very important. Our interchange over the past few days and returning to the texts of other inquirers in teacher education is pushing my thinking much further than my ritual personal reflection at the end of the semester. The questions that have been posed and the issues discussed help me to re-view the semester in additional ways. Talk is so powerful in learning.

From: Hamilton@kuhub.cc.ukans.edu

Karen, addressing the category you have labelled reflection, self-study, and collaborative inquiry, this fits right into the theme of social constructivism. These are the tools of the social constructivist. I always imagine myself as an archaeologist on a very important site — using toothbrushes and fancy tools to uncover what is really there. I look very carefully at myself and encourage others to do the same. I also realize that I am the lead archaeologist and I must explicitly model how to do the excavation for my students. My students like to hear how I struggle with issues because it relieves them to know they aren't the only ones.

From: Stefinee@byu.edu

I want to begin by responding to Karen. I think all three of us as well as Peggy hold social constructivism as a basic tenet of our beliefs about learning. However, we may have slightly different versions or emphases. Like me, you also use both Vygotsky and Piaget. From Piaget what is most important to me are his ideas of how change occurs. The idea that once we adapt and come to look at the world in new ways, so that it becomes part of our basic organization, is critical in working with people whose beliefs you hope will develop. The concepts of assimilation and accommodation are visible in our students' thinking as we try to move them. First they try to find ways to have what we are saying really be what they already believe. As we give them more and more disconfirming evidence they arrive at a time when they must accommodate. Mary Lynn has talked about bringing students to the point of choice. This is where that is for me.

Vygotsky is more helpful than Piaget because he has more to say about the process of change. His concept of the zone of proximal development is vital. Our students come to us with differing talents and at different points in their own development. His idea of the more capable other and the stages of development are helpful to me. Two of the most influential ideas from Vygotsky in my thinking are his notion that an important developmental move is the ability to make the simultaneous sequential: to tell a coherent story about an immediate situation. Reflective teachers can usually tell more than one story and provide both alternative and conflicting interpretations of each story. The second is Vygotsky's observation of children's need to talk and talk and talk in very repetitive ways about incidents to make this transition. I am becoming sadly concerned about the lack of opportunity for students to truly talk to us. My friend Arthur King once told me, 'I do not know what I know until I say it'. This means to me that my students need more and more chances to say what they know.

Finally, Piaget's idea of formal operational thinking points to the fact that students can construct and reconstruct experiences in their heads. They can replay a classroom experience or imagine it differently — incredible potential for plumbing their own thinking about past experience. I began thinking of this when I read Schön's (1983) chapter on Petra, the architect student. With her teacher she drew the site, destroyed it, created it again. The design and redesign worked like construction, demolition, reconstruction. Is this sort of what you are doing, Mary Lynn, as you push your students in their thinking by providing a demolition and reconstruction of the evidence they present?

From: Hamilton@kuhub.cc.ukans.edu

'Culture has you before you have it.' J. Garrison began his AERA presentation with that this year. He is right. Social constructivism. Yes, I am a social constructivist. I thought everyone was! I come to social constructivism from a sociological/ anthropological perspective. So, for example, I am most influenced by Berger and Luckman's early text as well as the work of Holland and Eisenhart and other anthropologists who look at the ways that we see our world and the ways our world creates us. I am always nudging my students to realize their places in the world. That means that we must do intense introspection, we must learn how to reflect, and we must be willing to tell the truth — as we see it — about experiences we have. So, for example, when a student says to me that he or she does not feel privileged, we probe that — what experiences did that person have/not have? What makes them up? I think that probing beliefs is an important part of the social constructivism stuff.

I have really not read much of the Piagetian perspective and I have read some of Vygotsky. I would say that I stumbled into alignment with their ideas rather than making a conscious choice. [*Stefinee — Here it is. This is where the experience comes before the theoretical knowing*] — even though the theoretical work could back it up. I do think that much of my understanding works that way.

Also, as Stefinee suggested, I advocate that my students deconstruct their world to understand it so they can reconstruct it from a more conscious perspective. Can I stop them from reconstructing a racist world? No. But I can make them more conscious of the incongruities in their lives, if they are there.

It follows then, and fits here, that 'teaching ourselves to teach' is important to consider because I believe that everything is social — the developmental learning-to-teach process is just another part. They have to put their ideas together. I can provide them with things to think about, but they live with themselves and they are inside their heads. What do you think?

From: kareng@uidaho.edu

I do see all of us using a social constructivist framework. Framework is how I do see it. I think where we differ is in the methods we use, but even then I would see our goals being the same because we all believe in the value of students constructing their own meaning. Discovering their own connections. Tobin says in one paper that if we say people who lecture are not social constructivist then we are treating it as a method not a philosophy. I see social constructivism being a philosophy that supports certain kinds of theories about learning and development, and practice/methods being the way we put them into practice.

While Vygotsky speaks a lot about the power of talk, I also see my understanding of language and how it supports learning, thinking, and literacy development as likewise grounded in whole language which has a lot of Dewey in it. Talk, for me, is the issue, but I do not think it needs to be repetitive. Actually, in whole language, that marks the difference between modelling and demonstrations. Teachers demonstrate and students take from that demonstration what connects with them at that time and place. There is no one-to-one correspondence between teaching and learning. Learners need to practice, but each time that practice is different, rather than repetitive, because they change, and the context changes.

I have been moving away from Piaget's stages as I have read research that shows that they do not cut across cultures. Instead, I have been playing with the concept of experience. Where learners are is relational to the experiences they have had rather than the stages they are moving through. I do see patterns in people's experiences but I also see learners who move through experience and construct meaning from it that does not fit the pattern. As a teacher, this means I need to focus on each learner and his/her journey. There is no one way to practice a philosophy, although I do believe that there are basic tenets which do run through practices that are based on this philosophy and that they might be the threads we focus on.

From: Stefinee@byu.edu

Talk — I actually think that as students move into new experiences like student teaching and sometimes their initial observation experiences, they have a great need to talk, and talk, and talk about what they are experiencing. They go on and on and on. When I say 'repetitive', I do not mean the same story over and over again — although it might be that. I mean that, in trying to understand what they are experiencing and turn it into a narrative they can live, students seem to need more space and time to talk about it than any context provides. My students talk about how their spouses and room mates say to them, 'I do not want to hear one more word about your teaching.' This is what I am talking about. The only people who seem willing to listen are others going through this experience. But Frank in the *Wounded Storyteller* talks about the importance of shaping narratives of experience into ways of acting in the world. Therefore, people willing to truly listen to the talk and question it can shape the tale and the teller. I think I'm not present enough during this time. I think we all agree that social constructivism, beliefs, and resistance are integrative themes. As a result, one part of walking our talk involves how we respond to students. I think my views about what social constructivism means are not the same as Peter McLaren's, for example. I think he particularly discounts the cultural heritage and diversity among white students. We also should not assume that it is only race, class, or gender issues that elicit our students' resistance.

I really like the idea of inquiry, reflection, etc. as the tools of the social constructivist, especially in learning. So if we want to create teachers whose practice I expect to develop far beyond mine, we know that if we help them use the tools it will free them from us in their learning. One of my beliefs about the role of the teacher is that the true teacher works constantly to become obsolete in the experiences of the students, so that the students necessarily, and hopefully, move beyond me. They get what I have to give for them and then they do not need me any more. I expect that helping my students link with each other, as more capable others, is also a part of guaranteeing that they will continue to learn beyond me.

From: Kareng@uidaho.edu

My strong efforts to create a community of learners to support my social constructivist views could also demonstrate the power of learning together. I often talk to my students about the need to find someone in their school to talk to. Maybe I need to talk more about the value this holds. For the past few semesters, I have presented theories/philosophy of whole language and social constructivism, involved the students in activities organized around these theories, and had them develop classroom activities that reflected these theories. For many this is hard. Using my understanding of social constructivism, I believe that this happens because they have limited experience to connect to — they have not been in social constructivism classrooms at any level. It is still difficult for them to understand that they can learn from reflecting on their own learning. Next semester, I am going to introduce the various philosophies of learning and development so that we have a common language. Then I am going to introduce activities and, after the theories are embedded, then we will discuss and explore their reactions.

From: Stefinee@byu.edu

One of the things I do is have them enact ideas or conceptions through role playing, through art, through posing. Then their beliefs become very visible and the contradictions reside in the presentation and not necessarily in the students.

Beliefs

From: kareng@uidaho.edu

I never really wanted to get involved with beliefs. They seemed so complex and not practical. I ignored the literature for a while but as a teacher educator, researcher, and staff developer, I found I could not discuss issues, ideas, without first grounding them in beliefs. Making changes seems to be associated with first becoming aware of our beliefs. Beliefs are sometimes difficult in methods courses because it is hard for beginners to see how beliefs connect with how they teach; hence statements of the kind, 'Why are we wasting time on them?'

From: Hamilton@kuhub.cc.ukans.edu

Belief is entwined in theory is entwined in philosophy and so on, Philosophy, theory, belief — walking our talk, living our beliefs, etc. Thomas Green talks about beliefs and philosophies in his *The Activities of Teaching*, a book upon which Fenstermacher based some of his work. Green is also the inspiration for Gary Fenstermacher's practical argument ideas. Anyway, Green talks about core beliefs and secondary beliefs. Core beliefs are those that mostly will not change and mostly remain very hidden from consciousness. The secondary beliefs can be in contradiction to the core beliefs, but, as humans, we compartmentalize very well and are often able to ignore the contradictions. So what I try to do is stay as aware as I can of my varying beliefs and consciously align them wherever possible. When we do not walk our talk, often it is a conflict between primary (core) and secondary beliefs. For example, I believe deeply in democracy and I am willing to stand up and defend it whenever I can. However, regarding [my son] Jesse, I want him to receive as much special attention as possible, so I consider him more equal than others. A contradiction? Yes. Justification? Well, I do not know for sure, but in this situation my beliefs about my child and his care definitely outweigh my beliefs about democracy. Importantly, this rule does not apply to anyone else. I will defend everyone else's right to attentive education, but I will do whatever I can — even put Jesse in the gifted program — if I think it will get him special attention. And that is not bearing out my belief in democracy. So, I am compartmentalizing my various beliefs. Is that good? No, I do not think so, but I do it anyway. I discuss the contradictory nature of this with my students to demonstrate the complexity of beliefs. I think burn-out occurs when we become routinized and automatic. To work against that, we must be reflective and interested in looking deeply into our experience.

From: kareng@uidaho.edu

As I have mentioned before, it was Giroux who opened that door. I did not really know what would happen but it made sense. Making our beliefs more visible helps us to critique them in a variety of ways. Uncovering my own beliefs and reflecting on inconsistencies between my beliefs and practice has been very powerful in helping me walk my talk.

In several texts I have read, the issue of practice not matching beliefs has been discussed. I think uncovering beliefs is one way to reduce the resistance. Sometimes, we do not know why we resist. Once we become aware of the source of our resistance, it is easier to critique it. I think this is hard for students as they feel they already have so little to guide them they do not want to let go of what they do have.

I continually tell students that they know a lot more about teaching than they think they do. Then, I try to think of activities that can help make this visible to them. I think much of it goes back to the transmission model they have been so immersed in. Being responsible for their own learning, their own questions, their own level of involvement, that is what we need to think about. Extrinsic motivation, grades, and the authority of the teacher have been the drive behind their learning. Learning to take control of their own learning or teaching themselves to teach seems almost impossible to some of them. Again, because of their experience, I think they see learning/teaching as an individual experience, something they feel they will have to do alone.

I still have much to learn about how to teach beginning teachers. I have not heard enough stories from the beginning teacher. Now that I kind of have my classroom figured out, I need to learn more about my students' classrooms. I am still learning how to use my framework to support my students. Through reading, talking, reflecting, and self-study, I more fully understand my framework. I am learning from listening to myself teach about how the different theories work.

From: Stefinee@byu.edu

A central principle that underlies all our work as teacher educators is our recognition of the power of beliefs. Part of that recognition means that in our teaching of future teachers we know that we will need to respond to their beliefs. Through a social constructivist stance, I think we respect and accept our students and their beliefs — even when we do not agree — because we know that we cannot change their beliefs, but we also know that they can choose to change their beliefs. Another part of this principle, or at least my response to it, is the recognition that we want students to recognize and know what their beliefs are. I am not out to change all of my students' beliefs or even all of any one student's beliefs. In most cases there is much that is fundamental in the thinking of my students that I value and that I want them to maintain. A central purpose of my teaching of teachers is helping them see what they know and think, and what they can build on from their experience and belief as they grow as teachers.

From: Hamilton@kuhub.cc.ukans.edu

Karen, I noted your comment, 'transforming student beliefs'. I suppose that comment caught me up short. Do you really want to transform their thoughts? Can you do that? Can we do that? When I hear language like that, I become concerned because I do not really think we can transform thought but we can take them up to the choice. Sometimes, maybe, we can offer people possibilities but they have to make the choice. I also think that opens us up for too much disappointment and we never know what will happen in their futures. I keep in mind the work I did with Richardson and Fenstermacher. They were definitely going to change peoples' minds, but the mind is the student's/teacher's social construction and the student's/ teacher's beliefs. Can we make them change? Why would they think our ideas are the correct ideas?

I have come to the point where I think that bringing them to the point of choice is my job; beyond that belongs to them, and if I can do that, I am satisfied. When my students were upset last summer by classroom discussions, I became upset because I thought they were closed-minded. I knew they probably wouldn't change, but at least I could present alternatives in a reasonable fashion. Some of the students still come up to me and talk about how their thinking changed as a result of the class. Did I transform them? No. If they did change, they changed themselves.

From: kareng@uidaho.edu

Yes, I too have come to realize that I cannot transform anyone's beliefs just as I cannot empower anyone. Lather has written well about the issues of resistance and how we interpret resistance. But I still present a transformative model of what I believe would support learning for all students. I think a social constructivist model provides a more effective frame for accommodating the history, culture, etc, learners bring to the classroom. I challenge students to rethink and review their schooling experience. I have them read texts about learners who did not succeed in the classroom. I do ask that they learn about the view of learning/teaching I am presenting so they can make an informed decision about how they want to teach and what is at stake with each model.

But I think I need to be honest. When one teaches using a transformative model, some students see this as making them change their views because of the authority they have always given the teacher and the difference in power they see between students and teachers. I agree with you, Mary Lynn: I feel I am responsible for presenting another way to 'look at' teaching, offering them choices, but I cannot make the choice for them. We never really know exactly how our work influences their thinking. It takes a lot of thinking to make choices that are not congruent with current beliefs. It takes a lot of courage. As Paul Heckman (in a personal communication) says, change in schools takes at least five years. I think for some teachers many things must happen in order to review their teaching. I have come to understand that experience is one of the keys because my experience had led me to believe that there needed to be changes in the classroom.

From: Hamilton@kuhub.cc.ukans.edu

Actually, I do not think it is hard to change all beliefs, just those beliefs that are core to us. We change tastes and beliefs about how to do things with some ease because we are quite able to compartmentalize many beliefs. I often ask my students, 'What do you think about this or that?' 'How do you know whether or not that is true?' 'What is your evidence?' I will also not hesitate to challenge them, but only after the ground rules are set.

From: Stefinee@byu.edu

I also feel that 'will' is an important part of change. This is not new, but the point I want to make is that I believe a 'will' to be different can lead to fundamental changes in world view. I just do not think it happens very often and I think that our lifelong experience may continue to play havoc with the reconstruction. One of the problems we constantly confront in our work with teaching teachers is that we can never do this work alone. We have collaborators we often disagree with who are central to this process — our colleagues on campus and in the public schools.

Our students become teachers in settings removed from our immediate support and influence. We work in settings where at best we share common ideas about learning and becoming a teacher and at worst where our beliefs about teaching and learning and our commitment to student development is completely at odds. We are not the only part of our students' learning experiences. I feel a constant responsibility to work with this larger arena.

I believe that people have the right to their own beliefs, and they deserve respect and acceptance even when I do not agree. I do not like to be marginalized for my beliefs. I do not like to work in circumstances where everyone is striving to change my beliefs, particularly when I do not feel accepted and I do not trust them. My brother, the construction worker, has a totally different belief system. As I struggle to understand the world from his perspective, I constantly gain new tools for understanding my world and for teaching my students. Not that I assume his beliefs, but I see how my action is interpreted by his belief.

Just as our students are limited in their ability to learn from us by the past experiences they have had, and their own beliefs which emerged from their experience, we are limited as well. My belief in the importance of creating community can be debilitating if I have a notion that communities must operate on consensus.

Resistance

From: Hamilton@kuhub.cc.ukans.edu

We should talk about resistance, then, because in many ways it has been part of our discussion. First, I must acknowledge that resistance is hard to deal with for me. Importantly, though, I must acknowledge that resistance is hard because I want those people to believe me and change their minds. However, since I know that will not happen, I have long given that up as a goal. In my classes, I simply want my students to be open-minded enough to consider the alternatives. From a beliefs perspective, once people become conscious of their beliefs, they can choose to change these or not. So, if they are open-minded enough to consider my ideas, I have to be open-minded enough to appreciate our differences in opinions. For example, last summer I had an amazing class of graduate students in a Foundations course. I had approximately twenty students, with a smattering of very, very vocal conservatives. By my estimation, the ideas in the class so threatened the students that some of them turned ugly from time-to-time, yelling in class, calling my house in tears, and threatening me with eternal damnation. All of this was hard to take, because I took it personally. When they attacked, I thought they were attacking me. Instead, they were grappling with their own beliefs and ideas. In retrospect, I think the students learned a lot of things — their language developed, their ideas expanded, and their ways of thinking broadened. Even the most vocal of the students called me the last day of class to say that there had been a misunderstanding on his/her part and that he/she was sorry for the outbursts in class. Interestingly, I received very high reviews from these students on a university survey, ranking me as an excellent teacher.

So, from my perspective, resistance can be hard to respond to in a positive fashion, but when I remember that my goal is open-mindedness, not changing everyone to think like me, I am more successful. What is also true is that their resistance is a function of their personal histories — and I really work on stirring that pot — and I must be ready to handle the results. (Of course, that does not mean I have to like it!)

From: Kareng@uidaho.edu

Over the past six years, I have continually asked myself why I teach the way I teach. Why do I challenge my students to review their beliefs about schooling and how they address race, culture, class, and gender? I think it would be less stressful for the students if, instead, I organized my practice to more closely match their past experiences. Practicing a critical, whole language, social constructivist's view of learning/teaching creates tension and resistance in my classroom as students have had limited experience with that learning environment.

From: Hamilton@kuhub.cc.ukans.edu

Think of the journey. We must assess ourselves and our students. This Spring in my Foundations graduate class I had them write a synthesis paper rather than a portfolio. In it, they discussed what they had learned. Then in class we discussed the class and their teaching and my teaching. Over and over, as they discussed my teaching, they talked about the modelling and the critical thinking — how it was not comfortable to be pushed in a variety of ways and how they appreciated it. Assessment is difficult to face some days, but necessary.

Karen Guilfoyle, Mary Lynn Hamilton, and Stefinee Pinnegar

From: Kareng@uidaho.edu

I think the issue of pain is one I struggle with. Learning is change. Piaget talks about disequilibrium when learning is taking place. New ideas and rethinking experience and beliefs create this feeling. Our students perhaps are seldom faced with 'real' learning so they do not know how to deal with the disequilibrium and take it out on us. Most were good students and did not have to struggle. Why should they have to struggle with ideas now. I know how to best run a classroom. Or do they? I think it was the book, *Teachers as Intellectuals*, by Giroux, that first introduced me to the ideas of putting pre-service teachers in the position of making visible their beliefs and theories about learning and teaching. It is very difficult to determine what you believe in and why. It is also very difficult to change your beliefs. I am often asking them to think about doing that in order to teach all learners in the classroom.

From: Stefinee@byu.edu

I want to move into other kinds of resistance that I experience. I often have problems with students who walk in on the first day of class and because of the syllabus, my authority as a female teacher, my manner — whatever — they want to argue and argue and be disruptive in the class but it is not always connected to their beliefs about the content of the course. I have had most of these experiences with men. For whatever reason they have felt threatened by me. I am finally learning to try to respond to their feeling of threat and powerlessness privately with them rather than continually confronting it in the classroom. I call them in to listen to them, to simply explore what they are thinking. This usually gives me ideas of how we might make the class a better experience for them and for everyone else.

What I have come to struggle with in my own experiences with resistance is how they reflect the students' feelings of being threatened or being betrayed or being made to be less than they are. As I begin to think about it this way, and as I listen to students talk with me privately, I get better ideas about how to proceed. I think in classrooms students have to trust the teacher. For meaningful learning to occur students need to feel that what the teacher asks for is worthwhile. I think this happens at a very personal level. My students look at me, and something I say or do, or my personal ethos, or aura, causes them to trust me. They see me as trustworthy. I must be trustworthy for them. The most disruptive thing to the learning process is when a student who initially trusted me feels betrayed when I break trust with them. But like Mary Lynn said about imposition, I do not control this, my students do. I can only try to understand it and try to make it not happen and respond quickly when it does. In contrast, I have to accept my students where they are if I am to teach them. If I want to teach students, I must accept them and they must feel that from me.

From: Hamilton@kuhub.cc.ukans.edu

I would like my students to transform their thinking, but I cannot make them. When I have a student who is conservative, I respect the difference and I keep trying to present alternatives. When a student resists, I attempt to respond to them as I responded to students when I taught high school. I look at their needs, I talk to them about alternatives. Yes, I want to shake them, but that will not work and it definitely will not change their ideas.

I think that I respectfully push my students to think about new ideas — if they will — and I hope that they will consider alternatives. Further, I see change as a natural process that is only painful when we resist it. Nothing remains the same: we are always changing. If they feel pain, it is, perhaps, because they are at the end, engaged in an intellectual act. Sometimes the feelings of exhilaration and excitement can be confused with pain when the unknown is involved. Frankly, I find the idea appealing.

If you want to create change, I think you must make students familiar with their beliefs and notions. They must understand where they came from in order to see where they are going. Before I talk about theories and philosophies, I have my students talk to me about their own theories and philosophies. Then, once they are aware of those, they can begin to compare in an explicit way what they like/do not like about what they read.

Of course our perspectives differ. We have had different lives. And so, when it comes to resistance, we each respond differently. I think that the issue of dominant culture could be carried over into teacher education. For example, we, as teacher educators, are the dominant culture. We think we know something and sometimes the students treat us as if we know everything, with all of the privileges. If we then think about the notion of needing to resist what you do not have, no wonder our students resist. Then if you add to that the notion that the students thought they knew something because they have always been in school, the situation is ripe for resistance.

Regarding imposition — if you think about it, we all impose our ideas on others. Some are more privileged than others. We all want to tell our stories and have our stories heard. Of course, we must be responsible for the power and privilege that we have, but there is always a power imbalance. As teachers we must offer students the tools to address marginalization and other related issues, but to some degree we could almost paralyze ourselves by trying too hard.

From: Kareng@uidaho.edu

The tension between these issues in the teaching of teachers pushes my thinking continuously. How to walk your talk, feel passionate and committed to your beliefs, and create a learning environment that respects the beliefs of all participants? For some, it creates resistance.

Karen Guilfoyle, Mary Lynn Hamilton, and Stefinee Pinnegar

From: Stefinee@byu.edu

I think there are several developmental tasks for beginning teachers. One is seeing themselves as a teacher — taking on the mantle of teacher and being comfortable with the responsibility and authority of that role. Last semester I had my students prepare five minute lessons and then we got together and talked aloud about those lessons. One of the students had a strong, relaxed classroom presence, but something bothered me about her interaction with her peers. I finally realized that, while she was comfortable presenting to the class, she mostly wanted to be a student not a teacher. As you both say, our students lack experience as teachers. I agree with Diane Holt-Reynolds that what they carry in their head is an image of themselves as teacher. This is a non-specific image. This image of themselves as a teacher is the image they are pursuing in their development. When what we teach connects to that image, supports it, or connects to truths about their own learning as students, this is when they pay attention. The image is usually nebulous. As Bob Bullough points out, the more complex and comprehensive that image or metaphor, the more likely the student is to be successful. Holt-Reynolds suggests that connecting to our students' experience as learners is the surest way to get them to learn the new things about teaching we want them to learn.

Another developmental task is what Tom Russell calls 'the content turn'. It is the move from being a learner and knowing a subject to a transformation of what we know as a student to enabling another student to learn. One of my student teachers said to me, 'I know how to write leads (newspaper). I know what a good lead looks like. In my student teaching, I'm having trouble taking what I know about leads and turning it into activities that will help my students write leads.' The move to curriculum is difficult.

Another developmental task is moving from being a friend in relationship to being a teacher in relationship. In their relationships with their friends, my students expect support. In their relationships with students, they must provide the support, and they must constantly strive to act for the long-term well-being of the child. Even during student teaching there is someone around who partially carries this responsibility. As a beginning teacher I thought of this as realizing 'I am the adult here.' In my interactions with students, with teachers, and with parents, I realized that no matter how immature or difficult, my major responsibility was to the learning and potential of the child and that I had to act mature. This is a difficult move. My students want to be kind.

From: Hamilton@kuhub.cc.ukans.edu

Experience is a key to a teacher's development. This is true for both the pre-service teacher and the teacher educator. As we gather experience and compare information among experiences, we decide what we like/do not like, what works/does not work. I also think that there is a shift from self-centredness toward an altruistic perspective. I do think that in 1969 Frances Fuller had it right. And I think her ideas fit with teacher educators as well. Remember in our initial development we talked about similar issues, and certainly Ardra Cole and Gary Knowles talked about having a similar experience.

How do I respond to that? My goal with my students as well as myself is reflection. I want my students to understand reflection and I want them to engage in reflective practice. I want that for myself as well. The more conscious we are about what we do, the more likely we are to change what we do, hopefully in the direction that best serves students.

Development

From: Kareng@uidaho.edu

Everything I do is an attempt to respond to the development of my students. Some of the strategies/structures I use to facilitate students' learning about learning/teaching are reflection, text set studies, field experience grade-level groups, study group, inquiry groups to explore personal interests and concerns, self-assessment, assigned activities to conduct in field experience, and student presentations. This semester, I also turned opening/closing of class over to the students. I organize the content of the course around three or four themes. I weave the pedagogical, social, and political together in exploring concepts. I share the assessment process with the students. They are responsible for maintaining a Learning Log over the semester; they write reflections and self-assessments critiquing both content and process. I do this to demonstrate another way to do teaching and support learning. I do it because I hope to transform the classrooms of students they will be teaching and open the learning environment for all students and voices.

From: Hamilton@kuhub.cc.ukans.edu

Just as the students are on a journey, so are we and we need to assess it. I keep my own portfolio of a class to help me do this. I know you do extensive journaling and write a letter to your students which assesses the semester you have shared. I am just struck here by the collision of our experience and theirs.

From: Stefinee@byu.edu

What I have questioned in my work is that I often do things with students because of experience that emerged in my first or second year of teaching — but then I wonder if there are things that I ought to be doing that are even antithetical to my current belief about teaching teachers that would be in better harmony with the current development of my students and would lead to stronger development across their lives as teachers or even increase the length of their lives as teachers? I am just not sure yet. I worry often about 'knowing what is best'. Do I really?

Karen Guilfoyle, Mary Lynn Hamilton, and Stefinee Pinnegar

From: Kareng@uidaho.edu

This is a journey. I am still learning how to use my framework to support the students in my classroom and how to teach teachers. Through reading, talking, reflecting, and self-study, I more fully understand my framework.

From: Stefinee@byu.edu

I like what Mary Lynn said about experience before theory. That is exactly what I think one of the relationships between theory and experience is. We come to understand something through experience or even through other theory and then we find theories that provide additional explanation. Therefore, I try to design class-room tasks that link to or develop experience. I try to capture public school experi-ence not just in the schools but in the things that I ask students to do. I try to be clear about my purposes in my assignments. I have some evidence that what I do works. During my curriculum assignment where my students are put into faculties and attempt to develop integrated curriculum, my students get into arguments about their subject matter and their students. Finally, someone reminds them, 'This is just an assignment.' I want my assignments to 'feel real' to my students. I want what I do with them to 'feel' like it is practical and has purpose directly related to what they will do as teachers. This is hard.

From: Hamilton@kuhub.cc.ukans.edu

I talked earlier about Stefinee's concept of 'making visible the practice in her classroom' (I think she got it from Loughran, 1996). I call this modelling. I model an idea or a way of being and talk to them about it, trying to make my actions and my beliefs about my actions more visible. I sometimes draw attention to my suc-cesses or failures as a teacher so we can talk about that. I ask them what worked, what did not, etc. kinds of questions. This, then, sets down the foundation for the times that they might model their own teaching strategies in the classroom. So, I attempt to live my principles in public and entwine my principles with my prac-tice. I want my students to realize how powerful and influential their roles are as teachers. They have the world at the touch of their fingers. I want them to realize and become responsible for that.

The Theory–Practice Relationship

From: Stefinee@byu.edu

For me philosophy (particularly if I embrace it) and theory are intertwined with belief. But I think — and this is where the relationship between theory, experience and practice becomes important — our philosophy emerges in our practice. It guides us in the selection of what we do with students. Our ways of being become routinized and automatic have within their purposes both functionalism and our beliefs. Experience and theory, if we articulate them, can be used to expand our practice because as they interact with each other we embrace more strongly some habitual practices and work like demons to eradicate others. It is in the practices that our experiences and our theories (beliefs/philosophy) are evident. Our immediate practice is also our experience. The differentiation I try to make is that practice is constructed with others, and therefore we never control what emerges completely. Our experience is what we experience in that practice.

From: Kareng@uidaho.edu

I feel I am just beginning to understand the issues of pre-service teachers. I try to listen to them carefully but, just as my words do not fit their experience, it is hard for me to remember exactly how I felt as a new teacher. I know they want more hands-on experience and to try out some of the ideas with children. I need to think more about how to tie together their experiences as students and teachers.

From: Stefinee@byu.edu

I was just thinking about the importance of remembering how we felt. In the piece we did for Tom and Fred's book (Russell and Korthagen, 1995) I learned two things that have transformed my thinking about what I am doing. One was from Mary Lynn: she taught me that my students will teach themselves to be teachers, just as I taught myself to be a teacher. I can help develop skills and prepare them for some things, but they will be in their own context with challenges and blessings unique to that context, and they are different from me — so their journey is their own — they will teach themselves. Peggy taught me about looking at myself as a beginning teacher (and therefore my students) with more loving eyes.

From: Hamilton@kuhub.cc.ukans.edu

In my early days of trying to 'teach myself to be a teacher', I drew upon my experience to figure things out. I knew that traditional strategies had failed miserably with these students of mine. So, I decided to talk with the students. I asked them what they wanted to learn. I talked to them about what they already knew. I implemented group work for assignments. Interestingly, now I can tie what I did then with the current literature — the use of prior knowledge, the notion of the student-directed classroom, the application of cooperative learning strategies — to demonstrate sound teaching practice. But at the time, I really did not have that knowledge. Then, I thought I was flying by the seat of my pants. Then, I thought

I was working overtime trying to figure out what would best interest my students. Those were wild days!

Community

From: Stefinee@byu.edu

When I think about myself as a teacher, I feel there are several things that come from my family background. The first of these is my commitment to community. I was raised in a small southern Utah community. My ancestors on my mother's side settled that community. They were the leaders of the community. My parents always made big purchases locally even when it cost more. This was a contribution to community growth and stability. Sacrificing for the community and its development has always been part of my ethos as a teacher. Mary Lynn's comments about her beginning as a teacher reveal how clearly her earliest decisions about what to do as a teacher emerge in her current practice as a teacher educator, not as a prototype for how all teachers should be but as a tool for promoting her students' learning. My family background and my earliest experience are crucial in my current work as a teacher educator.

From: Kareng@uidaho.edu

Community! I think that is central to our teaching, an essential part of our beliefs and maybe a reflection of feminist pedagogy and relational concerns. It is so much a part of what we do, it almost doesn't stand out because we see it is a given. But even Georgia (my feminist colleague here at the university) often makes the comment that 'They don't work at community like you do!' I think she sees herself as a social constructivist, does many group activities, yet does not focus on community. I see community as being important for a variety of reasons. First as a social constructivist, it seems to me you need a community to support your learning. Community implies a caring for one another, a sense of collaboration, as risk-free a learning environment as possible.

From: Stefinee@byu.edu

I think your example from your feminist colleague is a good one. She believes in collaboration and it points to the ways that collaborative effort is different from creating community. In collaborative efforts we can choose to only work with those who agree with us; those who disagree are more difficult. Also, part of what I see in our work is our commitment to those we are teaching and working with to create communities where their experience will be valued. When I teach people to do action research, I feel responsible that there be arenas where action research is published. This is all a part of community. This is what the S-STEP SIG has always been about. You mentioned you were giving the graduation speech at the high school where your first kindergarten class was graduating: that is about constructing community.

From: Kareng@uidaho.edu

I am on a committee to address a study (Sandler, Silverberg, and Hall, 1996) called *The Chilly Classroom Climate: A Guide to Improve the Education of Women*, published by the National Association for Women in Education. The study focuses on the tensions of women teaching in academia. I just received my copy in the mail so I'm not sure what it is all about but I do see it being an issue. For me, in elementary education, it is especially interesting because many of my students are women used to seeing men as the authority/expert. They 'behave' much better in the classes taught by men than they do in my classes. While they say that my class is the only one they can gripe in, they give little thought to how this affects me as a person. As women, we sometimes do not take care of each other. Once in a while I talk to them about this. It often gets woven in with our discussions on gender. Some women in my courses are not yet ready to address these issues. I think Patty Lather's chapter 'Staying Dumb' addresses this. My philosophy student was highly insulted when I talked about a masculine view of the world.

I think the issue with the philosophy students is more complex. I agree, I conference outside the classroom. I had about five conferences with her. I think she is a gifted student. She has been treated as a gifted student and been allowed to work on her own. She saw no value in the community and her colleagues. She often read when students gave presentations or worked in small groups. She had not learned how to support others' learning as well as her own. In my class, she wanted to go to the library, study on her own, and turn in a paper at the end of the semester. I suppose if content was my only purpose that might have worked. The experience makes more visible how important I see community being not only to learning in the college classroom but in the schools. Maybe our approach to gifted students in the public schools creates other problems. What kind of a colleague will she make? What kind of a learning environment will she organize. Actually, she believes she is smarter than most elementary education students. What does that mean?

This brings up another issue, our moral and ethical responsibility to the unseen children. While we want to support the learning of all students in our teacher education program, not all may make 'good' teachers. How does a teacher educator address this issue? In addition, I do not believe trust is a one-way street. Trust can only be built when both parties are willing to participate. Students as well as teachers play a role in establishing trust. I probably would lean to the role of teacher responsibility in trust but the student has to also play an active role in building that relationship. What do you think?

From: Stefinee@byu.edu

Since I think learning is a form of repentance and causes pain, I also think it is almost impossible to learn from someone you do not trust. But the trust can be in their knowledge of the subject, in their opinion about me, in their consistency and stability, in their acceptance of me as a learner.

From: Hamilton@kuhub.cc.ukans.edu

This reminds me of how we should talk with our students. Maybe we are not giving them enough power in our classrooms, even though we think we are. Maybe we are being narrow-minded when we think we are so open? What do you think? I struggle with this too and do not know the answers. I did talk with my students this semester and last, and in two out of the three classes they say to keep doing it. That felt good. In the other class, I need to give them more consideration for their experience or lack of it. I think we need to do that in order to address issues of power and control because those are critical issues at all levels. I certainly struggle with them.

From: Kareng@uidaho.edu

I am still working on talk in my undergraduate class. I think it may have to do with trust and feeling responsible for what they know which is something I have to let go of. Turning over opening/closing of class has helped in sharing the talk. More group work, activities that teach through doing, inquiry groups, text groups, etc. also help. I think I learned more about this in my writing to you. Talk with experts did not help us but talk with other beginners did. *That must be true for our students as well.* I think that is why my research class went so well this year. I was doing it with them. Our talk cuts across experience.

From: Hamilton@kuhub.cc.ukans.edu

My students are the same as Karen's: they appreciate the opportunity to talk. I value it as well because it gives them an opportunity to listen to themselves in a conscious fashion. I am not sure that talk cuts across experience. It gives voice to our experience and makes us conscious of aspects of our experience that might not ordinarily have voice. It helps us rethink our experience and add theoretical texture to it.

From: Stefinee@byu.edu

I believe that students need to talk and talk about new ideas. This is how an expert can talk to students, and the students get to hear what the expert says in response to the students' stories. Vygotsky is the expert on his own theory. As I talk and talk about it, I tell stories of my experience which do or do not support his theory; then I come to understand it better and to understand better what it means in my context. In 1978 Arthur King first told me learning was repentance. I thought it was, like, 'Nazism is romanticism gone crazy' — like, who cares? But as I came to terms with the way in which my teaching caused pain to my students in 1990, as I was writing to you and teaching in Michigan, I slowly began to understand how learning is repentance. The expert talk was superfluous but both experience and talk about it led me to understand it better.

I also want to put into the hopper of this conversation something else. For me the acceptance of divergent beliefs is a central part of the creation of a community. That is central for my teaching — making safe places for all participants in a community. In a learning community there is the added stipulation that the space allows growth.

From: Hamilton@kuhub.cc.ukans.edu

Beliefs and community: I think that the notion of 'acceptance of divergent beliefs' is a part of community, and a successful community can be formed and survive when people are willing to accept differences and not force one view upon an opposing view. As a family, we try to understand the other perspective in order to figure out where the other person was coming from. It does not make you agree with them, but it helps in understanding the motivation and the perspective.

Regarding finding someone to talk to — interesting. I think about my experience here. I really have no one. I have few people that are interested in my ideas and so I sometimes feel shrivelled up. But, I've managed to survive because I have colleagues beyond the four walls. Doing it alone? That is hard, and what is harder is that it makes me resistant to their notions. If they will not acknowledge my voice, why should I acknowledge their voices? Why should I work with them? Maybe that's it! Students need to have their voices acknowledged, but how can we do that and still teach the class? We would have to work with them on a more intimate level.

Community: the feminist perspective is strong in our work. Although women are not the only ones with community, we certainly find the notion of relations very important. There is an idealistic aspect of what we are saying — trustworthiness, acceptance, etc. Yes, all of that may be true, but we are not addressing completely the power relations of the classroom. What about grades? What about classroom ownership? It is a nice idea to put that aside, but they live in a world that does not really put that aside. So, what happens? They enter *fantasy* land for an hour three days a week. We propose alternatives, but they also deal with the real world and community is important here. Without a community — a strong community — they will not succeed. We have authority and we have power, and even when we try to give it up, it is still there. That is why obligations are important.

Obligation to Unseen Children

From: Stefinee@byu.edu

What has become most clear to me is my belief that my students' beliefs about schooling, teaching, students, and their talents and skills, are the bedrock that they will build on in moving from being a student to a teacher. I want my students to consciously consider who they are as a teacher, what they bring to teaching and how they can use the talents they have to develop as a teacher. I try to get them to see what they need to develop and how what we are doing with them can help in that process. As I listen to what Peggy said about looking at them with more loving eyes and responding in that way to them, I hope they will look at their future students with more loving eyes when those students confront them face-to-face.

What I learned from Mary Lynn [that they will teach themselves to be teachers] has given me increasing respect for their process and an understanding that, no matter how coercive I might like to be, the power to become a teacher resides in them. How they respond to their students will reside in part in the experiences we share together. If our experiences lead them to embrace better teaching practices, then I will meet my obligation to their students.

From: Hamilton@kuhub.cc.ukans.edu

I also want my students to think about their own contexts because I believe they must know themselves before they can make changes. I suppose this idea finally surfaced in my work with Virginia Richardson and Gary Fenstermacher. Although I had been thinking about these ideas before, I really developed these ideas clearly during my dissertation work.

I teach teachers the way I do because my experience, my readings, and my understandings suggest that people learn best this way. And how do I know it makes a difference? In the long-term, I'm not sure that I know. But, in the short-term, in class, I can see them developing their language and their understanding and I can hear them discussing with me and each other what they learned.

From: kareng@uidaho.edu

It seems to me that all three of us are not wanting to teach teachers to maintain the status quo. We have some ideas about what we envision the 'perfect classroom' to be and I feel that we have that vision in our mind when we struggle with what to present and support in our teacher education classrooms.

It seems that we are all trying to create more just and equitable learning environments for all learners regardless of race, gender, class, or culture. Our beliefs about how to do this are grounded in particular theories. I think one of the issues that makes teaching teachers tough for us is that we are attempting to transform thinking about teaching as well as prepare them for their future classrooms.

I had a particularly difficult time with a student this semester who had graduated in Liberal Arts in the field of Philosophy. She has been taught that philosophies are neutral and my belief in the social constructivist philosophy was wrong. She resisted interacting in that framework. She did not want to come to class, complete the assigned work, or read the assigned text. She did not believe in using 'I' in her papers and was very insulted when I challenged her to think in other than a masculine view of the world. One day in class, she said, 'If you believe in diversity, why can't I learn in whatever manner I want to?' As a student, I suppose she could have. As a teacher, I wanted her to explore other paradigms. I did give a lot of thought to her question. I finally replied that it was a *good* question and I would continue to think about it. If she were the only one that I was thinking about, it might not be an issue, but it was her future students I was also concerned with. Interesting. Teaching teachers adds complexity to our interactions.

But I think I need to be honest. When one preaches and teaches using a transformative model, some students see this as making them change their views because of the authority they have always given to the teacher and the difference in power they see between students and teachers. Like Mary Lynn, I feel responsible for presenting another way of looking at teaching, but I can not make the choice for them.

From: Hamilton@kuhub.cc.ukans.edu

In a methods class, I have the students talk about their experiences with different methods and their beliefs about certain methods and ways to teach. If they ask why we study these, I say that they motivate action and choices and they need to be conscious of them in order to make the truly best choices for *their students.*

And that is where my obligations lie. Always, when I am talking with my students, I am thinking about their future students. What would be best for them? What do my students need to know in order to be best prepared for their future students? I believe that having them understand their own histories and beliefs will best prepare them. I also believe in introducing them to teaching strategies that are different from their experiences in school, but I approach that with a lengthy discussion about what worked/did not work for them in school.

Also at the front of my mind is that, in a case of emergency, we always return to the ways we were taught. So, first I try to be a good model for innovation, and second, I have them analyze the models with which they are most familiar. History, background, context, experience — they are all important pieces for the preparation of a teacher. If we do not know our history, we are doomed to repeat it. Method and strategies are important, but you can be a racist using the inquiry method. So, for me, you need to look behind the method. After my class, you may still be a racist, but you *will* not be covert, and you will, hopefully, have seen the possibility of another way to think about things.

Karen Guilfoyle, Mary Lynn Hamilton, and Stefinee Pinnegar

From: Stefinee@byu.edu

One of the most difficult parts of being a teacher and now a teacher of teachers is that I have to make judgments. Grades are hard. But there are also several places where I decide whether students can proceed or not. For me there is an ongoing tension in my practice with students. This is the commitment I feel to helping my students succeed and have the opportunity to teach if they want, and the obligation I feel to the students they will teach. I first began to notice this in a very self-centred way. I found myself saying to students who were very difficult in my class something I began to think of as the Teacher Educator's Blessing: *May you have students just like you!* But then I started focusing on the students they would have.

I have tried to think hard about the implications of my practice with my students for their practice with theirs. It relates to a very strong belief about my responsibility as a teacher: to accept students where they are and hold them accountable for their best at that level. Then, second, to constantly work to expand the level of best with each student. It also relates to my discussion of personality and preparation. What is it that I am preparing them for? What is it that I want them to take away from that preparation? What are the implications for their work with their own students?

It also relates to the fact that our students will not always see in our teaching what we wanted them to see. They will interpret our actions. They will incorporate my practice into theirs just as I incorporated Mel Luthy's methods of teaching grammar and sentence analysis into my teaching of grammar and sentence analysis. But just as Mel did not get to choose what I would incorporate in my practice, I do not get to choose what my students will incorporate. So I think again and again about the possible negative consequences of what my students and I do together.

I am committed to educating an army of committed and gifted teachers because I think that is the only possible way to transform our society. The only thing we could do that would be more powerful is to educate an army of committed and gifted parents. In educating good teachers we are doing both.

To: Hamilton@kuhub.cc.ukans.edu

When I decided to become a teacher educator, I did not think about what it would mean in terms of academia. I thought about all the teachers I had observed and worked with and the students in their classrooms. I wanted to be part of making classrooms exciting, challenging, and meaningful, where all students were seen as learners, where race, class, and gender were addressed. I found that helping classroom teachers change after many years of routine practice was very difficult. I thought it might be more effective to support teachers in developing these kinds of classrooms before the 'system' got a hold on them. In thinking about teaching college students, I always thought about the students they would be teaching rather than them (pre-service teachers) as students.

I have had to rethink this assumption because they are students and teachers.

That is why being a teacher educator is complex. We are teaching on multiple levels. On days when I have had an especially difficult time in the classroom, I wonder if I want to continue. I think about becoming 'normal' and teaching like everyone else does (well, for a minute or two). In reality, the thing that keeps me centred is my obligation to the children in the classrooms my students will be teaching.

Based on my experience and knowledge, I believe that the kinds of classrooms I am promoting will make a difference for learners. I think they could be exciting places for both teachers and learners. I believe that just and equitable classrooms will support our democratic system. I think that learning to be a member of a community has many implications. But I feel a deep commitment to the unseen children our students will be teaching. It is often the 'bottom line' in my decision making.

Conclusion

Our writings suggest that we are serious, reflective teacher educators who honor the task of educating our students. Beyond acknowledging our approach to teacher education, we demonstrate through our writings that living by our principles is neither simple nor easy. Further, we assert a primary purpose for work is our concern for future generations. The unseen children in the schools ignite our passion for knowledge, our commitment to passion, and our desire to inspire future teachers. We feel a moral obligation to the students of our students. The faces of our students' future students haunt us when we see people we suspect are incompetent in our teacher education programs, when our classroom practices seem to be less than the best practice we know, when we respond to our students in ways that are disrespectful, demeaning, condescending or limiting to our students in any way, or when we require less than the best from our students. While we cannot control all the experiences our students have during their education as teachers, we can control our experiences with them. We aim for our interaction with our students to be exemplary in the kinds of relationships we want them to have with their students. Our understanding of the role of social constructivism and beliefs in the development of teachers and our responses to our own beliefs and those of our students are tools to help us meet the obligations we feel for the students of our students. We remember with tenderness the students we taught before becoming teacher educators. We remember the ways in which both our colleagues and ourselves fell short in preparing our students to develop their complete potential. We take these lessons seriously as we work to teach new generations to teach themselves to be teachers.

References

BERGER, P. and LUCKMAN, T. (1966) *The Social Construction of Reality*, Garden City, NJ, Doubleday.

BULLOUGH, R.V.JR., KNOWLES, J.G. and CROW, N.A. (1991) *Emerging as a Teacher*, New York, Routledge.

DEWEY, J. (1963) *Experience and Education*, New York, Collier.

FENSTERMACHER, G.D. (1986) 'Philosophy of research on teaching: Three aspects', in WITTROCK, M. (Ed) *Handbook of Research on Teaching*, 3rd ed., New York, MacMillan pp. 37–49.

FENSTERMACHER, G.D. (1994) 'The place of practical argument in the education of teachers', in RICHARDSON, V. (Ed) *Teacher Change and the Staff Development Process*, New York, Teachers College Press, pp. 23–42.

FRANK, A.W. (1995) *The Wounded Storyteller: Body, Illness, and Ethics*, Chicago, University of Chicago Press.

FULLER, F. (1969) 'Concerns for teachers: A developmental conceptualization', *American Educational Research Journal*, **6**, 2, pp. 207–26.

GARRISON, J. (1996) 'Deweyan approaches to dialogue across differences: A poetic of transactional listening', Paper presented at the meeting of the American Educational Research, New York.

GIROUX, H.A. (1988) *Teachers as Intellectuals: Toward a Critical Pedagogy of Learning*, Granby, MA, Bergin and Garvey.

GIROUX, H.A. and MCLAREN, P. (1994) *Between Borders: Pedagogy and the Politics of Cultural Studies*, New York, Routledge.

GREEN, T. (1971) *The Activities of Teaching*, New York, McGraw Hill Book Company.

GREEN, T. (1976) 'Teacher competence as practical rationality', *Educational Theory*, **26**, 3, pp. 249–58.

HOLLAND, D. and EISENHART, M. (1990) *Educated in Romance: Women, Achievement, and College Culture*, Chicago, University of Chicago Press.

HOLT-REYNOLDS, D. (1994) 'Starting with prospective teachers' beliefs about learning and self as learner: A teacher educators practical arguments', Paper presented at the meeting of the American Educational Research Association, New Orleans.

KING, A.H. (1986) *The Abundance of the Heart*, Salt Lake City, UT, Bookcraft.

KNOWLES, J.G. and COLE, A. (1995) 'Teacher educators reflecting on writing in practice', in RUSSELL, T. and KORTHAGEN, F. (Eds) *Teachers Who Teach Teachers*, Washington, DC, Falmer Press, pp. 71–94.

LATHER, P.A. (1991) *Getting Smart*, New York, Routledge.

LOUGHRAN, J.J. (1996) *Developing Reflective Practice: Learning about Teaching and Learning through Modelling*, London, Falmer Press.

MCLAREN, P. (1989) *Critical Pedagogy, the State, and Cultural Struggle*, Albany, NY, SUNY Press.

RICHARDSON, V. (1989) 'Practice and the improvement of research on teaching', Paper presented at the meeting of the American Educational Research Association, San Francisco.

RICHARDSON, V. (1994) *Teacher Change and the Staff Development Process*, New York, Teachers College Press.

RUSSELL, T. (1997) 'Teaching teachers: How I teach IS the message', in LOUGHRAN, J.J. and RUSSELL, T.L. (Eds) *Teaching about Teaching: Purpose, Passion and Pedagogy*, Washington, DC, Falmer Press.

RUSSELL, T. and KORTHAGEN, F. (1995) *Teachers Who Teach Teachers: Reflections on Teacher Education*, London, Falmer Press.

SANDLER, B.R., SILVERBERG, L.A. and HALL, R.M. (1996) *The Chilly Classroom Climate:*

A Guide to Improve the Education of Women, Washington, DC, National Association for Women in Education.

Schön, D.A. (1983) *The Reflective Practitioner: How Professionals Think in Action*, New York, Basic Books.

Tobin, K. (1992) 'Constructivist perspectives on educational research', Paper presented at the meeting of the American Educational Research Association, San Francisco.

Vygotsky, L.S. (1978) *Mind in Society: The Development of Higher Psychological Processes*, Cambridge, MA, Harvard University Press.

13　Storming through Teacher Education: Talk about Summerfest

Allan MacKinnon, Michael Cummings and Kathryn Alexander

Introduction

'Summerfest' is the name of a two-week Summer enrichment program for gifted elementary school children in the Burnaby School District of British Columbia, Canada. Approximately one hundred 6–12-year-old children from the city of Burnaby attend morning classes in science, technology, and the arts. Over the past six years (1991–6) this program has been interwoven with a Summer semester 'designs for learning' course in the natural sciences at Simon Fraser University. We regard this course as a 'teaching studio' in the sense that university instructors and teacher education students who are enrolled in the course teach children together. The early part of the semester is devoted to preparing lessons for the children, and sessions on campus during and after Summerfest are spent studying video-tapes of the lessons. Graduate students in science education and teaching assistants who have taken the course in previous years participate in the preparation and analysis of lessons. Thus the group of teachers involved in Summerfest consists of individuals with varying experience and expertise in the teaching of science.

Our work in Summerfest has led to a number of insights about learning to teach. In the main, we have developed a perspective on 'learning to teach at the elbows' as a form of apprenticeship (MacKinnon, in press). The metaphor of learning at the elbows focuses on aspects of practice — technique, manner, gesture, disposition — that are shared through work together, and which mediate the process of learning to teach. Our theoretical focus has been on a kind of 'embodied knowing' that could be characterized as tacit, unformulated, or even impossible to grasp (Polanyi, 1958; Ryle, 1949; Schön, 1983; Taylor, 1991). We assert that the practice of teaching is influenced by this type of knowledge and understanding, often acquired unwittingly by novices at the elbows of their sponsor teachers. Thus we are interested in socio-cultural elements of 'situated learning' (Lave and Wenger, 1991) that are frequently either missing in accounts of learning to teach or viewed pejoratively as a form of socialization akin to indoctrination.

Learning at the Elbows

We believe the metaphor of learning at the elbows helps to explain the development of 'teaching manner' (Fenstermacher, 1992) in a way that might extend more rational, mechanistic representations of learning in the professions. We claim that teaching manner can be observed 'rubbing off at the elbows' in studio work as though, in some of their actions, participants were chameleons of one another. In our interactions with students of education, teachers, and graduate students, we are compelled to use words such as 'manner' to describe elements of teaching behaviour that are sometimes passed from one teacher to another. Although Schön (1983, 1987) did attempt to deal with what he referred to as the 'non-logical processes' taking place in reflection-in-action and reflection-on-action, we see his ideas about learning in the professions as having paved the way to a deeper, contemporary discussion of socially embodied forms and communities of knowing that have great influence on learning practices.

In our view, the daily conduct of teachers is shaped by the communities of practice in which they have participated. While we agree with Schön's ideas about imitation being a highly constructive process, and with Aristotle when he writes of 'mimesis' as being foundational to learning in practical and productive human activities, we submit there is more to be said about the influence of work at the elbows on practices and identities that people appropriate through work together. There are occasions when seasoned teachers are able to 'see themselves' in the manner of their apprentices, when elements of style and character are passed on to novice practitioners. But to describe learning at the elbows in this fashion goes only part way; patterns of action form 'texts' that are not only 'written' and 'read', but which also function in 'writing' the co-workers. What may seem at first to be a simple gesture mimicked by a student may be the sign of a much larger development in *the way that person comes to see and hold himself or herself in practice*. Studio masters also acquire behaviors and traits of character found in others — sometimes students — who make an impression on them. There are also times when groups of students show in their practice how they have influenced one another's manner of working (MacKinnon and Grunau, 1994).

Although we believe the metaphor of learning at the elbows helps to draw out important empirical claims about learning to teach, it does not provide a complete framework for the improvement of teaching. Teacher education also requires the engagement of novice teachers in a wide variety of literature and study in the so-called foundations of education. Moreover, questions remain about the need to correct mistakes made in a teaching studio, or to inject theory at appropriate moments to enrich practice. In an attempt to understand these issues, MacKinnon (in press) draws on eastern philosophy to represent the dialogical relationship between apprenticeship and critical dialogue in learning to teach. He describes the analysis sessions of Summerfest in terms of the multifaceted task of:

1 establishing an evidential base for discussing scientific ideas with children;
2 determining how they regard such evidence, what they know already and

are able to reason independently, and how they use new experiences and information; and

3   investigating how the university students and instructors explore both their own reasoning and that of the children.

MacKinnon argues that the historical relationship between Confucianism and Taoism helps to gain a more holistic perspective on learning to teach through forming and 'retreating from' routines in teaching behavior, largely through ongoing, critical dialogue.

In this chapter we describe and illustrate the kind of critical dialogue about Summerfest that has engaged us over the past few years. We claim that much of our developing understanding of learning to teach is formed through our conversations. In an attempt to flesh out this notion, we draw from a conversation that took place immediately after the final class in the Summer of 1996, which we tape-recorded for the purpose of writing this chapter. We hope it will be instructive in terms of both the substance of our talk about learning to teach (*vis-à-vis* the experiences of our teacher education students in Summerfest) and the kind of perspectives and commitments each of us brings to our conversation. Our main goal is to portray the importance of a continuing dialogue in developing understandings of learning to teach. There are numerous occasions when our talk raises perplexing difficulties related to the Summerfest experiences. Although it is sometimes difficult to hear the critique of a good friend, the three voices in the following excerpts work together in moving toward understanding our experiences of learning to teach and teaching to learn.

Context

It will be helpful to provide some context surrounding the voices heard in the following conversation. Allan is the professor of the course. Michael is a graduate student of Allan's and has been the teaching assistant in Summerfest for the past four years. Kathryn is also a graduate student in education at SFU and, as Michael's partner, has been an interested bystander and participant in the debriefing conversations about Summerfest through the duration of Allan and Michael's teaching partnership. Our conversations about Summerfest are intense and ongoing. They reflect the often perplexing and rich challenges that arise in our informal, yet serious, inquiry into the meaning of our lives as educators. We do not usually tape our conversations, and we are somewhat at odds with presenting one of them here in a form which tends to flatten and fix the meaning of our inquiry. This is because we view our conversations, perspectives and understandings of learning to teach as being *in motion*. The vitality of our talk comes as much from the friction among our perspectives as it does from the negotiated consensus we sometimes experience.

The flow of ideas in the following conversation is accessible to readers without much interruption and elaboration by the authors. We do, however, wish to make certain analytic comments at intervals throughout the excerpt about the substance and character of the dialogue. To set the stage, we begin at a point in our talk where Allan is expressing concern about a group of three teacher education students' understanding and representation of science principles underlying their unit of study about 'storms'. Having observed their teaching at Summerfest and their accompanying unit plan assignment, his voice is one of frustration over what he sees as a lack of effort and research on the part of the students to design teaching approaches that would assist children in developing an understanding of storms. Michael's voice is typically one which is more empathic to the experience of *being a student*, in terms both of the children who participate in Summerfest and of the teacher education students. Further, Michael interprets the events of Summerfest through the lens of his growing philosophical appreciation of experience-based learning. Kathryn's voice is one which provides critical commentary of social reproduction in educational institutions. While she is more distant from the events of Summerfest in the sense that she has not experienced face-to-face interactions with participants, she has paid careful attention to various themes which emerged in conversation throughout the term. Her point of view often interrupts the shared beliefs of Allan and Michael, but usually leads to a broader, more critical awareness of the matter of learning to teach.

Discussion

Allan   I have questions about their understanding of storms. Yeah, they don't really involve questioning the causes of these phenomena . . . rather, they emulate them.

Kathryn   Well, in a sense what they've gone for is representations rather than actual like . . . the water is supposed to represent air and . . .

Allan   Right . . . So here is the big idea. This is a lesson titled 'Thunder and Tracking Storms'. The big idea for the lesson is [reading]: 'Lightning causes air to heat up and explode. The explosion is heard after the lightning strikes and is called thunder. The time delay between lightning and thunder is used to track the movement of the storm.' Okay. Lightning causes air to heat up and explode. Like where would that sound come from?

Michael   Well it's something probably that they might have read.

Kathryn   Do you think they got hold of a bad book . . . a bad kid's science book?

Allan   In a sense they are right because there is a huge . . .

Michael   . . . there is expansion . . . and so perhaps they didn't understand that part and they sort of filled in by themselves . . . you know. I know I read like that.

Allan   But for me it's almost the way the two sentences work together. 'Lightning causes the air to heat up and explode. The explosion is heard after the lightning strikes and it is called thunder.'

Kathryn	. . . Um hmm.
Allan	I wonder if they think the air takes a while to heat up and explode.
Kathryn	Yeah . . . There is a causality there. Is it the causality of the language that worries you?
Allan	Well, what bothers me . . . for some reason I think they don't really get it and they didn't really research it carefully.
Kathryn	You may be right. But is it in the language? Is it because they have simplified the language?
Allan	No, it's because they have reduced the lesson to the following . . .
Kathryn	Okay.
Allan	[reading] 'Teaching Approach: The equipment you need is a 30 centimetre by 40 centimetre sheet of paper and cookie sheets. The students will work in pairs and individually and relate the thunder sound with cookie sheets and paper folding. They will observe whether the distance between the observer and the source affects the sound and apply these results to our discussion about tracking storms.'
Michael	Oh man, oh man!
Allan	Okay that's it . . . then . . . 'Learning Outcomes', Okay? 'Students are expected to identify factors responsible for thunder.'
Michael	Sorry, can you read that again?
Allan	'Students are expected to identify factors responsible for thunder.' [continuing] 'To know how to track a thunder storm.'
Michael	Um hmm.
Allan	'And to describe the key features of thunder.'
Kathryn	Oh, that's bizarre.
Allan	And that's not the only time that happens in this unit. Then there's the assessment . . . 'Students will be able to describe the sequence of thunder and lightning.'
Kathryn	Isn't that strange. It's almost like magic . . . it's like a . . . kind of . . . almost animated . . .
Allan	[reading] 'Students will be able to use the sequence of events to explain how to track a storm.'
Kathryn	Gosh . . .
Allan	The thing about these statements is that they read like objectives or learning outcomes. There could be a lot more discussion about the kinds of strategies you would use to help students understand thunder, lightning and storms. I could pick another example if you'd like . . .
Michael	So that's one person. But *three* people are working on that unit.
Allan	[reading] 'Eye of the hurricane' — another lesson. Grade level 5, big idea: 'The hurricane is a vortex' . . . now before this

they have done bottles . . . 'it is circular in shape with winds flowing around its centre. There is no wind in the vortex as dry air sinks from the high pressure region.' We could go to the tornado lesson and find this bottle and this swirl of water, and they then say — 'Oh see, that's called a vortex.' Well, as a result of that, the kids are then able to say, 'Oh well, we can use this word "vortex", if they didn't know it already to describe the shape of a tornado funnel. But they have no idea *why* . . .

Michael   Yeah and they don't even . . .

Allan   . . . or why a tornado funnel occurs — they are not given that chance.

Kathryn   It's kind of like they've taken a consumer-based approach . . . like my sense is . . . they've gone to Science World (a science museum) or, you know, they have gone to Science and Nature Company (a science store), or whatever, and they have taken a consumer view of these representations. And from an adult perspective where you make these metaphorical leaps into . . . well it's like . . . they haven't done their research and they have a *kind* of a lesson . . . but they have a real lack of appreciation for children's thinking.

Allan   Yeah. Well that's my attitude [toward the unit].

Kathryn   But they also have a simplified notion . . . you know, on one hand, a simplified or a lack of appreciation for children's sophistication and, on the other hand, a very simple metaphorical, huh . . . script.

Michael   But there aren't even any links there and, uh . . .

Kathryn   No links . . .

Allan   Okay, here's another one. So this is a lesson on a hurricane as a vortex. Um, and they say [reading]: 'The Equipment: The students in pairs, each with two litre plastic bottles, duct tape, food coloring, water, scissors, mixer, modelling clay and a balloon. Attach modelling clay to one end of a piece of string. Remove the bottom of one of the bottles and secure the bottles together at the necks with balloon and tape. Place the string . . .' So this is just the instructions of how to join these two bottles. '. . . Plug the plug and then try to suspend weight in the eye of the vortex. Fill the bottle with coloured water and give it a circular stir to start the spinning motion. Pull the plug and then try to suspend the weight in the eye of the vortex.'

Okay, then they have a second experiment [reading]: 'Movement of the air inside the hurricane: Full class experiment using a large round tub or basin, water and ping-pong ball.' And they say, 'Fill the basin half full with water. With your hand begin to swirl the water around in a counter-clockwise

	direction. Remove your arm when the water is turning evenly. Pour a glass full of water into the eye of the hurricane . . .'
Kathryn	Hmmm.
Allan	'. . . and observe. Place a ping-pong ball in the eye of the hurricane and observe.'
Michael	So, pour a glass of water in and observe . . .
Allan	Yeah. Okay, you go like this [demonstrating motion of teacher]. Right, Okay. Just imagine this . . . you pour a glass of water in . . . and observe . . . and then . . . you're supposed to put a ping-pong ball in . . . and *it's going stay there?* [reading] 'Students will be able to investigate the inside of the vortex of a hurricane and infer why the eye of a hurricane is calm. Assessment questions: What just happened? What can you observe about the way in which the water is moving? Where is the water moving the fastest? slowest?'
Michael	So she's talking about, um . . . I am imagining Al, that water is moving around, I am thinking of eddies. I've done enough, been on enough streams, walked up and down enough streams, and you can have eddies, and then there's . . . at the very centre . . . there's like a dead calm . . . not a dead calm, but like I imagine it's less and less . . . it's like the centre of a record, right?
Allan	Yeah.
Michael	. . . and it's never . . . you see like, the size of that vortex depends on the size of the pan, and all that kind of stuff, right? And I guess what they are talking about is that, out there, it is moving faster than it is moving in here, and that is moving faster than this . . . so I guess you could sort of intuit . . . and eventually you get to a point where it's . . . I am not sure they go far enough with the argument.
Allan	Well I think that is really interesting and I think it is really useful, but, for me, the unit is not complete without an explanation of why air masses move in the way they do to create hurricanes. And, for me, you can't understand that until you really think about the spin of the earth.
Michael	Uh huh . . . And how cold air moves, and how warm air rises . . .
Allan	And how temperatures affect . . .
Michael	. . . yeah, affects condensation . . . holding water . . .
Michael	So you don't see the connection between the water and the hurricane, the eye of a hurricane?
Kathryn	I think that there needs to be some, uh . . . I think that it would give a child a very distorted notion of, um, movement of air. If I say it is a metaphorical representation, it's very incomplete, and uh, but I know that it's very visual, and it's a very available hands-on activity. But it contributes to a mythical understanding of matter.

Allan   Well I think it's . . . interestingly complex, and I think that . . .

Kathryn   But by simplifying it to this . . .

Allan   . . . but by simplifying it to this they are . . . missing part of the point. Now, I can appreciate what they are trying . . . and Michael certainly has a richer appreciation of this than I do. I can see what they are trying to do. But, for me, there is more to be said. But then, you see, it's interesting because I can think about what they are doing with children and it is sort of like, in part . . . 'Guess what is in the teacher's head.' And, in part, they are not really teaching . . . the concepts I'm really interested in. But, you see, nor am I teaching them . . . unless I do it here in my comments . . . but it is almost too late . . .

Kathryn   . . . teaching them the science, or teaching them how to . . .

Allan   . . . well inviting them to think a little more deeply . . .

Kathryn   . . . to think more deeply . . .

Allan   So when they made their presentation . . . they showed their video tonight and Michael was talking about me setting a tone, but really I was interrupting them because I was interested in what they understood about storms.

Kathryn   Um hmm. But you were alerted to the fact that there was like a lack of understanding.

Allan   Well, in their written work. Their presentation was a little better.

Kathryn   If . . .

Allan   But their written is really poor.

Kathryn   What about . . . now I don't have the language for this, uh . . . in your framework . . . but I would say *understanding where their knowledge base is* . . . like where they are coming from is important. And also . . . in a sense . . . I guess you could call it their objective but I guess it is their motive. Like to say . . . 'Why would you choose this?' 'What is it about this that excites you or interests you?' And, 'What is it that you know or don't know that would invite you to learn more, in order to teach it as a unit to children?' Like, I'm thinking that it has commodity value because of *'Twister'* [recent blockbuster motion picture] because of the . . . the availability of the materials. It's a fairly simple one to muster up. And if you didn't have a background in weather, or geography concepts, or climatology . . . that it would appear to be available material for the unit. So it is more like a performance in a sense than a representation of their knowledge.

Michael   But you know . . . they are *coming* to science . . . they are *coming to something* . . . to a subject . . . to a course to want to study science. Um, who knows why they went to weather. I mean maybe it was the activity, maybe the bottle of the activity, maybe it was something they read about the tornado activity

... it's interesting ... it would be interesting to know how they came to create the unit, but they are actually doing the best that they can ... they are not ...

Kathryn That is why I am saying ... that's why we don't know their background. Like here I am ... English, you know English major with an arts background and almost no science in my entire education. So how would I approach it? Earlier in our conversation you mentioned the Kinetic Molecular Theory.

Allan Yeah, because that would be ... that would be one of the theories that would allow you to understand storms. And also, there was no discussion of the effects of wind currents created by the spin of the earth.

Kathryn Yes, but, for you, these are very anchoring and important, conceptually.

Allan Well, they are concepts that are useful time and time again to think about events in science and to get down to a point where you can actually understand what occurs. You know, you, um ... you do need to think about these events ... and so here is a wonderful opportunity to do that, *but they missed it*.

Kathryn Yeah, but did they *know* that they missed it?

Michael Where else, where would you find that? I mean is it available ... the Kinetic Molecular Theory? I mean if you went through ten books would you be assured that you would find it? Now, they are looking at kid's books ...

Allan Well if you turn to 'weather' in any elementary science book you would find that. I mean ... Now, true ... I come out of this tradition and that is just commonplace for me, and it's not commonplace for everybody, and I admit that. But, see this assignment ... I can ... I can watch them work, and I spoke with Doug who video-taped them and, you know ... he and I talked about it. And so I was able to form some understanding ... I saw it take place and I saw the kids react — you know, engage or not engage in the activities ... you know, and, by that time, I am getting to know those kids too.

Michael Yeah, it seemed more like art activities ...

Allan But not only that ... I can take a look at what they have done here ... and then I've got seventeen, eighteen other units that I can compare it with. And I can see that some groups worked well together and other groups didn't, and, in other groups that didn't work well, certain individuals worked beautifully, and others ... you know, I can tell all that stuff ...

Michael But why would three people have, conceptually, almost the same sort of lack of connection? Why would three people have that? That's really odd ... that's really odd.

Kathryn Because, I guess ...

Michael	. . . they shared . . .
Allan	. . . and I am writing to the group [reading from remarks to group]: 'This activity is good for learning the name and shape of the funnel of the tornado, but in what sense does it help to understand how a tornado is formed. The cookie sheet activity has a similar quality, leaving me somewhat at odds about how the activity contributes to the understanding of storms.'
Michael	Uh huh.
Allan	And then . . . another comment for another activity. But you almost can read this like the other [reading]: 'Again the activity is an emulation of a hurricane . . . and a worthy one on those grounds, for it is interesting, after all, to notice the calm of the eye. In this sense the activity is really good, but it doesn't contribute to the understanding of how hurricanes are formed, how they are different from tornadoes, why air masses move in the atmosphere the way they do, and so on. That may be in your mind but it is not apparent to me.'
Kathryn	Yeah, and it is not expressed in the curriculum. It is not expressed in the conceptual . . .
Allan	And so that is the end of the specific comments, and this is my summary [reading]: 'I like the unit very much, but find that it focuses more on description and emulation than it does on developing understanding. The activities are interesting, for sure, but they could be more *sciencey*, if you know what I mean. An approach based on the latter intention would focus on heated air expansion, how it moves about as a mass, is influenced by the rotation of the earth . . . things like that. Not to worry too much about this, but I did want to point it out.' And then in parentheses . . . 'I actually did get a better idea, feel for your ideas during your presentation.' . . . which was tonight . . . 'The teaching approach, as I have pointed out, is somewhat perfunctory for me and I have indicated where I am curious how you will assist children in meeting the learning goals. The activities are good and I hope I can convince you to think about more investigative work in teaching approaches for the kids. The grade for the assignment is B.'
Kathryn	But you know part of it is group chemistry, but obviously they did not do their work. And I think that is something that we have been talking about in some sense — the going through the motions of the student teacher experience of . . . you know as if . . . simulating as if . . . you know you can manage the room and get people to meet your objectives. But there is not the . . . there is not enough attention sometimes placed on the integrity of the educative experience. And that is what you are picking up on. But what I'm picking up on in a sense

that has to do with, you know, receptivity, perception of your audience . . .

Michael But also just exposure to the whole idea of thinking about teaching that way.

Kathryn But I don't think that people learn to have that . . . I think that in fact that, if they start off like this, they are not going to develop a deeper appreciation of children's learning. I don't know.

Michael I don't agree at all. No.

Kathryn I think that they would . . . you know . . . tend to . . . take a more managerial approach . . . what they [children] look like, and are they having a good time — if they look like they are engaged . . . that's good enough . . .

Michael But I'm thinking, though, you know about the . . . talking about the whole idea of knowledge transfer. How *do* we teach? And how *do* children learn? And how can we . . . um, how can they develop an understanding of the eye of the storm, you know . . . or that whirling mass? To understand . . . I mean it's too ludicrous to think that [referring to the bottle demonstration] . . .

Kathryn But then you have to actually back it up . . .

Michael And then you actually have to back it up . . . absolutely. Yeah that's right.

Kathryn And then in a sense make very sure that, although the eye of the hurricane is *like* the middle of swirling water, it is *not* that. Air and water . . .

Michael Yeah, two different things . . .

Kathryn Dealing with, you know, dealing with different manifestations of matter . . . and that you just haven't, because you can't see air, that you are doing this just as a representation. And that you know, the notion of electricity and static, like you know, lightning is not . . . like, does lightning heat up the air and boom, it creates thunder? Is that really true? Is that really what happens? And . . . did anyone get into the folk . . . the folk understanding that you count seconds between the lightning and thunder?

Michael No . . . it hasn't been thought through. But what I find interesting about it is that . . . when you talk about constructivism . . . there is this idea that we hang onto our early beliefs . . . that we have these . . . unfortunate word . . . *native* notions . . . or early understandings and beliefs that we sort of hang on to. I can relate to that . . . we have these ideas that we remember as children having learned something . . . you create an understanding for yourself that works. Somehow, your conception works. And then you try that out in the world and it works and then you come to a science program where you are asked to write and think about that. You know . . . you are bringing that notion . . . And somehow, even though you are reading other stuff, that old notion is still alive.

Kathryn I know, but what they have done is they have reinforced that . . .

Michael Of course, of course they have reinforced that because they know only *that* as the truth, you see . . . That is what is so fascinating . . . that they are actually passing that on . . . yeah right on. They are passing that on as teachers. But it is based on a lack of real investigation of their own. But they are coming to a course on science to look at that, themselves. You keep on . . . you keep your old ideas . . . you just imprint everything, your old idea on to the words . . . and that's why it's so difficult to come to the subject as a graduate student because you are continually coming to this place of non-understanding because of the way you interpret the world. The way you *see*, the way you have come to visualize things is often broken down.

The Nature of Learning to Teach

Michael delineates the contradictions of being a student in two distinct communities of practice — one as a student teacher, the other as a graduate student. In the former community there is more pressure to appear competent and knowledgeable in all contexts. In the latter, one is continually examining one's assumptions and beliefs. Although student teachers are frequently encouraged to be reflective about their practice in 'journals', simultaneously they are expected to perform in classrooms where it would be devastating to suspend one's judgment over subject-matter or a decision that requires immediate action. This leads to a crucial dilemma about the nature of learning to teach.

Although it is not fully elaborated upon in this particular conversation, one of the troubling themes for Allan throughout the semester was the teacher education students' apparent resistance to critical talk and inquiry about the nature of children's learning at Summerfest. According to him, the teacher education students' concerns had more to do with gathering a repertoire of activities and a 'bag of tricks' for science teaching. This feeling was especially troubling, given Allan's emphasis on modelling a critical analysis of teaching in his own handling of the children at Summerfest, and in his debriefing sessions with Kathryn and Michael. Of course, it is interesting and perplexing in itself that teacher education students have no access to the ongoing dialogues that sustained both Michael and Allan throughout the semester.

Kathryn's concern is with the 'hidden curriculum' of teacher education that forecloses on students' deeper investigations and understandings of content areas and children's learning. She is well aware of the need for the appropriate conceptual tools required for accomplished teaching, but acutely aware of the lack of conditions and occasions for genuine and critical engagement in teacher education programs. In particular, Kathryn conceptualizes this dilemma as the institutional mediation of student teachers' identity as knowers, given that the focus on teaching competency, classroom management and mastery of content leaves little room for ambiguity and exploration. This theme is brought out in the remaining excerpts of the conversation, as the discussion turns to the issue of grading and assessing students taking the Summerfest course.

Kathryn   The thing that is interesting is this notion of good conceptual models to work side by side with both a scientific concept and a metaphor for the activity. And that is kind of what you are asking your students to do. And that is the pedagogical challenge . . . to take that and package it in a way that is both . . . um . . . has complexity and simplicity in it. I mean, you know, that can contain the facts but be an appropriate model to facilitate learning or understanding. I think that it comes down to one's notion of appreciation for the child. I guess from my ever-cynical perspective about how people think of children, I feel that they've often got a childish notion of what children are, they have an almost simulated notion of children's understanding, and so they have misread their audience, they have misread, um, you know, kids' savvy. You know, I am thinking back to my own brother . . . you know . . . when he was six or seven years old, as soon as he was able to read he was reading about protozoa, planets, dinosaurs, minerals . . . and all those kinds of things. And children have this great philosophical capacity; they think very deeply about things. And yet they are so cooperative that they will go for shallow understanding to cooperate with what's going on in the room, right?

Michael   Yes, that's right.

Kathryn   That's why they will foreclose on their intuitive wisdom, in order to accommodate the structure in the room.

Allan   Sometimes they won't tolerate it.

Kathryn   Yeah.

Allan   And, we certainly had kids at Summerfest who gave me that impression . . . that they didn't tolerate any silly work.

Kathryn   But, you see, they're science camp kids, so they've got an identity that is already formed, you know, that they are good at this . . . or it's okay for them. I am thinking of the time I was a kid in elementary school. I don't know if you had this experience, but there was this whole series of films on science concepts . . . things like weather. They were really entertaining and fascinating films. And I remember sitting in a gym with, you know, three hundred or something kids all day watching four of these things in row. I still remember the stuff explaining the, um, the water cycle, and another one on photosynthesis [laughs]. The weird thing was that they had added animation and Greek representations of what we used to think . . . 'and now we think this . . .'

Allan   Right, uh-huh.

Kathryn   And I remember it was full of jokes and it was of very high entertainment value. And I still carry these bizarre images of what I think the cycle of water is, and what I think photosynthesis is. They're still with me to this very day.

Michael   And in that cartoon form?

Kathryn   In that cartoon form, right.

Michael   And to some degree it works for you, right? I mean that gets reinforced?

Kathryn   Yeah. I mean . . . I guess you could say that is the constructivist thing. That seems really interesting to me. Why do people choose their units? It's like you have got to have a hook in . . . you know, some kind of passion or reason for choosing something. So someone who says, 'Oh yeah, we'll do storms, you know', or 'We'll do dinosaurs . . .' You know, without having some real passion . . .

Allan   Well, it could be something like that with those two bottles (water vortex demonstration). A person could have seen it at Science World or any number of places . . . those two bottles. And you think, 'Oh, that's science.'

Kathryn   Yep.

Allan   'Oh well . . . what can I do with that? Gee . . . well, you know, I could study storms . . .'

Michael   Yeah.

Kathryn   But you see, that is the difference between going from a *real* interest in the phenomena . . . or going from a viable activity, and *scavenging* activities.

Allan   This whole idea . . . that um, we are grading. I sometimes think that is where it comes from. In a way it is a manufactured thing. I just want to have meaningful pedagogical relationships with my students. But we put ourselves into this position where we, you know . . .

Michael   There has to be the assessment and the products.

Kathryn   But the culture of this student teacher experience may not lead to meaningful pedagogical relationships if they are concerned about lesson plans. They can manufacture a facsimile of that. And thus, in some sense, appease your demands, and yet not know how to . . .

Michael   You know . . . what is interesting, um, we are talking about this unit on thunder and hurricanes and . . . I don't know, I still

	think it is only one or maybe two of them . . . the odd thing is that there could be three teachers who would think like that, or who would teach like that . . . it's pretty ludicrous.
Allan	Yeah . . . well I think it is quite intriguing.
Allan	I think what I am trying to do kind of backfired. I am trying to be more constructive.
Kathryn	But constructiveness has to come from a position of critique.
Allan	Being constructive and critique go hand-in-hand. But when I say it has backfired, I mean that it's really damaged people in unanticipated ways. Ways that I would have never imagined that hurt people deeply, you know, taking it personally, taking it, in a very vulnerable state.
Kathryn	How do you get around that, it just . . .
Allan	Right. Not grading, but establishing . . .
Kathryn	. . . like, a rapport — a trusting rapport . . .
Allan	Yeah, well, it's such a sensitive topic, that any shortcomings I think I experience in my relations with students usually re-volve around . . .
Kathryn	. . . grades?
Allan	A lot of stress about grades and assignments. We keep them busy . . . we definitely keep them busy with make-work projects.

Conclusion

For the time being, this last utterance rests as our substantive conclusion about the nature of learning to teach. We would like to re-emphasize the importance we place on our continuing critical dialogue in negotiating understandings about learning to teach. If the conversation above concluded here, we might begin to see the whole Summerfest experience as contributing to the maelstrom of teacher education. The events of Summerfest and our conversations over the entire semester, however, build on those of Summers past and anticipate those of Summers-to-come, mutually resonating and informing each other in a way that we believe leads to better and more just practice as teacher educators. Although partial and ephemeral, this crit-ical dialogue and negotiation is what sustains professional and intellectual growth.

The metaphor *learning to teach at the elbows* puts forward claims about learning to teach that focus on the development of 'teaching manner'. Our particu-lar interest here is in characterizing and understanding aspects of teaching that seem to be acquired, shared, mediated, and changed through teachers' work together — a shaping that we believe occurs initially through a kind of mimicry in the practice setting and in many cases appears to take place independent of rational delibera-tion. If so, *how do we understand this kind of learning?* How do we then represent our work and knowledge as teacher educators? How do we understand the vulner-ability of our students and the necessity of their developing critical perspectives in their practice? These questions are raised in a way that underscores the fragile interplay between learning as socio-culturally-mediated activity and critical dialogue, both in the initial preparation of teachers and in our own growth as teacher educators. This rendering of teacher educators' knowledge may differ from the usual representations found in research literature, but we remain committed to the notion that our knowledge and understanding resides *in formation* in such critical conversations as that presented and discussed in this chapter.

References

FENSTERMACHER, G.D. (1992) 'The concepts of method and manner in teaching,' in OSER, F.K., DICK, A. and PATRY, J.-L. (Eds) *Effective and Responsible Teaching: The New Synthesis* (Ch. 7), San Francisco, Jossey-Bass.

LAVE, J. and WENGER, E. (1991) *Situated Learning: Legitimate Peripheral Participation*, Cambridge, Cambridge University Press.

MACKINNON, A.M. (in press) 'Learning to teach at the elbows: The Tao of teaching', *Teaching and Teacher Education*, **13**, 1.

MACKINNON, A.M. and GRUNAU, H. (1994) 'Teacher development through reflection, community, and discourse', in GRIMMETT, P.P. and NEUFELD, J. (Eds) *The Struggle for Authenticity: Teacher Development in a Changing Educational Context*, New York, Teachers College Press, pp. 165–92.

POLANYI, M. (1958) *Personal Knowledge: Towards a Post-critical Philosophy*, Chicago, The University of Chicago Press.

RYLE, G. (1949) *The Concept of Mind*, London, Hutchinson and Co.

SCHÖN, D. (1983) *The Reflective Practitioner: How Professionals Think-in-action*, New York, Basic Books.

SCHÖN, D.A. (1987) *Educating the Reflective Practitioner: Toward a New Design for Teaching and Learning in the Professions*, San Francisco, Jossey-Bass.

TAYLOR, C. (1991) 'The dialogical self', in HILEY, D.R., BOHMAN, J.F. and SHUSTERMAN, R. (Eds) *The Interpretive Turn: Philosophy, Science, Culture*, Ithaca, Cornell University Press, pp. 304–14.

TREMMEL, R. (1993) 'Zen and the art of reflective practice in teacher education', *Harvard Educational Review*, **63**, 4, pp. 434–58.

Section 5

Conclusion

14   Becoming Passionate about Teacher Education

Tom Russell

This concluding chapter of *Teaching about Teaching: Purpose, Passion and Pedagogy* is intended for those who turn first to a book's conclusion as well as for those who have already examined the preceding chapters. By volunteering to prepare the introductory chapter, my co-editor has given me the unique opportunity and challenge of looking back and consolidating. When John and I approached the contributors nine months ago, as John was completing his term as a visitor at Queen's University, we recognized this collection as more than a chance to express our shared passion for the importance of pedagogy in teacher education. This volume would also be a way to gather together a special community of teacher educators who have become treasured professional colleagues. That they share our passion for purpose and pedagogy is apparent in their responses to our invitation; these chapters were produced in less than six months. One further statement serves to express my personal assessment of the quality and significance of these contributions: Although my retirement is still a decade away, I would be more than content if this were my last professional publication. This collection issues an important and, we hope, compelling invitation to teacher educators to enhance their contributions to future generations of teachers and students by joining us in becoming passionate about teacher education.

'Passion' is not a term readily associated with either teacher education or the academic enterprise more generally, but we see it as an essential way of signalling the work that lies before us. Teacher educators have developed and embraced many important new ideas in the last two decades, yet new ideas are easily lost, diluted, and marginalized when the overall framework of a teacher education program is not modified to support them. This collection displays and celebrates the vitality of teacher educators who see and accept the inherent challenges, contradictions and dilemmas of teacher education, and who are working to ensure that significant changes at the course level and personal level are extended into significant program-level changes that permeate a teacher education community. We have come to see 'passion' as a term that should take its place beside terms such as 'relevance' and 'rigour' as we continue to improve the discipline of teacher education.

Pre-service teacher education programs face many dilemmas, and one central dilemma involves the tension between preparing new teachers to succeed in schools as they are and preparing new teachers to be welcome and support the changes that are on the horizon. With the best of intentions, teacher education programs run the risks of asking new teachers to do some or all of the following:

- to 'run before they walk';
- to transform the teaching–learning relationship, even though schools and universities have been unable to make that transformation;
- to rethink the content they teach as they also rethink the manner in which they teach;
- to understand the difference between collecting others' teaching resources and learning to prepare one's own;
- to reflect on teaching before they take charge of a classroom; and
- to write before they have anything to write about.

The contributors to this collection share a number of strategies for minimizing these potentially frustrating elements of pre-service programs. They understand that actions speak louder than words, and so they focus on the pedagogy they use in their own classrooms. They understand that learning is a personal experience and so they share their own learning with those they help to learn to teach. They understand that reflection is inseparable from experience, and so they attend to how people learn by doing. They understand that successful teaching depends on a community of professionals in a school and so they foster learning communities within their own classrooms.

After considering several approaches to preparing a closing chapter for this collection, I settled on letting the authors speak for themselves. As I reviewed each chapter to appreciate again its passion for pedagogy in teacher education, I searched for a quotation that expressed a central theme. Others will certainly select different quotations as their personal favourite, but the ones assembled here serve to remind the reader of the journey just completed or, for those about to begin, to signal the journey that lies ahead.

The chapters by Cynthia Nicol and Peter Chin show the remarkable intensity and passion of the teacher educator in the early stages of work in this field, and they provide rare access to the thought processes and sustaining rationales of individuals committed to extracting sound principles from personal experience and then enacting them in their pre-service classrooms.

1 Cynthia Nicol

Listening for what we expect might happen provides us with a framework through which to interpret events. As a teacher with desired goals and intentions I listen for the various mathematical concepts and ideas that my students are required to know and understand. But at the same time I want to listen to and attend to students' experience. A focus only on listening *for* makes it difficult to listen *to* students' experiences, to focus on the meaning of the experience from the students' perspective, and to act upon events that are unanticipated. Listening *for* affects what the teacher finds as valuable information, while a focus on only listening *to* may make it difficult to interpret students' experiences. Listening *to* means shedding preconceived agendas, being responsive and attending to what students say and do. Listening *for* involves listening for worthwhile subject-matter content within educational goals and intentions. The challenge remains for me as I struggle to remain suspended and attentive on a fine balance between accomplishing my own teaching goals and experiencing teaching from prospective teachers' eyes.

2 Peter Chin

As I reflect upon the core beliefs that I have about what it is that I stand for as a teacher educator, it becomes abundantly clear that I advocate the importance of articulating, critiquing, and understanding one's beliefs about teaching and learning. These beliefs serve as the foundation that informs one's practice as he or she designs curriculum for students. Finally, the importance of establishing frameworks for understanding so that one can monitor the effectiveness of one's teaching leads to an iterative process of professional development and the improvement of one's teaching. These same core beliefs that I have about my role as a teacher educator have been mirrored in this chapter — as I have applied these beliefs to my own role as a learner.

The chapters by Vicki LaBoskey and Anna Richert reveal the achievements that become possible in a small, intense community such as Mills College, where a unique program of pre-service teacher education has developed in the last decade.

3 Vicki LaBoskey

I design my program and my practice to be relentless in the modelling of, and requirement for, purpose and passion in teaching. I try to have all of my assignments and all of my activities provide opportunities for everyone, including me, to examine, from a variety of perspectives, our beliefs, attitudes, reasons, intentions, emotional reactions, and intellectual processing. We learn together how to appreciate the complexity and live with the uncertainty as we construct and reconstruct our belief systems.

4 Anna Richert

Perhaps the longest persistent challenge of teacher education is how to teach theory and practice together in ways that promote the use of theory to illuminate practice, and the use of practice to challenge and extend theory. These coupled practices are the mainstay of reflective teaching, and therefore, the basis of inquiry-based teacher education as I have been describing it in this chapter. Existing theory helps teachers both frame and explore problems by helping them to ask pertinent questions, to know which questions to ask, to examine data that will help them answer their questions, and so forth. In a similar way, everyday practice challenges teachers to examine theory by looking for confirming and disconfirming evidence, and to construct new theory as a result of their reflective work. By definition, teachers who approach their work in this reflective and inquiring way necessarily embrace the uncertainty of the work of teaching because they do not take as *given* but as *problematic* the conditions of school. They see their work as guided by a process of coming to understand more fully what is, in order to determine what needs to be as the work proceeds. Understanding what is in relation to what might be, requires these teachers to examine the purposes of the work of school in the first place. In the process, they necessarily engage the moral questions of their work.

The chapters by Garry Hoban and Tony Clarke focus on aspects of teacher education that are quite unique to the enterprise. Garry illustrates how his own classroom becomes a model for the kinds of attention to 'learning about learning' that he hopes will lead new teachers to see how much potential there is for genuine innovation in the classroom. Tony uses his personal experiences as a student teacher and as a new teacher receiving student teachers into his classroom to illustrate how important it is to develop a coaching role during practicum placements.

5 Garry Hoban

There is, however, another spin off to using this teaching strategy — you are getting a weekly evaluation of not only *what* you are teaching but also *how* you are teaching. This is risky business — you are exposing yourself to criticism from your own students. But how can you expect trainee teachers to take your recommendations about being a reflective teacher seriously when you do not do it yourself. Encouraging your own students to analyze their positive and negative teaching experiences gives you the opportunity to discuss aspects about learning when students are supposed to be doing it. By reading the students' reflective journals I realized that I should be more specific about the purpose of the class and provide a more conducive learning environment. But this teaching method depends on developing a level of trust within the class. You will know that this has been established when pre-service teachers are prepared to discuss their negative as well as their positive learning experiences in your class. Furthermore, many pre-service teachers commented throughout the course that seeking their views about my teaching demonstrated that I valued their opinion and that I was 'practicing what I was preaching'. I think it is important that we, as teacher educators, model procedures to establish a dialogue between teachers and students to engage in discussions about the quality of teaching and learning.

6 Tony Clarke

I believe we need to conceptualize the way we think about the role of practicum advisors. I suggest that the notion of teacher educator is a far more appropriate conceptualization than those currently in use in teacher education. Further, the notion of coaching has much to offer in terms of capturing the level of engagement that we expect of advisors as they work with student teachers. The advisor as coach notion also provides a useful heuristic for explicating the relationship between advisor and student teacher in practicum settings. I have argued that there are certain principles that are common to exemplary coaching practice in site-based educational settings and that these are worthy of consideration in our work with student teachers. Finally, our *modus operandi* as we prepare sites for student teaching practica should be to ensure that advisors are professionally ready, carefully selected, and provided with ongoing support for their work with student teachers. Each of these points is important if the work of practicum advisors is to feature more significantly than is currently the case in our discussion of, and contribution to, pre-service teacher education.

Two chapters in this collection develop and convey their messages in the form of conversations among three contributors. Allan MacKinnon, Michael Cummings and Kathryn Alexander used a face-to-face conversation and my eyes were drawn to the passage about 'meaningful pedagogical relationships'. Karen Guilfoyle, Mary Lynn Hamilton, and Stefinee Pinnegar used electronic mail for their conversation, and my eyes were drawn to their summary.

7   Allan MacKinnon, Michael Cummings and Kathryn Alexander

Allan This whole idea that we are grading: I sometimes think that is where it comes from. In a way it is a manufactured thing. I just want to have meaningful pedagogical relationships with my students. But we put ourselves into this position where we, you know . . .

Michael There has to be the assessment and the products.

Kathryn But the culture of this student teacher experience may not lead to meaningful pedagogical relationships if they are concerned about lesson plans. They can manufacture a facsimile of that. And thus, in some sense, appease your demands, and yet not know how to . . .

8   Karen Guilfoyle, Mary Lynn Hamilton, and Stefinee Pinnegar

The unseen children in the schools ignite our passion for knowledge, our commitment to passion, and our desire to inspire future teachers. We feel a moral obligation to the students of our students. The faces of our students' future students haunt us when we see people we suspect are incompetent in our teacher education programs, when our classroom practices seem to be less than the best practice we know, when we respond to our students in ways that are disrespectful, demeaning, condescending or limiting to our students in any way, or when we require less than the best from our students. While we cannot control all the experiences our students have during their education as teachers, we can control our experiences with them. We aim for our interaction with our students to be exemplary in the kinds of relationships we want them to have with their students. Our understanding of the role of social constructivism and beliefs in the development of teachers and our responses to our own beliefs and those of our students are tools to help us meet the obligations we feel for the students of our students. We remember with tenderness the students we taught before becoming teacher educators. We remember the ways in which both our colleagues and ourselves fell short in preparing our students to develop their complete potential. We take these lessons seriously as we work to teach new generations to teach themselves to be teachers.

Continuing the pattern of grouping excerpts in pairs, I turn to the chapters by Bob Bullough and by Jeff Northfield and Dick Gunstone. These teacher educators have many years of experience, and their contributions to this collection complement those by individuals who are relatively new to the enterprise.

9 Bob Bullough

By necessity and by design, I have become a student of teaching and teacher education. The work has become more interesting and challenging than I ever imagined it could be, especially when I think back to when I was fleeing from it. I am now convinced that the future of teacher education is dependent on the willingness of teacher educators to practice theory and to theorize our practice and to put the results of our efforts before a frequently hostile public. We must make a compelling case that what we do has value.

10 Jeff Northfield and Richard Gunstone

Our personal learning has been long and difficult as in our teacher efforts we tended to overestimate what we were able to tell teachers and underestimate the importance of, and our ability in, providing conditions for teachers to be learners about teaching. Our challenge has been to develop teacher education courses (both preservice and in-service) in ways that reflect this developing insight, that it is teachers who have to be learners, and then appreciate the nature of their knowledge.

Finally, for consistency, I accepted the potentially awkward challenge of selecting passages from the editors' own contributions to the collection.

11 John Loughran

This desire to be able to articulate my understanding about my pedagogy has become increasingly important to me because I want my student-teachers' learning to be more than the absorption of propositions about teaching. If learning about teaching *is* simply the absorption of a teacher educator's pedagogical knowledge, then it seems to me most likely that it will be learnt in a manner that encourages digestion and regurgitation in practicum experiences then, more likely than not, rejected in their own post-university teaching practice when the pervading influence of their being assessed is removed. I want my student-teachers to be engaged in their learning about teaching. I want them to consider their own developing practice and to make informed decisions about their teaching, and I want this to be based on an explicit 'knowing about practice' which they develop through their own active and purposeful learning about teaching.

12 Tom Russell

I have found it useful to think in terms of getting our practices to catch up to what we say and write, and to catch up to what we say we believe about teaching and learning. It is also a matter of learning how to make our beliefs influence our practices, recognizing all the while that the central matter is 'listening to our practices' learning what words mean when we express them in our actions, and learning what ideas do to the people we are teaching. These are major challenges for experienced teachers and teacher educators. Those who are new to teaching may not even see the issue, because they have not had access to the experiences of teaching that are essential to understanding just how easy it is to separate actions from beliefs and goals at the front of a classroom.

These are some of the ways in which we see pedagogy as central to the purpose of teacher education, and passion as central to the manner in which teacher education is conducted. We share our teaching and learning with new teachers as we also develop teaching strategies and program structures that will engage new teachers. Recognizing the power of experience, we attend as fully as possible to the impact of new teachers' experiences in school classrooms, but we also work to make our own university classrooms settings that will extend their learning from experience.

Notes on Contributors

Kathryn Alexander is a doctoral candidate in the Faculty of Education at Simon Fraser University. Her research interests explore the dynamics of documentary texts and identity construction in institutions, and includes critical ethnography and the politics of writing 'up' others.

Robert V. Bullough, Jr. is Professor of Educational Studies, University of Utah, Salt Lake City, Utah. His most recent books include the co-authored volumes, *A Teacher's Journey*, due out shortly with Teachers College Press, *Becoming a Student of Teaching: Methodologies for Exploring Self and School Context* (1995) and, the co-edited volume *Teachers and Mentors* (1996). His research focuses on teacher education and development and curriculum studies.

Peter Chin is an Assistant Professor in the Faculty of Education at Queen's University where he teaches in the area of science teacher education. His research interests centre around the complexities of the practicum setting and the issues of teaching and learning that affect the pre-service teachers and the school associates. From a constructivist perspective he also focuses on metacognition, multicultural/inclusive science, and issues within the philosophy of science.

Anthony Clarke was a secondary school teacher of mathematics, computer science, and physical education, now specializing in the more general area of the professional development of teachers and teacher educators. He is affiliated with the Centre for the Study of Teacher Education at the University of British Columbia. Current research interests focus on reflective practice in teacher education, school/university partnerships, and the work of school and university advisors in the practicum.

Michael Cummings works as a teaching assistant and sessional instructor at Simon Fraser University, where he is completing his Masters Degree in curriculum studies. His thesis focuses on how children and teachers understand science experiences.

Gary D. Fenstermacher is a philosopher of education currently serving as Professor of Educational Foundations at the University of Michigan. He is formerly the Dean of the College of Education at the University of Arizona, and Past President of the American Association of Colleges for Teacher Education. His research interests include normative theories of teacher reasoning, and educational policy analysis.

Karen Guilfoyle is an Associate Professor in Teacher Education at the Univeristy of Idaho. Her field is literacy, language, and culture, and her research focuses on learning and teaching using a critical social-constructivist framework.

Richard Gunstone is the Professor of Science and Technology Education in the School of Graduate Studies, Faculty of Education, Monash University. He has devoted a great deal of time and effort to pre-service teacher education and in collaboration with Jeff Northfield developed and extended the 'Stream 3' science teacher education program at Monash University from the late 1970s through to the early 1990s.

Mary Lynn Hamilton, an Associate Professor in the Department of Curriculum and Instruction at the University of Kansas, studies her own teaching practice and encourages her students to do the same. She is currently the chair-elect of the Self-Study of Teacher Education Practices SIG within the American Educational Research Association. Mary Lynn recently spent time in Australia as visiting Professor for the pre-service teacher education program in the School of Graduate Studies, Faculty of Education, Monash University.

Garry Hoban is a lecturer in Science Education at Charles Sturt University in Bathurst, Australia. His research interests focus on teacher professional development and improving his own practice in teacher education. In both of these areas he is exploring ways to access student data to improve teacher learning.

Vicki Kubler LaBoskey is an Associate Professor of Education at Mills College in Oakland CA and Director of the elementary portion of their Teachers for Tomorrow's Schools Credential Program. Her current areas of interest are in elementary pre-service education with a focus on reflective teaching and teaching as a moral and political act. She is also interested in action research, portfolios, and teacher educator self-study — and also new teacher support (teacher development as a vehicle for school reform).

John Loughran is the Director of Pre-service Education and Professional Development in the School of Graduate Studies, Faculty of Education, Monash University, Australia. John teaches prospective science teachers in the Graduate Diploma in Education and his research interests include reflective practice, teaching and learning and science education. He has written extensively about learning to teach (*Developing Reflective Practice: Learning about Teaching and Learning through Modelling*, Falmer Press, 1996) and is an active member of the S-STEP SIG within the American Educational Research Association.

Allan MacKinnon is an Associate Professor in the Faculty of Education at Simon Fraser University, where he teaches in the area of science education. His interests include the philosophy of science, teacher education, and the use of interactive television and video technologies in science teacher development.

Cynthia Nicol is an experienced teacher, who, after teaching mathematics for seven years in a remote coastal village of northern British Columbia, has moved to Vancouver (BC) to further her study of teaching and learning mathematics. She is currently a doctoral candidate at the University of British Columbia studying her own practice of, and challenges associated with, teaching elementary prospective teachers to teach mathematics for understanding. Her research interests also include the learning of mathematics and learning to teach mathematics.

Jeff Northfield is a Professor of Education and Head of School at the Peninsula Campus, Faculty of Education, Monash University. Jeff has been involved in pre-service teacher education throughout his academic career and recently returned to school teaching for a year in order to genuinely pursue a purposeful way of gaining 'recent and relevant' high school teaching experience. This return to school also gave him a long awaited opportunity to practice what he preaches in teaching and has led to the development of a book from this experience co-authored with John Loughran; *Opening the Classroom Door: Teacher, Learner, Researcher* (1996, Falmer Press).

Stefinee Pinnegar, born of pioneer stock and reared in the once small town of St. George, Utah, has always been interested in examining the connections between abstract ideas and concrete experience. Through her undergraduate education at Dixie College, Southern Utah University, her teaching in Arizona and Indiana, her graduate education at Brigham Young University and the University of Arizona, she came to see these as the relationship of theory, experience, and practice. Currently, as an Associate Professor of Teacher Education at Brigham Young University, she works to create experiences with her students that develop and investigate their learning concerning these relationships.

Anna E. Richert is an Associate Professor of Education at Mills College in Oakland, CA and co-director of the Teachers for Tomorrow's Schools. Her research continues to focus on teacher learning; she is currently completing a longitudinal study on teacher learning in the context of school change. Her co-authored book with Linda Lambert, Karen Kent, Michelle Collay and Mary Dietz entitled *Who Will Save Our Schools: Teachers as Constructivist Leaders of Change*, will appear in December 1996.

Tom Russell is a Professor in the Faculty of Education at Queen's University, Kingston, Ontario, where his teaching responsibilities include pre-service methods courses in secondary science. He co-ordinates the Waterloo-Queen's Science Education Program, which provides extensive teaching experience both before and after pre-service education courses.

Author Index

Aikin, W.M., 16
Alberty, H.A., 16

Baird, J.R., 42, 120, 125, 135
Ball, D., 96, 98, 99, 114
Baratz-Snowden, J., 162
Barnes, D., 40, 136, 145
Belenkey, M.B., 79
Bell, B., 49, 50, 54, 124, 133
Berger, P., 186
Bird, T., 19, 90, 159
Blakey, J., 176
Bode, B.H., 16
Borrowman, M.L., 4
Brookfield, S., 117, 118, 123
Brown, J.S., 76, 134
Browne, C., 168
Bruner, J., 84
Buchmann, M., 97
Bullough, R.V., 18, 19, 21, 22, 23, 26, 27,
    29, 54, 196

Calderhead, J., 97
Ceci, S.J., 134
Chin, P., 120, 121, 127
Clark, C., 114
Clarke, A., 176
Cobb, P., 133, 134
Cogan, M., 170
Cole, A., 197
Connelly, M., 117
Costa, A., 173
Cuban, L., 96, 115

Darling-Hammond, L., 75, 133
Dewey, J., 15, 20, 63, 153, 187
Driver, R., 133, 134

Eisner, E., 20
Erickson, G.L., 133

Faire, J., 133
Farnham-Diggory, S., 54

Fensham, P.J., 56
Fenstermacher, G.D., 27, 189, 211
Fine, M., 81
Frank, A.W., 187
Freire, P., 14, 16, 20
Fullan, M., 75
Fuller, F., 68

Garland, C., 168
Garrison, J., 186
Gilbert, J., 49, 50, 54
Giroux, H.A., 189, 194
Glickman, G., 170
Goldhammer, R., 170
Goodlad, J., xii, 16, 17, 20
Gore, J., 97, 153, 162
Green, T., 189
Greene, M., 161
Griffiths, M., 20
Grossman, P., 75
Gunstone, R.F., 133
Guyton, E., 170

Habermas, J., 17
Hall, G., 50
Halsall, N.D., 40
Hargreaves, A., 8, 173
Hatton, E., 13, 20
Hawkins, D., 85
Heckman, P., 191
Hennessy, S., 134
Hoban, G., 134
Hodson, B.L., 65
Holland, D., 186
Hollingsworth, S., 40
Holt, J., 37
Holt-Reynolds, D., 97, 196
Hunt, D., 20

Ireland, D., 40

Jackson, P.W., 89
Johnston, C., 168
Joyce, B., 170, 173

Katz, L., 96
Kessels, J.P.A.M., 48
Kilbourn, B., 118, 170
Klohr, P., 16
Knowles, G., 97, 197

LaBoskey, V., 150, 151, 153, 154, 159, 162
Lampert, M., 96, 98
Lanier, J.E., 9
Lather, P.A., 191, 201
Lave, J., 134, 173, 210
Levinson, D.J., 13
Lieberman, A., 75
Lortie, D., 22, 97, 118, 145, 146
Loughran, J.J., 3, 62, 63, 121, 147, 198

MacKinnon, A.M., 210, 211
May, W., 170
McDiarmid, W., 97
McIntyre, D., 168
McLaren, P., 188
McNiff, J., 40, 96
Meier, D., 74
Mitchell, I.J., 42, 59, 120, 125
Munby, H., 8, 53, 135
Murray, J., 5

Northfield, J.R., 42, 120, 125

Osborne, R., 133

Patton, M.Q., 136, 141
Piaget, J., 185, 187, 194
Pinar, W., 18
Polanyi, M., 19, 210

Posner, G., 122
Prawat, R.S., 134

Richards, J., 114
Richardson, V., 18, 191
Rogoff, B., 133
Russell, T.L., 42, 58, 196, 199
Ryle, G., 210

Sandler, B.R., 201
Sarason, S., 75, 145
Saxe, G.B., 134
Schön, D.A., 3, 39, 40, 44, 63, 81, 110, 111, 117, 121, 122, 171, 186, 210, 211
Scribner, S., 134
Shulman, L.S., 61, 65, 75, 82, 98, 159, 175
Smyth, J., 48
Spradley, J.P., 24

Taylor, C., 210

van Manen, M., 5, 6, 19, 58, 150
von Glaserfield, E., 133
Vygotsky, L.S., 185, 186

Walker, J., 61
White, R.T., 58
Wideen, M., 124, 176
Wilson, S.M., 75
Wineburg, S., 96
Wolf, K.P., 159
Wolfe, D., 168

Zeichner, K.M., 153

Subject Index

Action Research, 25, 40
Advisor, 164–6, 169, 170, 176
Alissa, 107
Analogy, 120, 121
Andrea, 101
Apprenticeship, 54, 97, 118, 134, 145, 210
Assessment, 57, 154, 223
Attitude, 65, 144
Authority of experience, 39, 135
Autobiographical, 118, 164

Backtalk, 34, 42
Behaviour model, 54
Beliefs, 17, 92, 105, 129, 184, 188, 189,
    195, 203, 207
  about learning, 127, 155, 157, 185
  about teaching and learning, 123
  systems, 151, 192, 231, 234
Beth, 107

Careers, 79
Carol, 89
Carole, 107, 110, 111, 114
Carolyn, 136
Carrie, 150, 162
Case studies, 53
Challenge, 9, 61, 81, 98
Change, 73, 74, 76, 92, 97, 192, 194, 195,
    206
Classroom, 67, 84, 193
  environment, 138
  ethnography, 24
  experiences, 122
  practice, 120
Coach(ing), 172, 173, 232
Collaboration, 82, 86, 114
College of Teacher Educators, 178
Community, 29, 73, 89, 184, 200, 203
Complexities of teaching, 39, 114, 161
Concept(ion), 78, 84, 119, 220, 221
Concerns, 52, 200
Confidence, 66, 114
Constructivism, 121, 122, 133, 134, 156,
    185, 186, 188, 190, 193, 220

Content, 133
  knowledge, 65
  turn, 44, 196
Context, 65, 66, 75, 88, 93, 102, 115, 118,
    122, 123, 133, 135, 147, 151, 173,
    187, 212, 221
Conversation, 81, 92
Corrine, 101
Credibility, 114
Critical incidents, 119
Culture, 93, 193
Curriculum, 15, 84, 196, 231
  assignment, 85
  hidden, 221
  knowledge, 65
  methods course, 127
  planning, 78, 126
  project, 77, 84, 87, 88, 90
  symposium, 84, 85
Cynthia, 109
  journal, 99, 103, 104

Dan, 106, 108
Debriefing, 66
Decision-making, 97, 135
Development, 184, 196, 197
  model, 54
Dilemma, 96, 97, 221, 222
Discourse, 67, 84, 175
Discover(y), 67, 103

Education
  complexity of, 154
  outcomes, 21
  researchers, 134
  settings, 179
  theory, 145, 146
Elementary
  school students, 106, 110
  science classes, 135
  teacher, 96, 142, 151
English, 74, 83, 151, 218
Evaluation, 160
Experience(s), 63, 64, 67, 118, 140, 122

Feedback, 120, 154
Feminist pedagogy, 183, 200, 203
Field experience, 197
Ford Teaching Project, 40
Freedom of expression, 103
Frustration, 102

Gary, 106
Generating meaning, 78
Genevieve, 87, 88, 90
Gloria, 141, 143, 146
Goals, 118
Group work, 5, 57, 143

Hands-on investigations, 135
Hermeneutics, 16
Heuristic, 178
Horse Problem, 105, 108, 110
Hurricane, 214, 215, 220

Ilana, 87, 88
Inquiry, 98, 99, 188, 197
Instructional strategies, 112, 133
Internship program, 119
Interpretive discussions, 5
Iterative process, 120

Janan, 92
Janet journal, 101, 103
Jigsaw activity, 57, 125
Journal, 95, 98, 99, 135, 221
  Jill, 102
  Karen, 99
  Kathy, 101
  Ken, 101, 105
  Kendra, 95, 101, 105, 114
  Tanis, 102

King, Arthur, 186, 203
Knowing/Knowledge, 76, 79, 114, 117, 210
  about teaching and learning, 51
  acquiring new, 75
  construction, 135
  existing, 61, 134, 140
  nature of, 234
  representation of, 217
  significance of, 49
Krall, Flo, 15

Learning, 8, 49, 111, 126, 196, 219
  about learning, 21, 66, 232
  about teaching, 6, 49, 58, 61, 63, 65, 66

active role in, 119, 123, 125
  as a teacher educator, 122
  by doing, 66, 127, 128
  context, 76, 147, 201
  documenting own, 136
  facilitator of, 154
  from experience, 20, 68
  inhibited, 136
  lack of, 144
  mathematics, 97
  narrow understanding of, 134
  outcomes, 60, 214
  to teach, 41, 79, 93, 115, 122, 166, 221, 224
Life history, 19, 23
Linda, 109
Listening, 59, 109, 111, 123
  for, 105, 109, 111, 230
  to their voices, 126

Marginalization, 195
Martin, Ann, 107
Mathematics, 95, 97, 98, 99, 114, 230
Mathew, 173, 174
Matt, 77, 79
Metacognition, 120, 137
Metaphor Analysis, 23, 216
Mimesis, 211
Model(ling), 62, 66, 155, 193, 198, 232
  teaching and learning approaches, 49, 54, 138
Monster Problem, 100, 101, 102
Moral and ethical
  dilemmas, action, question, 17, 79, 83
  imperative, 77
  implications, 161
  obligation, 207

Narratives, 115

Passionate creeds, 161
Pedagogical
  challenge, 97, 222
  choices, 86, 91, 126
  content knowledge, 61, 65
  justification, 90
  knowledge, 58, 64, 234
  purpose, 62
  reasoning, 63, 86, 98
  tasks, 96
  turn, 44
Pedagogues, 9

Pedagogy, 6, 56, 61, 69, 133, 151, 234
  of teacher education, 55, 97
PEEL, 42, 43, 59, 120, 125
Personal
  feelings, 138
  growth, 96, 124
  histories, 193
  identity, 19
  interests and concerns, 197
  pedagogies, 135
  teaching text, 19, 22, 26
Philosophy, 16, 21, 157, 187, 198, 205
  of teaching and learning, 117, 123
Physics teachers, 83
Piaget, 185, 186, 187, 194
Portfolio, 151, 152, 154, 158, 159, 197
Practical(s), 135, 140, 142
Practice
  boundaries of, 64
  better understanding of, 119, 121
  illuminate, 231
  knowing about, 234
  what they preach, 4
Practicum, 33, 164, 169, 173, 179
Pre-service
  programs, 68, 230
  teachers, 8, 106, 117, 124, 126, 135,
    138, 140, 147, 199, 206
Prediction-Observation-Explanation
  (P.O.E.), 42, 43, 57
Principles, 19, 21, 29, 49
  in practice, 22, 97
  of pedagogy, 3, 58
Problem(atic), 80, 83, 111
  the conditions of school, 231
Processing and synthesising, 61
Profession(al), 53, 68
  development, 23, 49, 51, 96, 118, 122,
    129, 168, 178
  education, 22
  knowledge, 4, 117
  readiness, 176
  researchers, 145
  role, 76
  voice, xiii
Program
  alternative, 14
  consecutive, 121
  continuity, 22
Purpose, 61
  of teacher education, 235
Puzzling, 113

Question(ing), 5, 54, 67, 79, 109, 122, 153

Reflect(ing), 9, 53, 68, 90, 96, 124, 138,
  175, 190
  catalysts for, 120
  conditions for, ix
  on teaching, viii, 124
Reflection, 63, 65, 144, 147, 150, 153,
  158, 185, 197, 211
Reflective, 221, 231
  deliberation, 161
  practice, 39, 80, 97, 151, 171
  practitioners, x, ix, 83, 145, 157, 161,
    185, 232
  professional growth, 120
  teacher educators, 207
  turn, 44
Reframing, 3
Relationship(s), 117, 121, 201
  between teaching and learning, 6
  between theory and experience, 198
  between theory and practice, 5
  pedagogical, 223
  with teacher, 138
Research(ing), 112, 114
  in teacher education, 134
  own practice, 98
Resistance, 88, 92, 184, 192, 194, 221
Return to the classroom, 33, 41
Risk taking, 64, 67, 114

S-STEP SIG, 33, 201
School
  advisor, 165, 174
  experience, 73, 198
  learning, 57
  structures and systems, 21, 74, 75, 81
Science, 140, 215, 217, 222
  classes, 143
  demonstrations, 124
  education, 120, 210
  lessons, 141
  methods course, 122, 136, 142
  teaching, 36, 118, 119, 141
  teacher educator, 57
Secondary school, 145
Self
  analysis/awareness, 22, 125, 137, 138,
    139, 146, 197
  monitoring of learning, 136
  study, 185, 198
Sheryl, 89
Shoshana, 78, 79
Social
  and cultural conditions, 133
  constructivism, 134, 184, 200, 207

influences, 138
studies, 85, 151
theory, 15
Sponsor teachers, 210
Standardised tests, 74
Story telling, 19, 115, 119
Student
eyes, 118, 199
needs, 153, 161
personal lives, 77, 78
resistance, 188
shadow studies, 24
teacher, 28, 64, 68, 152, 167, 169
teachers' pedagogical knowledge, 63
thinking and understanding, 105, 204
Sue, 143, 145, 146
Summerfest, 210, 211, 222
Supervision, 170, 178
Support, 52, 177
Systemics of schooling, 27

Tacit knowledge, 4, 19, 58, 184
Teach
mathematics/science, 105, 140
with tact, 150
Teacher education, 17, 22, 41, 43, 52, 54,
55, 65, 75, 80, 83, 115, 117, 224
curriculum, 76
for change, 21, 82
practices, 117
programs, 54, 233
purpose of, 48
Teacher educator(s), 38, 59, 95, 120, 128,
129, 134, 137, 177, 200, 206, 231
as Coach, 170
as learners, 54
in collaboration, 54
families of, ix
Teacher(s)
and learners' perspective, 59, 117
as learner/coach, 52, 119
beginning, 4, 68, 196, 199
conceptions of good teaching, 25
development, 196
elementary and secondary, 83
explanations, 138
for tomorrow's schools, 151
History/Geography, 167
identity, 21
interaction, 52
interviews and classroom ethnographies,
24
knowledge, 49, 52, 56

of mathematics, 96
of student-teachers, 58
preparation, 74
professional knowledge, 8
prospective, 39, 66, 95, 97, 98, 100,
112, 113, 129
voices, 8
Teaching and learning, 24, 62, 79, 117,
122, 123, 124, 129, 147, 183
environment, 60, 65
experiences, 49, 123
monitoring, 127, 128
Teaching, 140
about teaching, 4, 65, 66, 68
approach, 64, 214, 219
as a moral and political act, 78, 150
as a relationship, 58
as inquiry and learning, 96, 97
assessing practices, 97
images of, 34
methods, xii
ourselves to teach, 186
philosophy, 157
pre-service teachers, 4, 113
resources, 126
settings, 123
strategies, 64, 65, 124, 125, 146
teachers, 73
Tensions and dilemmas, 96, 115
Textbook Analysis, 25
Theory/Theoretical, 83, 188
literature, 118, 121, 198
propositions, 96
texture, 202
Private and public, 20
Thinking aloud, 63
Transition to teacher, 51
Transmission, 143, 145
Trial and error, 138, 142
Trust(ing), 21, 59, 60, 147

Uncertainty, 76, 97, 153
Understanding, 60, 61, 62, 78, 83, 96,
119, 123, 125, 126, 127, 133, 140,
145, 220

Validity, 110
Videotaping, 25, 125
Voices of teacher educators, viii

Wait-time, 5

Zone of proximal development, 185